Michael Rysbrack

Sculptor 1694–1770

KATHARINE EUSTACE

CITY OF BRISTOL
MUSEUM AND ART GALLERY
1982

Published by the Friends of Bristol Art Gallery
on behalf of the City of Bristol Museum & Art Gallery
for the exhibition: 6 March–1 May 1982

ISBN 0 900199 16 4

Designed by Sally Rose and Peter French
of the City of Bristol Museum & Art Gallery

Planned and produced by Pisces Press London

Contents

Foreword

Few citizens in Bristol realise that Rysbrack's William III statue in Queen Square is Western Europe's finest eighteenth-century equestrian monument. We are fortunate to be richly endowed in Bristol and the West Country with the work of one of the greatest sculptors ever to work in England. Because of this it is reasonable and fitting to concentrate on Rysbrack's work in this area. Although the exhibition is to some extent limited geographically, it is still able to provide the first extensive and revealing survey of the works of this sculptor.

Such an exhibition is beyond the resources of the City of Bristol Museum and Art Gallery and we are dependent upon the very generous support of

The Arts Council of Great Britain
Sun Life Assurance
Paul Mellon Centre for Studies in British Art
Smith Kline & French Laboratories Ltd
Osmond, Tricks & Son, Chartered Surveyors, Fine Art Auctioneers and Estate Agents
The Gane Charitable Trust, Bristol.

These sponsors have understood that our public's knowledge and appreciation of sculpture lie far behind those of painting and the applied arts. We hope that the exhibition will provide many visitors with the special sense of discovery which can occur when a new subject of enduring interest and reward is first encountered. I am sure the exhibition will encourage a popular reappraisal of the great wealth of eighteenth-century sculpture, one of the outstanding achievements of British art.

Her Majesty The Queen has graciously allowed us to include Rysbrack's superb terracotta bust of Queen Elizabeth I. We are greatly indebted to all the lenders and especially to His Grace the Duke of Beaufort, the Earl of Harrowby, Viscount Cobham and the National Trust, Stourhead. The staff of the Department of Sculpture, Victoria and Albert Museum, have given us invaluable help and guidance, both as lenders and in many other matters. Dr Charles Avery of Christie's has been of particular assistance to us.

Dr Terry Friedman's interest and advice were vital to the genesis of the exhibition and we are very grateful to him and to the other contributors for their introductory essays: Malcolm Baker of the Victoria and Albert Museum, Mary Greenacre of the Area Museum Council for the South West and Michael Liversidge of the University of Bristol's Department of History of Art. Katharine Eustace, Assistant Curator of Fine Art has selected the exhibits and written the catalogue.

Arnold Wilson,
Director, City Art Gallery

January 1982

Acknowledgements

My first thanks are to my Director and my Curator who entrusted me with such an undertaking. To Francis Greenacre in particular who has been a constant source of encouragement and enthusiasm throughout, I owe a debt for the opportunity he gave me to do something so exciting. Together we have worked on the organisation and without his experience and financial acumen the project would have floundered. Then there are the host of supporters within the institution whose roles too often go unsung, but without whom any exhibition would be impossible: Karin Walton who read through the manuscript and proofs of the entire catalogue; Lesley Cottle and Louise Hillard who typed and patiently retyped it, Lillian Jackson who typed much of the vast correspondence; the conservators Mary Greenacre, Mark Norman, Brian Boyd and Fred Lester, who found themselves with more than they had bargained for, and who were a forum for stimulating discussion and ideas. The exhibition and catalogue were designed by Peter French and Sally Rose, and the construction of the displays was in the capable hands of Ken Fussell and his team. That every item in the catalogue is illustrated, together with many photographs of monuments, is largely due to the intrepid work of Ron Mason, the Museum's own photographer, and also of Derek Balmer and Royston Walters; John Trelawny-Ross took the excellent photographs of 'William III'.

Outside the institution many, many people have helped in a myriad of ways with knowledge and advice, academic and practical. The contributors to the catalogue, whom my Director has thanked, did far more than that. Without the help of the Victoria and Albert Museum much would not have been attempted or achieved. My special thanks go to Anthony Radcliffe, whose support was unfailing and to Lucy Cullen and Ben Curran of the Sculpture Department. Michael Kauffman and his staff in the Department of Prints and Drawings were patience itself in organising an exceptionally large loan at what must have been a particularly trying time for them. Paddy Daley and the sculpture working party spent an afternoon demonstrating the handling of half a ton of marble and Charlie Harris taught me the art of packing, in that inimitable V & A way. Elsewhere, I received much valuable assistance from: Geoffrey de Bellaigue, Judith Harland and Mrs Gell at the Lord Chamberlain's Office and Kensington Palace; Patrick Noon and Susan Carstairs at the Yale Center for British Art; Charles Avery and the Department of Sculpture at Christie's; Maureen Attrill at Plymouth Art Gallery, Ian Rutherford at Hull, Ian Lowe and John White at the Ashmolean; Miss Scull at the Soane Museum, Ivor Heale, and Beck and Pollitzer. In Bristol I had the help of Mary Williams and the staff of the Bristol Record Office, particularly Judith Close and Shelagh Laing; of Anthony Beeson and his colleagues in the Fine Art section and Geoffrey Langley and Ann Smith in the Reference section of the Central Library. Many helped on individual points: William Agnew, Jonathan Barry, Kenneth Beaulah, Sarah Bevan, Anne Buddle, Frances Collard, Elizabeth and Michael Darby, Mrs Elgar, John Harris, Reginald Humphris, Richard Jenkyns, Francis Kelly, Edward King, John Larson, Bryan Little, Jennifer Montagu, Howard Nixon, Nicholas Penny, Elizabeth Ralph, Michael Snodin, Sheena Stoddard, Glen Taylor, Nicolette Vincent, Lisa White and Thomas Wiedemann.

I, too, would like to thank the lenders, not just for lending, but for the time they gave me. Finally I would like to record my admiration for those redoubtable women, Katharine Esdaile, Margaret Webb and Margaret Whinney, without whose pioneering work no one could have attempted such an exhibition.

Katharine Eustace
Assistant Curator, Fine Art

"No vain man"

Katharine Eustace

Michael Rysbrack was born in 1694, at Antwerp in Flanders, then a Spanish province, now part of Belgium.[1] Almost nothing is known for certain of his early years, save that he was a Catholic, his father and brothers were painters and he trained under the sculptor Michel van der Voort.[2] There is no known work by him in Flanders, yet when he arrived in London in 1720 he was already an independent master with a distinctly individual and innovatory style. He achieved almost immediate recognition and until his retirement in 1764, nearly fifty years later, maintained a position as the leading sculptor during a period when sculpture, alone of all the arts in England, could compete with the continent, and when, in England, the status of sculpture outshone that of painting.

It has been customary to see English culture in the first half of the eighteenth century as a series of politically and aesthetically divided camps. This may have been exaggerated, particularly when talking of Rysbrack; so too has the question of his religion in so far as it affected his work.[3] Rysbrack could not be said to have worked predominantly for any one set or faction. He worked for both James Gibbs and Lord Burlington. The former had introduced the baroque architecture of Fontana from Rome, and carried on the tradition of Wren, while the latter was the leader of the so-called 'Burlington House Set', with its strict adherence to the tenets of Palladio. Party seems to have meant little or nothing to him. In 1726 he was doing the "large head, broad face" of Sir Robert Walpole, the great Whig Prime Minister.[4] At the same time he was working on the figure for the monument to the High Tory, Edward Colston (Cat. No. 6), who, it was generally understood, had opposed the Whig-supported Hanoverian succession in 1714, to the point of sedition. *The Free Briton* pointed out on 16 August 1733: "we should never take Party into the affair, nor prefer a bad or indifferent hand to a good one on the score of Politics. I know not whether Rysbrack be a Whig or a Tory, I know him to be a good statuary, and I believe him to be an honest man and impartial Sculptor". Only once could Rysbrack's patronage perhaps be said to have been affected by factionalism. During the 1730s art and sculpture, and Rysbrack in particular, had "Protection in the Court of great Britain".[5] With the death of Queen Caroline in 1737, artistic circles found a new centre in Frederick, Prince of Wales, who until his own death in 1751 became the arbiter of royal taste and patronage.[6] He had earlier employed Rysbrack but had been so entirely at odds with his father and mother, George II and Queen Caroline, that he determined to differ in everything political and aesthetic. This may have resulted in the temporary decline in the number of Rysbrack's commissions in the early 1740s.[7]

Rysbrack's own letters and the accounts of three perceptive contemporaries, George Vertue, Charles Rogers and Horace Walpole, present a detailed and personal account of the sculptor. Vertue, the engraver, antiquarian and diarist, was a particularly close friend. The insights he provides in the 'Notebooks' are beyond those of mere acquaintance or hearsay and on occasion Rysbrack actually speaks through him. This is in strict contrast to Vertue's entries for the French Huguenot L. F. Roubiliac, where, though his admiration for the sculptor's work is unstinting, his information is no more than might be gleaned from the *Gentleman's Magazine* or town gossip.[8] Vertue was a Catholic, and though one must be wary of over-emphasising religion, this may well have been an initial cause of their friendship. It is Vertue who tells us that Rysbrack's father had been in England with the painter Largillière "but the troubles & disturbances to Catholics about Oates's plot, caus'd these two painters to go to Paris".[9] This same inside information is apparent in the long and detailed obituary he gives Rysbrack's brother Peter, a not very considerable still-life painter.[10] Very early on, in 1723, Vertue tells us, in recounting the ill-usage received by Rysbrack at the hands of James Gibbs, the architect (Cat. No. 10), that "the poor Man has oppend his mind to me" on the subject.[11] The same protective tone is present in Vertue's comments on Kent's part in the Newton monument:

> April. 1731. Sett up in Westminster Abbey the Monument of Sr Isaac Newton. a noble and Elegant work of Mr Michael Rysbrack. much to his Reputation. tho the design or drawing of it on paper was poor enough, yet for that only Mr Kent is honourd with his name on it (Pictor et Architect inventor.) which if it had been deliverd to any other Sculptor besides Rysbrack, he might have been glad to have his name omitted.[12]

Vertue for all his catholicity of taste and Rysbrack for all his great knowledge, may both have felt at a disadvantage for not having been to Rome. Rysbrack's model and design for the chimney-piece relief in East India House, initially failed to please the directors. They turned to Arthur Pond, who, as Vertue cynically records, was briefly a pupil of the painter Vanderbank, and had been to Italy at the expense of his father. Pond submitted a design "on a half sheet of paper.-heightned". One can almost hear Rysbrack's irritation in Vertue's concluding comment: "who ever thinks that travelling will qualify a painter, tho' it may as a Gentleman."[13]

Vertue died in 1756, and his place as 'biographer' was taken by Charles Rogers, the Custom House official whose important collection is now at Plymouth City Art Gallery. Rogers was a much younger man but he was clearly very fond of Rysbrack and a great admirer of the sculptor's work. Rogers deemed him, alone among his contemporaries, worthy of being included in his book *A Collection of Prints in Imitation of Drawings*.[14] He reproduced Rysbrack's design for a sundial engraved by James Basire in 1768, which had been given to Rogers by the artist "as a New Year's Gift" in 1765.

Our third important source is that doyen of aestheticism, the creator of Strawberry Hill, Horace Walpole. He certainly knew Rysbrack, though perhaps only in the capacity of patron, for he entrusted the sculptor with the plinth for the statue commemorating his mother, Lady Walpole, in Westminster Abbey; the statue by Valori he had imported from Rome. In *Anecdotes of Painting in England* Walpole relied almost entirely on Vertue for his facts, which perhaps accounts for the length of his entry on Rysbrack and the brevity of that for Roubiliac.[15] Walpole nonetheless, particularly in his use of adjectives, is enlightening. We know Walpole was not an admirer of Rysbrack's 'Flora' at Stourhead (fig. 50 and Cat. No. 74), yet he averred Rysbrack to be "the best sculptor that has appeared in these islands since Le Soeur".

One of the keys to Rysbrack's long working life was, as Walpole put it, "his deep knowledge of his art and singular industry". Rogers, paraphrasing Vertue, and *The Free Briton* of 16 August 1733, says that "he never undertook any great work but with an Industry which far exceeded his Reward." His capacity for hard work, the thoroughness with which he approached every aspect of it, and his attention to detail are all borne out by the sources. He was, Charles Rogers relates "an early riser, attending to his workmen, and working with them from five or six in the morning till late at night". This care for his workmen is apparent too from his letters to Sir Edward Littleton.[16] On two occasions it is clear that his men and the workshop prevent him from beginning work on some models.[17] Rysbrack's constant supervision of his men may explain why it has been difficult at times to distinguish his work from that of his studio. Mrs Webb was tempted to conclude that he did nearly all the work.[18] Though his clay models were always entirely his own work, it would have been a physical impossibility for him to have undertaken the great number of marble works attributed to him.[19] It is also clear from the letters that he continued to be much in demand and very busy, and that ill health alone stopped him and drove him into retirement in 1764, when he was already over seventy. From 1757 he appears to have been almost constantly ill, but his remedy was to "go into the Shop" and work.[20]

The numerous and beautiful, highly finished designs which he presented to prospective clients, were recognised in his own day as works of art in themselves, and were collected and mounted like Old Master drawings (Cat. No. 39). For many commissions he worked through several stages of scale model before the marble was begun and each stage was an end in itself; thus the little 'Hercules' (Cat. No. 72) and the model for the statue of John Locke at Christ Church, Oxford, are finished objects in their own right, as are the full-size terracotta busts for the same projects.[21] The letters reveal a careful man: when sending a design for a chimney-piece at Teddesley Hall, Staffordshire, he writes: "I do not think it proper to Enclose it in a Letter, because it will spoil it, but I shall send it Rolled on a Stick, in a Very little box, by Kirk and Saunders's Waggon on Monday Next."[22] Evidence of his conscientious nature, even after his retirement, is clear in the anxiety he expresses over the fate of the Beaufort monuments. In a letter written to the Duchess in 1766 he lists the number and contents of the boxes, asks that they be collected and concludes with a note of urgency, "I am not well, and if I should Die, I know not will become of the Monument."[23]

Rysbrack was perhaps sensitive to the fact that he had never been to Rome. But there was never any suggestion that he was not fully acquainted with the "Beauties of the Antique". Commentators, contemporary and latter-day, have been at pains to demonstrate his complete mastery of the principles of classical sculpture. Rogers tells us that "his great abilities were not acquired without great application; for he had studied very assiduously in his youth". His sale catalogues are a mine of information on his sources. They show that he had marbles, plasters and bronzes "after the antique" and not a few antique works. He owned all the great seventeenth- and eighteenth-century engraved publications of antique sculpture, too. He had copies of Bartoli, Bellori, Perrier, and Sandrart (see Cat. Nos. 27, 73, 75, 84 and 85, and figs. 52 and 53) all of whose engravings are surprisingly poor. He also had the infinitely superior *Signorum Veterum Icones* by Bisschop,[24] as well as Rossi and Maffei's work, both of which convey very well the three-dimensional character of sculpture, and finally Montfaucon's *L'Antiquité Expliquée* of 1714, described in the catalogue as "*Antiquities* with the *Supplement*, in fifteen volumes".[25]

Rysbrack's collecting instincts were very pronounced and extremely catholic. His assiduity and "the fury with which he made his Collections", were, Rogers averred, besides his generosity to his less successful relations, the cause of his relative poverty. Rysbrack's name is found several times among the successful bidders noted in the margin of a sale catalogue of the collection of Arthur Pond, his rival in the India House chimney-piece dispute.[26] He owned a large number of works by and after François Duquesnoy, 'Il Fiammingo', the Flemish seventeenth-century sculptor, whose reputation and influence were then so much greater than they are today. He had examples of works after Michelangelo and Giambologna, by Algardi and Bernini, by Quellien and Rusconi, and by his contemporaries Plumière, van der Voort, Scheemakers and Roubiliac. His collection of prints and drawings was vast. The dispersal took ten days at the first sale at Langfords' in 1764, and Christie's held a further three-day sale ten years later. There were works by and after Michelangelo, Raphael, Titian, Veronese, Palma, Pietro da Cortona, the Carracci, Rubens, Van Dyck, Le Brun, Claude and Poussin and many others. Perhaps more remarkable were those after Watteau, Bouchardon, Lancret, Vien, Greuze, and Teniers, Ostade and Wouvermans. He owned complete sets of Hogarth's 'Apprentice' and 'Election' series, engravings after Gainsborough's 'Gypsies' and West's 'Angelica and Medora', and other engravings by McArdell and Bartolozzi. One could go on at length listing the intriguing oddities, but the following must suffice: "a set of views of Asia, Africa etc. by Zeeman and Hollar, and Johnston's ornaments",[27] the latter being a very important rococo pattern book.[28] That he kept abreast of changing fashion is borne out by other items listed in the catalogues: for example Sir William Chambers' *Designs of Chinese Buildings*, Robert Wood's *Ruins of Palmyra*, and Piranesi's *Antichita Romane* of 1756.[29]

In a small way he may have dealt in antiques, casts after the antique, and Old Masters. Jacob Bouverie was paying Rysbrack eight guineas for a "Holy Family of *Carlo Marat*" in 1738.[30] Charles Rogers writes in his account book for 23 September 1765: "Paid Mr Rysbrack for a Cast of Gior. di Bologna's Samson Killing the Lyon, Do. ditto Anatomical Figure Mich. Angelo's Do. Do. Torso."[31]

One of the most remarkable features of Rysbrack's long career was the extraordinarily cordial terms on which Rysbrack conducted matters with all his patrons. In 1732 Vertue clearly felt that "as he gaind acquaintances friends. & business" so he prospered.[32] Many of his patrons like the Bouveries, the Beauforts, Henry Hoare and Cox Macro were with him from very early on, and supported him at the end by buying liberally at his retirement sales. He stayed on the best of terms with anyone he worked with or for. Contrary to general opinion, an opinion probably fostered by Vertue's diatribe, he continued to work with James Gibbs well after he had established an independent reputation. They are seen in company in the 'Conversation of Virtuosi' (Cat. No. 1) in 1735. From drawings in the Gibbs Collection, now in the Ashmolean Museum, it would appear that he worked closely with Gibbs on the latter's last and greatest project, the Radcliffe Camera at Oxford.[33] Rysbrack was undoubtedly a gregarious individual. His clubbable nature is clear from his membership of the various clubs of the day, from the "Grand Virtuosi Clubb"[34] and St. Luke's to the Rose and Crown Club, which, on Vertue's account, held very lively, somewhat ribald meetings.[35] He was an associate of the Foundling Hospital and a founder-member of the Royal Academy, though ill health prevented him attending the first meetings in 1769. But even at the end when he "had scarcely strength to rise from his chair", Rogers tells that he "was very sensible of his approaching dissolution of which a slow Dropsy had given him long notice: but he spoke of it, not with the affected disregard of a Stoic Philosopher, but with the easy indifference of Man of sense; nor would he even now refuse to laugh when the conversation took a gay turn".[36] His letters reveal a man of charm and humour as well as common sense; that to Sir Edward Littleton of 10 November 1759 begins "How to write to Your Honour, I don't know. If I had the Assurance of an Irishman, a Swiss, or a Gascon; I would do it without any fear."[37]

Sir Edward Littleton was a patron of Rysbrack s later years, at a time when he was already bowed "by the dropsical disorder" which finally killed him, and their exchange of letters tells of their warm regard for each other. On 5 July 1757 Rysbrack writes: "I am Extreamly obliged to You and Your Good Lady for the honour you do me in Expressing so great Regard for me in Your last most Complaisant letter and am Rejoyced to hear you are both in Exceeding Good health."[38] Eight years and much work later he concludes a letter of 30 November 1765; "I wish You and Your Good Lady that Good Angel who has so much regard for me all the happiness of this Life."[39] Littleton responded to an appeal by Rysbrack by distributing the sale catalogues of 1765 among the gentlemen of his acquaintance. Rysbrack thanks him for his trouble and concludes the letter and the correspondence, "I think the Esteem which You and Mr. Hoare have for me, I shall never forget."[40] "Mr. Hoare" was Henry Hoare, the creator of Stourhead, that most classical of English gardens. He had been a patron of Rysbrack's from as early as 1727,[41] and continued to give Rysbrack work right up to the year of the sculptor's retirement. It would appear that Hoare never once commissioned Rysbrack on his own initiative, but that he saw models in the studio and ordered full-scale versions. Patron and artist clearly held each other in mutual trust and esteem bordering on affection. Hoare wrote to his daughter Lady Bruce in October 1762: "I thought old Rysbrack would have wept for joy to see his Offspring placed to such advantage."[42] On at least one occasion Rysbrack accompanied his patron to Stourhead.[43] Rysbrack in a letter asked that he might draw a subject or two of Hoare's choosing, and the implication is that these would be a present.[44] In his will he left Hoare the little 'Hercules' (Cat. No. 72).[45]

Rysbrack's reputation was founded on his skill as a modeller in clay. Vertue notes in his very first entry on the sculptor in October 1720 that his "moddels in Clay are very excellent & shows him to be a great Master *tho' young*".[46] In 1732 Vertue recalls this and enlarges upon it "when he first came to England [Rysbrack] imployd his time in Moddelling small figures to show his skill in the plastic Art",[47] and there then follows a list of sixty-eight busts which Rysbrack had modelled, often from the life; clearly his intentions had succeeded. When his popularity was temporarily eclipsed by that of Peter Scheemakers in the early 1740s, it was to clay models that he resorted. The 'Rubens' of 1743 (Cat. No. 57), and the 'Hercules' (Cat. No. 72) of 1744 are supreme achievements in the medium of terracotta and demonstrate his outstanding technical virtuosity. Again, it is Vertue who, in describing the terracotta relief for the Foundling Hospital in 1746, goes straight to the point when he says "therein shows his great Skill in the plastic Art wherein as the Materia is moleable, still permitts the Artist to express his mind more Artfully & with greater freedom. than on the laborious or durable marble".[48] He was quite capable of virtuoso feats in marble, such as he achieved in his busts of Rubens and Van Dyck (Cat. Nos. 53 and 54). Nonetheless it is quite apparent that he loved terracotta and delighted in its responsive nature. His pleasure and pride in his little models continued throughout his life. He was obviously distressed by the damage to the goat, modelled in the 1720s for a life-size version for Lord Burlington at Chiswick, and which he only parted with to Littleton in 1765.[49]

Rysbrack was an acknowledged master of the portrait bust; as Vertue says, "His superior meritt to other Sculptors is very aparent in his Modells of portraits – from the life none equalling for truth of Likeness and property of ornaments or head-dress &c,"[50] which gives added interest to such otherwise rather anonymous men as Henry Blaake (Cat. No. 90) or the Innys brothers (Cat. Nos. 19 and 20). It is, however, with the historical portraits, those busts of Queen Elizabeth, Milton, Rubens and King Alfred, and many others that Rysbrack set new standards. Both he and Vertue were exceptionally careful of their documentary sources, in an age which had developed a strong sense of history, and an antiquarian patriotism. But Rysbrack is perhaps more faithful to the spirit of his sources: thus his 'Milton' has all the sobriety of Faithorne's engraving, in which there is a definite hint of puritanism, but not so Vertue's (see Cat. No. 77). By contrast Rysbrack's 'Rubens' and 'Van Dyck' echo in a most subtle way the flamboyant elegance characteristic of pre-Commonwealth painting (Cat. Nos. 59 and 60). From two-dimensional sources, prints and paintings, he conjured up images in the round that are remarkable for their veracity and conviction.

Rysbrack, though "no vain man", as Walpole points out, was confident of his own merit. His sarcasm over the reception of Scheemakers' 'Shakespeare' in 1741 which Walpole justly condemned, stemmed from more than wounded pride. Vertue recorded that the event "provokes him to say. that he believes whereever he goes in what part of the world so ever, he shall be able to live, if here, the run of the whole posse, or multitude – follow the outcry without distinction – or judgement of the degrees of merit".[51] Such apparent confidence was well founded, for his patronage by people of all persuasions over the entire length of a long working life is remarkable.

From the beginning, Rysbrack had demonstrated a complete assimilation of the classical ideals of early-eighteenth-century aesthetics, but his versatility is quite remarkable. In his work there is always an appropriateness of style to the subject, be it the domesticity of busts like those of the Innys brothers, the bravura of the 'Rubens' and 'Van Dyck' or the *gravitas* of the 'Milton'. His work is very much an expression of himself, a man of wit, of order, elegance and balance.

[1] He invariably signed himself "M". "Ml." or "Mich. Rysbrack". Vertue, with that endearing lack of pedantry so characteristic of the eighteenth century, spelt the surname a multiplicity of ways, the most bizarre being "Ricebrake" and "Rysprake". Horace Walpole must be held responsible for the widespread use of the spelling "Rysbrack".

[2] For a fuller account see Webb, 1954, Chapters I and II.

[3] As a foreigner there would have been no bar to his practising his religion, though always at the Embassy chapels. I am grateful to Bryan Little for pointing out that he probably attended the Portuguese Embassy Chapel, at Lincolns Inn Fields until 1736, and thereafter in South Street, Mayfair. He was a witness there at the marriage of Francis Sesarego and Mary-Anne Boterbeaugh, 8 July 1753: *Catholic Record Society*, XXXVIII, 1941, p. 123, entry 347. This same Mary-Anne Sesarego was left money in his will: Webb, 1954, p. 190.

[4] Vertue, III, p. 31; the marble bust is at Houghton Hall, Norfolk, the terracotta model in the National Portrait Gallery, London.

[5] Vertue, III, p. 66.

[6] Sutton, 1981, The Age of Sir Robert Walpole, *Apollo*, CXIV, p. 333; Sudbury: Gainsborough's House, 1981, *Frederick, Prince of Wales and his circle*.

[7] Vertue, III, p. 116.

[8] Vertue puts Roubiliac's place of birth as Switzerland, Normandy and finally Lyons.

[9] Vertue, III, p. 37.

[10] Vertue, III, p. 142.

[11] Vertue, III, p. 17.

[12] Vertue, III, p. 50.

[13] Vertue, III, p. 37.

[14] Published in 1778. All further references relating to Rogers are taken from this book.

[15] Walpole, 1798 edn., *Works*, Vol. III, *Anecdotes of Painting*, pp. 477–80, *passim*.

[16] The letters were published in transcript in 1932 when the Rysbrack terracottas from the collection at Teddesley Hall, Staffordshire, were sold at Spink & Son Ltd; catalogue and introduction by Mrs Esdaile. The quotations here are taken from Webb, 1954, Appendix One, complete transcripts.

[17] Webb, 1954, pp. 194 and 200: Letters II and XII.

[18] Ibid., p. 68.

[19] Of the only two men who we know worked with Rysbrack, Peter Classins is described by Vertue as a "Foreman" and Vanderhagen would appear to have achieved something of the status of a partner: Vertue, II, p. 152, and Cat. No. 57.

[20] Webb, 1954, p. 202: Letter XIV.

[21] Cat. No. 72 and V.A.M. 33. 1867: fig. 48 and illustrated in Esdaile, 1932, pl. V.

[22] Webb, 1954, p. 196: Letter IV. The chimney-piece was to contain Rysbrack's terracotta relief, the model for 'Charity' in the Foundling Hospital, now in the Victoria and Albert Museum (V.A.M. A58–1953).

[23] Appendix 3.

[24] Described in Langfords' sale catalogue as "Bishop's statues", he apparently had two sets, lots 57 and 55 on 20 and 21 February 1764, but it is more likely that the cataloguer has split the two-volume edition of 1669.

[25] Lot 55, 25 February 1764.

[26] Langford Sale Catalogue, 25 April 1759; a copy among the Cottonian papers, Plymouth City Museum and Art Gallery. Lot 72, the Guercino of "the Virgin and Christ giving the rosary to a saint", was purchased by Rysbrack and later included in Mr Roger's Prints in Imitation of Drawings.

[27] Christie's, 7 February 1774, lot 55.

[28] H. Hayward, 1964, Thomas Johnson and the English Rococo.

[29] Christie's, 8 February 1774, lot 54, and 9 February, lots 56 and 57.

[30] Longford Castle Muniment Room: 'Extracts from the Private Account Book of Jacob, 1st Viscount Folkestone 1722–1761'.

[31] Plymouth City Museum and Art Gallery: Cottonian papers.

[32] Vertue, III, p. 56.

[33] See Cat. No. 13.

[34] Vertue, III, p. 73.

[35] Vertue, VI, pp. 31–7.

[36] Rogers, 1778, A collection of Prints in Imitation of Drawings.

[37] Webb, 1954, p. 203: Letter XV.

[38] Ibid., p. 197: Letter VI.

[39] Ibid., p. 208: Letter XXI.

[40] Ibid., p. 209: Letter XXIII.

[41] W.R.O. Stourhead papers 383.4: 10 October 1727, an agreement between Hoare and Rysbrack for a marble bust of Inigo Jones.

[42] Quoted in Woodbridge, 1965, Henry Hoare's paradise, The Art Bulletin, XLVII.

[43] See Cat. No. 74: W.R.O. T.O.T.2411, letter to Lord Bruce.

[44] Appendix 4.

[45] Quoted by Webb, 1954, p. 190.

[46] Vertue, I, p. 76.

[47] Vertue, III, pp. 56–7.

[48] Vertue, III, p. 132.

[49] Webb, 1954, pp. 207–8: Letters XXI and XXII. The stone version is now at Chatsworth, Derbyshire, the terracotta model at Anglesey Abbey, Cambridgeshire.

[50] Vertue, III, p. 84.

[51] Vertue, III, p. 116.

Rysbrack and Gibbs

Dr Terry F. Friedman

George Vertue, the diarist and engraver, makes one of the earliest contemporary references to Michael Rysbrack in England. In October 1720 he records the arrival from Antwerp of the 26-year-old sculptor whose "moddels in clay" are already "very excellent & shows him to be a great Master *tho' young*". Vertue adds that "he was recommended to Mr. Gibbs. Architect."[1]

James Gibbs (1682–1754) had introduced into this country the idea that the designing of church monuments could be the legitimate pursuit of the professional architect, where previously it had been almost exclusively the preserve of sculptors and master-masons. He had inherited this idea during his years of training in Rome (1704–8) under the Papal architect, Carlo Fontana, who had been a pupil of the great baroque sculptor and architect, Bernini. Late in 1708 Gibbs set up practice in London and rapidly established a reputation as a talented and erudite designer with his church of St. Mary-le-Strand; later came St. Martin-in-the-Fields, numerous country houses and collegiate buildings, including the Radcliffe Library at Oxford. By the early 1720s he had designed several of the most important new monuments in Westminster Abbey. The figures on the Duke of Newcastle's tomb (1714–23) were carved by Francis Bird (1667–1731), an Englishman who had also trained in Rome before 1700 under the leading baroque sculptor of the period, Pierre Le Gros the younger. But Bird had limited technical ability and lacked imagination; a rival sculptor, Peter Scheemakers (1691–1781) "spoke slightingly" of him and told Lord Harley, who paid for Newcastle's monument, that "there was indeed a great deal of fine marble which was well, but there was such figures that disgracd it, that to do right, his Lordship shoud take them away".[2] So Rysbrack's appearance in London in 1720 must have been especially welcome.

In 1723 Vertue hinted that Gibbs had patronised the sculptor only "for his own advantage not for Encouragement". He reported a conversation with "poor" Rysbrack who "told me of his [Gibbs'] extravagant exactions on his labour that he coud not possibly live had not other busines come in to help him of more proffit". Vertue cited the case of Matthew Prior's monument (1721) in Poets' Corner, which Gibbs had chosen Rysbrack to carve (fig. 1). He offered Rysbrack "no more than 35 pounds" for each of the two principal statues "when others have above a hundred pounds, & Gibbs is to have . . . upwards of a hundred pounds for each". Vertue considered this "an unreasonable gripeing usage to a most Ingenious Artist".[3] Nevertheless, the commission had brought both immediate and enormous success:

> While Gibbs displays his elegant Design
> And Rysbracks Art does in the Sculpture shine
> With due composure, & proportion just
> adding new lustre to the finish't Bust
> Each Artist here, perpetuates his Name
> And shares with Prior, an Immortal Fame.[4]

Of their other early collaborations, much less is known. A sketch by Rysbrack of the 5th Earl of

fig. 1 Monument to Matthew Prior in Westminster Abbey, plate CXII in Gibbs' *Book of Architecture*, 1728.

fig. 2 "A Design for a Monument for His Grace the late Duke of *Buckingham*", plate CXVI in Gibbs' *Book of Architecture*, 1728.

17

fig. 3 Monument to William Hilliard by Thomas Paty in the Lord Mayor's Chapel, Bristol, *circa* 1750.

Exeter's monument in St. Martin's, Stamford, designed and carved (1704) in Rome by Pierre-Etienne Monnot (Cat. No. 38), resembles so closely the composition Gibbs proposed for the Duke of Buckingham's monument in Westminster Abbey (1721–2, unexecuted; fig. 2) that it is reasonable to suggest that Rysbrack had been employed to record the work for him[5] and, furthermore, that this was one of Gibbs' methods of building up his repertory of forms. Like most of his drawings Rysbrack's sketch is more accomplished and lively than those of his English contemporaries. By 1723 he had also carved Gibbs' Westminster Abbey monuments to John Smith and to Ben Jonson, whose bust in relief is of "great Spirit, Ease, and Happiness".[6] These were followed in 1727–8 by the monuments to Dr John Freind and to Katherina Bovey of Flaxley in Gloucestershire (one of the founders of The Three Choirs Festival), which Gibbs described as having "Figures . . . very well handled by Mr. *Rysbrack*."[7] During these years he supplied a set of historical portrait busts, including one of William III, for Gibbs' building in the celebrated landscape garden at Stowe in Buckinghamshire.[8] Rysbrack also executed portraits of the architect in terracotta and marble (Cat. No. 10). The success of the partnership is demonstrated by the purchase of houses in St. Marylebone, where they lived in considerable splendour and carried on their respective businesses. So, in 1725, for example, we find Gibbs, who lived at the corner of Wimpole Street and Henrietta Street, giving directions to Alexander Pope, of whom he wished to have a portrait carved in marble that "Mr Rysbracks house is in the further end of Bond street Just cross Tyburn Rode in Lord Oxfords ground upon the right hand, going to his Chaple".[9] The sculptor subscribed to *A Book of Architecture* and the two men, bound further by their interests in collecting works of art and, albeit secretly, their adherence to Roman Catholicism, later appear together in Gawen Hamilton's 'Club of Artists' (Cat. No. 1).

Their commissions for church monuments came from various sources. Among the most lucrative were those from the governors and staff of St. Bartholomew's Hospital in Smithfield, London, where Gibbs served as a governor himself from 1723, and as architect for the rebuilding from 1728 to his death twenty-six years later. John Freind was a celebrated physician there and Humphry Parsons, who was elected a governor in 1727, was the son-in-law of Sir Ambrose and Lady Mary Crowley, for whom Gibbs designed a wall tablet with double profile portraits (sculptor unrecorded) in Mitcham church, Surrey, sometime after 1727–8 (Cat. No. 14). Francis Colston, who was elected a governor in the same year as Gibbs, and Thomas Edwards, who followed several years later, together commissioned the monument to their kinsman, Edward Colston, the great Bristol philanthropist, who had also served as a Bart's governor and at his death in 1721, at the age of eighty-five, had bequeathed £500 to the hospital. The Colston monument in All Saints', Bristol (Cat. No. 8) is not only Gibbs' most important achievement in this field outside London but provides a particularly complete picture of the complicated activities involved in designing, carving and erecting a major monument in the early Georgian period (figs. 4 and 5).

Although in his will Colston requested burial "without any manner of Pomp or Ostentation"[10] as befits the Augustan humanitarian, his heirs erected a tomb which is larger and more splendid, both in design and materials, than the conventional wall tablets previously set up by the family. And, since the commission came several years after his death, Rysbrack, who had been selected to carve the effigy, probably began by preparing the life-size terracotta bust, now in the City of Bristol Museum and Art Gallery (Cat. No. 6).

fig. 4 Monument to Edward Colston, 1728–9, All Saints Church, Bristol.

Rysbrack's terracotta bust is one of his early masterpieces; the pliable, warm-coloured clay is modelled with that remarkable combination of authority, sensitivity and alertness which confirms a contemporary verdict that "his superior meritt to other Sculptors is very aparent in his Modells of portraits . . . none equallizing for truth of Likeness and property of ornaments or head dress".[11] Although, unfortunately, no document has come to light to suggest when the bust was made, it bears a close resemblance to the marble portrait of Gibbs (1726), which Vertue proclaimed "extreamly like" (Cat. No. 10), and even more to the terracotta bust (dated February 1727) of the elderly Richard Miller (Queen's College, Oxford), a benefactor of St. Martin-in-the-Fields' Charity School, and has an almost identical treatment of the full-bottomed wig and casually-buttoned shirt.[12] This group of early portraits shows both Rysbrack's debt to the Flemish baroque tradition of his teacher, Michel van der Voort (1667–1737), and also the beginning of a new, livelier and more naturalistic direction in English portrait sculpture.[13] This development was to have astonishing success and R. Campbell was accurate in reporting in *The London Tradesman* in 1747 that the "Taste of Busts . . . prevails much of late Years, and in some measure interferes with Portrait Painting: The Nobility now effect to have their Busts done that Way rather than sit for their Pictures".[14]

For the recumbent effigy of Colston, Rysbrack 'adjusted' the terracotta bust merely by turning the head slightly downward and adding a neck tie. In 1728 Gibbs and Rysbrack again experimented with this pose, the figure now set against a more elaborate architectural background, in the monument to Sir Edward Seymour at Maiden Bradley in Wiltshire (Cat. No. 13); and independently Rysbrack used it in Dean Drelincourt's monument in Armagh Cathedral.[15] The relaxed quality of the figures owes something to French taste. François Girardon's famous tomb of Cardinal Richelieu in the Church of the Sorbonne (1675–94) was particularly admired by British artists; the painter, Joseph Highmore, on a trip to Paris in 1734, thought it "the finest piece of sculpture I have ever yet seen", adding that "ye print of it is known".[16] Significantly, copies were owned both by Rysbrack, who later turned again to Girardon in connection with the equestrian statue of William III at Bristol, and by Gibbs. Colston, however, is portrayed in the everyday clothes of the modest, secular philanthropist, his right hand placed gently against his breast. This imbues the figure with directness and an absence of pomposity which, although not universally admired – Lady Luxborough told William Shenstone of The Leasowes that she "cannot like Mr. Coulston's dress and full-bottomed wig on a tomb"[17] – was evidently the message intended to be conveyed to the congregation and visitors. In an unusual, popular engraving issued in 1751, two groups of figures, representing Charity and the succoured poor, pay homage to Colston's beneficences, which are listed in detail on the monument (Cat. No. 9).

Gibbs illustrated his design in *A Book of Architecture* (Cat. No. 8), which was published in May 1728, where it is referred to as "now making". The white marble effigy and *putti* were almost certainly carved in Rysbrack's studio in London and then transported by sea; perhaps not coincidentally, the governors of St. Bartholomew's opened negotiations in 1730 with the Bath entrepreneur and philanthropist, Ralph Allen, for the shipment of huge quantities of stone needed for rebuilding the hospital, via Bristol, where the docks then came to within a short distance of All Saints'.[18]

Meanwhile, the black-and-white-veined marble tomb-chest and beautiful Ionic columns and pediment surrounding the effigy were being carved in Bristol by a local mason named Michael Sidnell, who signed the work "SIDNELL BRISTOL Fecit 1729". Little is known about him. Made a burgess in 1718, he signed a number of local monuments, assisted Thomas Paty at Redland Chapel and independently built Westbury Court in Gloucestershire; although declared a bankrupt in 1742 he was well enough established by 1728 to have subscribed four guineas for a copy of *A Book of Architecture*.[19] His links with Rysbrack are especially apparent in the wall monument to Thomas Edwards (died 1727), one of Colston's executors, and Jane Edwards (died 1733) in St. James's church (fig. 30), which clearly derives from Rysbrack's monument to Andrew Innys (1726) in St. John-on-the-Wall (fig. 29). Even more interesting is the wall tablet to Mary Edwards, who died in 1736 and was also buried in St. James's (fig. 31); it is copied from Plate 123, left, in *A Book of Architecture* (Cat. No. 11). For some reason this design also attracted other sculptors besides Rysbrack.

The Colston commission firmly established Rysbrack's reputation in the West Country, as the great variety of his later works in this exhibition shows. The Seymour monument, for example, was praised as "beautiful" by a popular London weekly, the *Grub-Street Journal*.[20] In Thomas Paty's monument to William Hilliard (died 1735) in the Lord Mayor's Chapel at Bristol (*circa* 1750, fig. 3), a fine Rysbrack-like portrait bust is set against an ambitious

fig. 5   The effigy of Edward Colston from his monument in All Saints' Church, Bristol.

architectural background inspired by the Westminster Abbey monument to Matthew Prior (fig. 1), which appears as Plate 112 in *A Book of Architecture*. So both Gibbs' and Rysbrack's influence persisted in the region.[21]

However, by the time the Colston monument was erected in about 1729, the two men had parted professionally. Gibbs devoted less energy to monuments; the designs in his book were serving their purpose as being "of use to such Gentlemen as might be concerned in Building, especially in the remote parts of the Country, where little or no assistance for Designs can be procured [and] which may be executed by any Workman who understands Lines".[22] At the same time Rysbrack's brilliance as both a carver and independent designer was becoming increasingly apparent.

[1] Vertue, I, p. 76, and "from the time of his first comeing . . . [Gibbs] has much imployd him" (III, p. 17). The information relating to Gibbs is taken from the author's forthcoming book; for a brief life and list of works, see Colvin, 1978, *A Biographical Dictionary of British Architects 1600–1840*, pp. 337–45.

[2] Vertue, III, p. 108. The Newcastle monument is in Gibbs' *A Book of Architecture* (1728) p. xxii, pl. 111, and Whinney, 1964, *Sculpture in Britain 1530 to 1830*, pp. 77–8.

[3] Vertue, III, p. 17.

[4] Vertue, III, p. 21 (1724). The "finish't Bust" of Prior is by Antoine Coysevox.

[5] Gibbs, *op. cit.*, p. xxiii, pl. 116; see also Cat. No. 44.

[6] *The London and Westminster Guide, Through the Cities and Suburbs* (1768) p. 55. Gibbs, *op. cit.*, pls. 122 centre, 124 middle.

[7] Gibbs, *op. cit.*, p. xxiii, pl. 115.

[8] By 1735 transferred to Kent's Temple of British Worthies in the Elysian Fields: P. Willis, 1977, *Charles Bridgeman and the English Landscape Garden*, pls. 135, 153.

[9] G. Sherburn, 1956, *The Correspondence of Alexander Pope*, II, p. 298. The Oxford or Marylebone Chapel, now St. Peter's, Vere Street, was designed by Gibbs in 1721–4, (Gibbs, 1728, *op. cit.*, pp. vii–viii, pls. 24 and 25). The bust, 1729–30, in The Athenaeum, London, is discussed in W. K. Wimsatt, 1965, *The Portraits of Alexander Pope*, pp. 97–106.

[10] H. J. Wilkins, 1920, *Edward Colston: A Chronological Account of His Life and Work . . .*, p. 136.

[11] Vertue, III, p. 84 (1738).

[12] Rysbrack's marble bust of Miller is in St. Martin's Vestry Hall; J. P. Malcolm, 1807, *Londinium Redivivum; or, an Ancient History and Modern description of London* IV, p. 195; K. Esdaile, June 1944, The so-called aged Wren, *Architectural Review*, pp. 142–3; M. I. Webb, 1954, *Michael Rysbrack, Sculptor*, pp. 53–4, 221, pls. 16 and 17.

[13] H. Gerson & E. H. Ter Kuile, 1960, *Art and Architecture in Belgium 1600 to 1800*, pp. 42–3, pls. 26 and 27; Brussels: Musée d'Art Ancien, 1977, *La sculpture au siècle de Rubens dans les Pays-Bas meridionaux et la principauté de Liège*, pp. 219–42. Rysbrack owned "Two figures, of *Religion* and *Lucretia*, by Mr. Vandervoort" (British Library, *A Catalogue Of the Genuine, Large and Curious Collection of Models, &c. of Mr. Michael Rysbrack*, 25 January 1766, p. 5, lot 37) and "A *Layman* as large as life, by Mr. *Vandervoort*," (Messrs Colnaghi, *A Catalogue Of the Curious and Well-chosen Collection of Plaster Figures, Heads, Hands, &c. of Mr. Michael Rysbrack*, 18 April 1767, lot 86).

[14] R. Campbell, 1747, *The London Tradesman* (reprinted in facsimile, 1969), p. 139.

[15] H. Potterton, 1975, *Irish Church Monuments 1570–1880*, p. 76, fig. 40.

[16] E. Johnston, 1970, Joseph Highmore's Paris Journal, 1734, *Walpole Society*, Vol. XLII, p. 73. Lot 16 of *A Catalogue of the Capital and Entire Collection of Prints, Drawings, and Books of Prints, of Mr Michael Rysbrack*, Langfords', 16 February 1764, was "Cardinal *Richelieu's* tomb, by *Girardon*".

[17] H. Knight, 1775, *Letters Written By the Late Right Honourable Lady Luxborough, To William Shenstone, Esq.*, p, 167 (1749).

[18] B. Boyce, 1967, *The Benevolent Man, A Life of Ralph Allen of Bath*, pp. 40–5.

[19] Colvin, *op. cit.*, p. 735; Little, Jenner and Gomme, 1979, *Bristol, an architectural history*, p. 439; R. Gunnis, 1953, *Dictionary of British Sculptors 1660–1851*, p. 351; A. Wilson, 1976, Rysbrack in Bristol, *Apollo*, CIII, p. 24.

[20] No. 56, 28 January 1731, p. 2.

[21] Gunnis, *op. cit.*, pp. 294–5; W. Ison, 1952, *The Georgian Buildings of Bristol*, pp. 11, 41. William Cole mentions Rysbrack's work in Bristol in 1735 and the William III equestrian statue in 1768 (BL, Add. MSS. 5957 fo. 3v, 5842 fo. 128v, respectively).

[22] Gibbs, *op. cit*, p. i.

William III, Queen Square, Bristol, 1731–1736

Katharine Eustace

"This prince, like most of those in our annals, contributed nothing to the advancement of arts"; this harsh judgement was made of William III (1650–1702) by Horace Walpole in 1763. He went on to declare: "In England he met with nothing but disgusts. He understood little of the nation . . . Reserved, unsociable, ill in his health, and sowered by his situation",[1] for William III was not a popular King. It is all the more remarkable therefore that this much maligned monarch should, after his death, have become the subject of numerous public monuments of which the one in Queen Square is surely the finest.

This change of attitude is a reflection of the extraordinary complexity of politics in the early eighteenth century, politics which were entirely coloured by religion, for, as Trevelyan put it, "religious differences were the motive force behind political passions".[2] Nowhere was this more true than in Bristol, which at the end of the seventeenth and beginning of the eighteenth centuries, was the mirror image of Tawney's "bourgeois republic", a city state. The oligarchy was superficially Whig, that is to say, in the very simplest terms, it was Low Church to the point of non-conformity, and had supported the Hanoverian succession. Latimer, the nineteenth-century Bristol historian, therefore interpreted the commissioning of an equestrian statue to William III, as a demonstration of loyalty by the Whig merchants.[3] It would appear, however, that the affair was much more complex, for all the individuals who can be associated with the commission seem to have been Tories or members of the Church Party. Party loyalties were not, however, rigidly adhered to and Walpole's Excise Bill of 1733 was equally disliked by Tory and Whig merchants whose import trade it so affected.

Tawney suggested that the loyalties of cities continued to be suspect for a generation.[4] The commissioning of the equestrian statue of William III may well have been a demonstration of loyalty. Bristol's common council proceedings are full of petitions of loyalty at this period, such as that of 3 April 1723 "to congratulate Your Majesty on the Happy discovery of the most detestable Conspiracy against your person and Government",[5] or on occasions such as the

fig. 6   Queen Square, Bristol, from William Halfpenny's *Perspective Made Easy, circa* 1730.

fig. 7   William III, bronze, erected 1736, Queen Square, Bristol.

marriage of the Prince of Wales in 1736.[6] There were constant alarms of invasion and though the merchants may not have cared for the Hanoverians, the dynasty did represent stability and continuity, and was without taint of catholicism. The petitions are full of such phrases as "Bigotted popish ffugitive" and the "Abjured popish Pretender", for such matters were "Injurious to Trade".[7] George II on his accession in 1727 was exhorted to "maintain those valuable blessings, the Religion, Laws and liberties of this Nation . . .".[8] When the Prince of Wales visited the city on 11 November 1738 he declared: "This great City may always depend upon my particular Wishes for its prosperity, and the advancement of its Trade, which is so Valuable an Effect of Liberty, and so strong a Support to the Honour, and Happiness of this Nation".[9]

The inscription on Buck's engraved 'Prospect of Bristol' (1734) reads: "This City is most valuable for it's extensive Trade, to all Parts of the World; in which it exceeds, all other Cities and Towns in Great Britain, except London . . . it appears to be a Place full of rich and Industrious People."[10] Bristol built itself a Council House in 1702, a Custom House in 1712, St. Mark's was designated the Mayor's Chapel and restored in 1722, and in 1740 work began on the new Exchange. All visitors to Bristol commented on the similarity of the city to London and this was due to the merchants' desire to display a magnificence worthy of the second city in the Kingdom.[11] Bristol had its state coach, sword and scabbard and a mayoral chain. One of the chief manifestations of civic pride was the development of Queen Square which, as later guide books proudly recorded, was, at seven and a quarter acres, the largest in England, excepting only Lincolns Inn Fields. In the 1720s it looked rather bleak and open (fig. 6) but by the end of the century it was to be much admired for its leafy walks (fig. 14). This was the outcome of corporation policy and as early as 1705 a committee had been appointed to consider the area which had formerly been called the Marsh, and the inhabitants were ordered to clear it of timber "and all other nuisances".[12] The Square had its own keeper whose salary was paid by the Chamber,[13] and the lighting was to be at the expense of the Chamber where elsewhere it was to be at that of the householders.[14] It was the site, too, of the New Custom House.[15] Many of the inhabitants of the new and handsomely-built houses were aldermen and members of the common council; their names appear regularly on the corporation rent rolls as tenants. The city's accounts show regular payments for planting trees,[16] for gravelling, and for painting the railings. What more fitting place to raise an equestrian statue, a form of monument which had for so long been a symbol of the struggle of Christianity against paganism (see Cat. No. 27) and which had later been revived as a symbol of civic liberties and civic pride.[17] While London argued the merits of equestrian statues, metropolitan rivalries encouraged Bristolians.[18] The sense of competition is very well expressed in a poem of 1731 addressed by one Bispham Dickinson to the Mayor and common council, which ends:

> *BRISTOL, thy Fame should be the Poets Theme*
> *Since thou art influenc'd by a power Supreme,*
> *Henceforth let London blush whilst Bristol shines,*
> *And all the World applaud their great designs;*
> *BRISTOL, thy Wealth does no such Honour bring*
> *As will the Statue of so great a King.*[19]

figs. 8 and 9   Details of the statue of William III, Queen Square, Bristol.

The circumstances surrounding the actual commissioning of the statue from Rysbrack and the raising of the subscription to pay for it are obscure. On 4 December 1731 a memorial "Subscribed by a great Number of Gentlemen" was produced and read in the Chamber. The form of proceeding was not the usual form of motion moved by the Mayor.[20] The Chamber agreed to allow the statue to be erected in Queen Square, and to contribute to "so agreeable a Design", though not the thousand pounds at first suggested. On 14 December, Thomas Freke was proposing a statue of George II to the Society of Merchants; it was turned down but money was to be forthcoming for the statue of William III already proposed by the corporation.[21] On 6 May 1732 Alderman Becher argued that three members of the house should be chosen to join a committee, together with three others from the Society of Merchants and three of the subscribers.[22] James Stewart in a footnote to his history suggests that the memorialists were none other than the Mayor and corporation.[23] A long piece of verse entitled *Queen Elizabeth's Ghost* and purporting to come from the "Free-Women" of Bristol, mocks the "ungrateful Town" for choosing "Great Nassau" instead of Elizabeth; it suggests a venal interest on the part of Aldermen Becher, Taylor, Fry and Elton, particularly the first-named who had an interest in Bristol's brass works.[24]

The man behind the undertaking, or at least the man with the organisational ability and financial expertise, would appear to have been John Elbridge, "Treasurer to King Williams Statue".[25] Born at Pemaquid or Penequid in what was then Essex, Massachusetts, he was sent to England with his sister Elizabeth to live with a cousin, Thomas Moore, Controller of the Customs in Bristol. Descended on his mother's side from the Aldworths, he owned one of the great sugar houses that refined the cane from family plantations in Jamaica. It is not clear when he himself went into the Custom House, but at his death in 1738 he was Deputy Controller, Receiver of the Society of Merchants' duties of Wharfage and Tonnage, and a very rich man; on his own calculation he left £77,669.3.4.[26] Like Edward Colston (see Cat. No. 6), he was inspired by a charitable and missionary zeal for his own city. The books listed in the inventory to his well-appointed house in the Royal Fort in 1738 are indicative of his attitudes: *The Whole Duty of Man, Grounds and Reasons for the Christian Religion, The Cause of Decay of Christian Piety*, to cite but three.[27] He founded a school on St. Michael's Hill for twenty-four poor girls who were to be taught the principles of the "Christian Protestant Religion".[28] On 7 January 1736 he was elected Treasurer at the second meeting of the subscribers to the British Infirmary, which took place at the Council House.[29] According to Richard Smith, the historian of the Infirmary, most of the furnishing of the new institution was at his own expense. Until 1780 it was called "Elbridge's Ward", and the first and all subsequent annual sermons were addressed to him.[30] He left £5,000 to the Infirmary in his will. He nominated Dean Creswicke, who was also behind the foundation of the Infirmary, John Scrope, the Whig MP, and Recorder of Bristol, John Cossins of Redland (see Cat. No. 15), as executors to his will, and left substantial sums of money to these, his "good Friends".[31]

That John Elbridge and John Cossins were friends is a very important piece of information. It may explain a great deal about the choice of Rysbrack as the sculptor for the equestrian monument. The earliest work by Rysbrack in Bristol is signed and dated 1726. It is the monument to Andrew Innys in St. John the Baptist (figs. 28 and 29). Innys was Cossins' father-in-law and Cossins, his wife and two brothers-in-law were sitting to Rysbrack at just this

28

fig. 10 Detail of the statue of William III, Queen Square, Bristol.

fig. 11   Detail of the statue of William III, Queen Square, Bristol.

fig. 12   William III, marble, *circa* 1736, Yale Center for British Art, Paul Mellon Collection.

time (see Cat. Nos. 15, 16, 18, and 19), while Jeremy Innys was a past-master of the Merchant Venturers'. Elbridge did business with the Edwards family (Cat. No. 11) and as a Custom House official would almost certainly have known the Town Clerk, Henry Blaake (Cat. No. 32), who died just as the idea for an equestrian statue gathered momentum.

Nothing is known of the competition for the commission other than what Vertue recorded in August 1732:

> The Moddels of King William on horseback being some time in hand & partys animating the Artists to out vie each other. one was made being the larger by Mr Rysbrack. and an other by Mr Schemaker – both the Moddels or casts guilt with Gold [see Cat. No. 25], being first Viewd by judges of Art & horses was sent to Bristol. where the Subscribers for erecting this Equestrian Statue. had collected about 2000 pounds to pay the expence of it.[32]

Vertue was very optimistic about the sum raised by subscribers. Beyond council proceedings, very few papers have survived which tell us anything about the progress of the subscription, and the work of the committee. The list of subscribers referred to in council proceedings has not survived. Aldermen and councillors were frequently Merchant Venturers as well, and because the economy of the city was highly complicated, it is difficult to relate loans between individuals and the city, to specific projects. Only one set of vouchers has survived for payments for the statue. On 25 August 1733 the Chamberlain is instructed to pay John Elbridge £500 "towards the erecting a publick Equestrian Statue of our Great and Glorious Deliverer the late King William the Third."[33] In 1734 the Merchant Venturers' accounts record the payment of £300 to John Elbridge, towards the statue.[34] That was not the end of the subscription. Vertue noted in 1735 that "it was expected on account of his extraordinary care. & skill. and several losses. by casting – the Bristolians woud have made him a voluntary present. over and above the contract. but no such thing. was done."[35] The reason that no present was forthcoming was not that the Bristolians did not recognise the quality of their monument but that they were having difficulty raising the original sum. On 25 September 1736 Lyonel Lyde, the Mayor, informed the Chamber that the equestrian statue was erected in Queen Square "in the handsomest manner & as he believed to everybodies' satisfaction", and then appealed for a further contribution as the balance outstanding was £709.10.3.[36] After some demur the Chamber agreed to pay a further £500, on the advice of a special committee.[37] The City Audit records the payment to John Elbridge in 1737, "toward defraying the Expense of Erecting the Equestrian statue".[38] The year before, the Merchant Venturers' had paid a further £200 to Lyonel Lyde "towards finishing King Williams Statue".[39]

The making of the statue is almost as ill-documented as its commissioning. We have nothing to match Mariette's description, published in 1768, of the casting of the equestrian statue of Louis XV, though from that, we can understand it to have been a considerable undertaking.[40] Vertue's mention of losses in casting and the fact that Scheemakers had finished a similar commission in "a composite hard mettal Lead pewter &c",[41] which had been set up in Hull two years earlier suggests that bronze, as well as being "the rarest and costliest of all materials at all periods" was also the most difficult to cast. Vertue is again our informer. In 1733 he records that "the great Model" was begun on 1 May and "finisht in Clay horse and Man. and cast in plaster of Paris. and Sett up in his work house. on Aug. 1."; he adds "much approvd on.

and by the Criticks skilfull in that Art thought to be the best statue ever made in England".[42] In 1734 he tells us that on 1 August "the brass horse Cast all at once. that is, all the horse (excepting the tail) and the leggs of the figure on each side of the horse. the statue it Self being cast before as far as the middle down to the thighs".[43]

The finished statue differs little from the model (Cat. No. 25), save in one important respect: William III no longer wears a victor's crown of laurels. His rival Scheemakers' 'William III' (fig. 13) wears a laurel wreath, as does Cheere's version at Petersfield. Rysbrack must have changed his mind very late for a bust of William III, now at Yale (fig. 12), probably done at about the same time, has a laurel wreath. Perhaps he felt it created a rather absurd air, as it certainly does on Rastrelli's 'Peter the Great' in Leningrad; perhaps it was difficult to cast satisfactorily. Whatever the reason, his solution of an athlete's headband is simply and elegantly effective. Though Vertue records the model as gilt there is no evidence that the finished statue was ever gilded, unlike Cheere's 'William III' at Petersfield which was gilded until well into the nineteenth century, and Scheemakers' version at Hull which is gilt to this day.

The London *General Evening Post* reported in 1735 "Yesterday [Monday 7 July] the famous Equestrian statue of King William the Third cast in Brass by Mr. Rysbrack, the famous Statuary, was put on board Ship in the River in order to be carried to Bristol".[44] Queen Caroline had been specially to see it less than a month before.[45] There was a postscript to the casting and erecting of the statue. In 1749 it was reported to be in need of repair.[46] The Town Clerk was instructed to "write to Mr. Rysbrach and acquaint him with the Defects in that Statue that the

fig. 13   William III, gilded metal, erected 1734, by Peter Scheemakers, Kingston-upon-Hull.

same are of such a kind as if not soon remedyed will absolutely ruin a Statue which well deserves to be as lasting as it is elegant and beautiful: that it is expected some care be taken about this affair because the present condition of the Statue is a Standing Reflection not only upon the Gentlemen who were at a considerable Expence in paying for Erecting this Statue but also upon the Statuary himself that the work is not Substantially executed."[47] The city was then at some expense to have it restored,[48] and today the statue is in remarkably good condition.

fig. 14   Queen Square, Bristol, from the north-west corner showing the statue of William III and the spire of St. Mary Redcliffe; watercolour by T. L. S. Rowbotham, 1827, City of Bristol Museum and Art Gallery.

1. Walpole, 1763, III, pp. 105–6.
2. Trevelyan, 1942, p. 329.
3. Latimer, 1893, pp. 178–9.
4. Tawney, 1922 (Pelican edn 1948), pp. 202–5.
5. B.R.O. Common Council Proceedings, 1722–38, fo. 17
6. *Ibid.*, fo. 425.
7. *Ibid.*, fo. 127.
8. *Ibid.*, fo. 135.
9. *Ibid.*, fo. 552.
10. 'The South East Prospect of The City of Bristol', engraved by S. and N. Buck, 1734. (City of Bristol Museum and Art Galley, Mb 378).
11. Ralph, 1973, p. 22.
12. B.R.O. C.C.P., 1702–22, fo. 95.
13. *Ibid.*, fo. 122.
14. B.R.O. C.C.P., 1738–45, fo. 10.
15. *Ibid.*, fo. 221.
16. *Ibid.*, fo. 276.
17. Panofsky, 1964, pp. 83–5.
18. For a discussion of the controversy that surrounded the erection of an equestrian statue of William III, see Glen Taylor's thesis (1981) towards a degree in Fine and Decorative Arts at Leeds University.
19. Quoted by James Stewart (see Cat. No. 23), 1733, MS. 'History of the Famous City and Port of Bristol', Vol. 1, fo. 167: Bodleian Library, Oxford, Gough MSS, 'Somerset 2'.
20. B.R.O. C.C.P. 1722–38, fo. 265.
21. A.C.R.L. Microfilm: Merchants' Hall Books of Proceedings, Book 4.
22. B.R.O. C.C.P. 1722–38, fo. 276.
23. Stewart, 1733, fo. 166: Bodleian, Gough MSS, 'Somerset 2'.
24. S.R.O. DD/S/WH Box 59. Another version is in the Bodleian, and Jonathan Barry suggests it may be by Alexander Catcott.
25. B.R.O. Vouchers, 1797 Box.
26. B.R.O. AC/WO 10 (15) j.
27. B.R.O. AC/WO 18.
28. B.R.O. 28049(25).
29. Smith MS. II, p. 13.
30. *Ibid.*, II, p. 138.
31. B.R.O. AC/WO 10 (14) b.
32. Vertue, III, p. 61.
33. B.R.O. C.C.P. 1722–38, fo. 329.
34. I am grateful to Miss Elizabeth Ralph, Honorary Archivist to the Merchant Venturers', for this information.
35. Vertue, III, p. 76.
36. B.R.O. C.C.P. 1722–38, fos. 446–7.
37. *Ibid.*, fo. 455.
38. B.R.O. 04026(105), fo. 65.
39. I am grateful to Miss Ralph for this information.
40. Mariette, P.J., 1768, *passim*.
41. Vertue, III, p. 72.
42. Vertue, III, p. 66.
43. *Ibid.*, p. 72.
44. B.M., Burney 313b.
45. Vertue, III, p. 75; 11 June, *Daily Journal*; 10–12 June, *General Evening Post*; B.M. Burney 309b.
46. B.R.O. C.C.P., 1745–54, fos. 90/100 and 116a.
47. B.R.O. Proceeding of Mayor and Aldermen, 04418(1) fo. 31.
48. B.R.O. Vouchers, 1750 Box, Voucher No. 202.

Sculpture for Palladian Interiors: Rysbrack's reliefs and their setting

Malcolm Baker

Charles Rogers, who visited Rysbrack in his old age, concludes his account of the sculptor's achievement, by asserting that "none of his works merit greater attention than his Basso-relievos & Models in Clay, which will be esteemed by every one who is sensible of true Elegance & the Beauties of the Antique".[1] Although Rysbrack's terracotta models are highly regarded today, the reliefs are not usually given the same attention and, as a genre of sculpture, have been neglected in favour of the sculptor's monuments and portrait busts. Nevertheless they constitute a substantial part of Rysbrack's work and illustrate many of the essential characteristics of his style.

The reliefs were of course intended for use in an architectural context, either set in walls above doorways or placed above chimney-pieces. In subject and composition they vary from copies of antique reliefs (Cat. No. 81) to adaptations of baroque sources and new inventions by the sculptor himself (fig. 15). Although Rysbrack executed such work throughout his long career, the majority of surviving examples date from the early years, during the 1720s and early 30s. The earliest is the 'Roman Marriage' in the Cupola Room at Kensington Palace, commissioned in January 1723;[2] this was followed by the series of classical reliefs at Houghton Hall, Norfolk (1726–30, fig. 17), the chimney-pieces at Elm Grove, Roehampton, Surrey (*circa* 1725), the East India Office (completed in 1729, fig. 15), Clandon Park, Surrey (1731–5, fig. 19), Godmersham Park, Kent (*circa* 1735), the Foundling Hospital (*circa* 1746) and the classical subjects at Woburn Abbey, Bedfordshire (1755).[3]

When Rysbrack came to England about 1720 he evidently arrived as a mature artist with a thorough training in the Antwerp workshop of Michel van der Voort. This training would have made him familiar with the strong tradition of relief sculpture in the Netherlands that was obviously well developed in the work of Giambologna's master, Jacques Dubroeucq, in the mid-sixteenth century and was continued in the sculpture carved by the Antwerp-born Artus Quellien and his assistants for the Town Hall in Amsterdam.[4] Quellien's work at Amsterdam, which formed the most celebrated sculptural complex – the garden figures of Versailles excepted – in northern Europe during the later seventeenth century, was well known to Rysbrack. His sale catalogues show that he owned not only engravings[5] of all these reliefs but also terracotta casts of a number of them.[6]

Like van der Voort, Quellien drew on two traditions in seventeenth-century Flemish sculpture: on the one hand, the rich baroque manner based on Rubens and best exemplified by the work of Lucas Faydherbe and, on the other, the style developed in France from a close study of antique sculpture by François Duquesnoy and introduced into the north by his brother Jerome.[7] Elements of both can be seen in Rysbrack's own style and his reliefs in particular show an indebtedness to Quellien. The debt to this Flemish tradition is especially evident in the relief made for the East India Office (fig. 15). The *putti* on the left are of a type associated with

Duquesnoy while the figure of the recumbent Neptune, the female allegories standing with camel and lion and the figure on the left bending to lift a bale, all derive from the 'Four Continents' relief on the back pediment of the Amsterdam Town Hall.[8] The relationship between the main figures in high relief and the delicately executed details of ship and landscape in the background, similarly recalls Quellien's handling of the relief form.

Rysbrack's thorough training as a baroque artist in the Flemish tradition is also suggested by the engraved works in his own collection, the sale catalogue of which lists an impressively comprehensive range of sixteenth- and seventeenth-century pictorial sources. These engravings were frequently used as sources for reliefs. The 'Sacrifice' scene above one of the chimney-pieces at Clandon, for example, is freely adapted from Pietro da Cortona's painting in the Pinacoteca, Rome[9] while the 'Choice of Hercules' relief at Carlton Towers, Yorkshire[10] (for which a drawing survives in the Victoria and Albert Museum[11] and a terracotta model was included in the 1767 sale catalogue[12]) is taken from Annibale Carracci's composition in the Palazzo Farnese. Elsewhere Rysbrack draws on Poussin and Polidoro da Caravaggio[13] who decorated the facades of many sixteenth-century Roman *palazzi* with scenes of classical sacrifices and processions. In the range of his sources Rysbrack provides an interesting parallel to another Flemish sculptor, Francis van Bossuit (1635–1692) whose ivory carvings are frequently based on similar compositions, although he, unlike Rysbrack, apparently knew the originals at first hand.[14] It is significant, however, that Rysbrack's choice is marked by a predilection for the more classicising

fig. 15   Chimney-piece, East India Office (now Commonwealth Relations Office), London, completed 1729.

fig. 16   Plate LXXIII (reversed) from Montfaucon's *Antiquity Explained* II, 1721.

of sixteenth- and seventeenth-century artists, and exuberant baroque compositions such as the East India Office chimney-piece remain exceptional.

Many of Rysbrack's reliefs were indeed based directly on antique reliefs known to the sculptor through the engravings of Perrier, Bisschop, Montfaucon and Bartoli all of whom are listed in his sale catalogues. In the Stone Hall at Houghton, for example, the 'Sacrifice of a Bull' (fig. 19) is based on Montfaucon's *L'Antiquité Expliquée* (fig. 16) of which Rysbrack owned the English edition of 1721, while the source for the terracotta model of another 'Sacrifice' at Stourhead (Cat. No. 82) was Bartoli's engraving (Cat. No. 85) of a relief on the Arch of Constantine which was included in the first edition of Bellori's *Admiranda Romanorum Antiquitatum*.[15]

These classical reliefs were conceived very much as part of the interiors in which they were placed and the architect, rather than the sculptor, was probably responsible for the choice of subject and composition as well as the setting. This is certainly suggested by a sketch in William Kent's hand, dated 1726, for the chimney-piece in the Stone Hall at Houghton, showing essentially the same composition as that carved by Rysbrack. Reliefs of this type were employed in some of the most impressive and influential interiors by Campbell, Leoni and Kent and their use in such a context appears to be quite new. Bas-reliefs of baroque subjects were of course often placed in architectural settings during the seventeenth century.[16] But although antique reliefs were well-known and much admired they seem only rarely to have formed part of an architectural interior[17] until later in the eighteenth century as when for example, in the 1760s Marchionni set the famous 'Antinous' relief above a chimney-piece in the Villa Albani.[18] The use of reliefs copying antique compositions as a prominent and integral part of a domestic interior would appear to be an innovation of the English Palladians in which Rysbrack was closely involved.

A precedent for employing reliefs in an interior could be found in Palladio's *Architecture* which appeared in Leoni's English edition in 1715–16.[19] An interest in the use of reliefs in interiors is however already seen in a drawing of 1711 by William Talman which includes at least one relief by Edward Pearce.[20] Fourteen years later Colen Campbell, in Volume III of his *Vitruvius Britannicus*, shows reliefs in his engraved design for the Hall at Houghton[21] and in the same year reliefs after Bartoli had been executed for Gibbs' interior at Ditchley, Oxfordshire.[22] The culmination of this development, however, is the interior of the Stone Hall as it was designed by William Kent, where the role to be played by sculpture in the Palladian interior is fully exploited for the first time (fig. 17). The sacrificial themes depicted here would have been familiar from Virgil to any educated eighteenth-century spectator while the serious manner in which the reliefs exemplified classical virtues would have been seen as completely in accord with the precepts of Lord Shaftesbury and Joseph Addison whose writings exercised such influence on early-eighteenth-century English taste.[23] Similarly the restrained style and accomplished execution of Rysbrack's marbles would have been wholly in keeping with the ideals of the English Palladians.

The development of a form of relief sculpture closely modelled on antique sources but employed in a modern setting is a phenomenon that in some ways parallels the contemporary evolution of the classicising portrait bust first seen in Rysbrack's 'Earl of Nottingham' (1723). Just as Rysbrack's classicising portraits anticipate the fully classical busts of Wilton, Banks and

fig. 17   North-west corner of the Stone Hall, Houghton Hall, Norfolk, 1726–30.

Nollekens so the use of relief sculpture in settings such as Houghton looks forward to interiors such as that of Robert Adam's Newby Hall, Yorkshire.

This development of relief sculpture appears to have taken place primarily during the 1720s and early 30s and the availability of a sculptor such as Rysbrack must surely have encouraged the use of this type of sculpture by architects such as Kent. Arriving in England around 1720 Rysbrack could claim a real mastery of relief sculpture in the Flemish tradition and a thorough understanding of the classicising style derived from Duquesnoy. These two attributes could hardly have been better suited to the needs of the English Palladians at this time. The extent of Rysbrack's contribution to the success of their interiors is indeed made clear by comparing the effect of the classical subjects executed in plaster by Bagutti at Ditchley with the same compositions in marble by Rysbrack at Houghton.

Although Rysbrack continued to produce reliefs throughout his career the most important and impressive date from his first fifteen years in England. The Kensington Palace 'Roman Marriage' was among the first of his important commissions and his collaboration with Kent probably played an important part in establishing him as the preferred sculptor of Lord Burlington and the Palladians. But the reliefs perhaps played a further role in Rysbrack's development as a sculptor. The classicising manner which he had learnt originally from van der Voort is far more pronounced in Rysbrack's work than in that of his teacher. The small terracotta of a 'Sacrifice' at Stourhead (Cat. No. 83) probably dates from before 1728, since it is related to a chimney-piece relief at Elm Grove, Roehampton which is illustrated in Gibbs' *Book of Architecture*.[24] But even in this early work, with its still quite Flemish female figures and its clear

fig. 18   Chimney-piece at Cams Hill, Hampshire.

reminiscences of Cortona, the treatment of the figures and drapery is far less baroque than that in van der Voort's approximately contemporary relief of the 'Raising of Lazarus' in St. Jacobskerk, Antwerp.[25] This tendency to emphasise the more classical elements in his style no doubt represents Rysbrack's response to the taste of his English patrons; perhaps it also reflects the experience of executing classical reliefs to meet the requirements of Palladian architects?

Although the major responsibility for the choice of the reliefs' subjects probably lay with the architect concerned, Rysbrack's own role in the creation of these reliefs should not be underestimated. His drawings, though apparently done for his own amusement,[26] show how accomplished he was in pictorial design and the full-scale cartoon (British Museum) for the Houghton chimney-piece relief suggests that it is the sculptor, rather than Kent, who should receive credit for the strength of the detailed composition. The reliefs adapted from baroque engravings share many distinctive compositional features with the drawings, again indicating that it was Rysbrack himself who was responsible for modifying his sources.

The sculptor's contribution is also evident in the reliefs derived from classical sources which in their details are far from slavish copies, sometimes combining motifs from several different engravings as well as having features that are in no way classical. In the terracotta model (Cat. No. 81) for one of the Houghton 'Sacrifices', for example, the somewhat grotesque profiles given to the two kneeling figures are here discarded in favour of the richly bearded heads derived from the Flemish baroque.

It was also presumably Rysbrack who was responsible for the variations between different

fig. 19   Chimney-piece relief in the entrance hall at Clandon Park, Surrey, 1731–5.

reliefs employing fundamentally the same composition in different contexts. In a chimney-piece relief (fig. 18) formerly at Cams Hill, Hampshire,[27] the two *putti* holding a wreath, taken from Montfaucon (fig. 16) and used first in one of the Stourhead terracotta models for Houghton (Cat. No. 81), are combined with a priest pouring libations on to an altar, a motif taken from one of the large reliefs at Clandon (fig. 19). The exact responsibilities of sculptor and architect, however, require further investigation. So, too, does the part played by the assistants in Rysbrack's workshop. The surviving bills for work at Woburn[28] indicate that although Rysbrack may have carved the reliefs, the chimney-pieces were produced by Delvall. Furthermore, references in Rysbrack's sale catalogues to reliefs by van der Hagen "after Mr Rysbrack"[29] raise the possibility that some of the surviving reliefs were in fact executed by assistants.

Whatever may be the detailed division of responsibility between architect, sculptor and assistants for their design and execution, Rysbrack's reliefs form a significant part of his work and together with the monuments and portrait busts represent a distinctive aspect of Augustan taste.

[1] C. Rogers, 1728, *Prints in Imitation of Drawings*, II, p. 228. For kind help in the preparation of this essay I am grateful to Kate Eustace, Terry Friedman, John Harris, John Kenworthy-Browne, who is preparing a full study of the reliefs, Alastair Laing, Andrew MacLelland and Jennifer Montagu.

[2] H. M. Colvin *et al*, 1978, *A History of the Kings Works*, V, p. 198; M. I. Webb, 1954, *Michael Rysbrack, Sculptor*, pl. 7.

[3] Details of these commissions and their chronology are given in Webb, *op. cit.*, pp. 126–35.

[4] K. Freemantle, 1969, *The Baroque Town Hall of Amsterdam*, Utrecht, chapter VI.

[5] 20 February 1764, lot 53.

[6] 24 January 1766, lots 37, 44–6, 61–2; 25 January 1766, lots 15 and 20.

[7] For these sculptors see the exhibition catalogue *La sculpture au siècle de Rubens*, Brussels, 1977.

[8] Freemantle, *op. cit.*, pls. 181–200.

[9] G. Briganti, 1962, *Pietro da Cortona*, Florence, pl. 115.

[10] Mark Girouard in *Country Life*, 26 January 1967.

[11] John Physick in *Country Life*, 2 May 1974.

[12] 14 February 1767, lot 54.

[13] 24 January 1766, lot 73.

[14] C. Theuerkauff, 1975, Zu Francis van Bossuit (1635–1692) "Beeldsnyder in Yveer", *Wallraf-Richartz Jahrbuch*, XXXVII, pp. 119–82.

[15] These sources are identified in Webb, *op. cit.*, p. 128, pls. 57 and 58.

[16] For example, in Webb's design for the Music Hall, Lamport Hall, Northants, illustrated in O. Hill and J. Cornforth, 1968, *English Country Houses. Caroline 1625–1685*, p. 101.

[17] One notable exception is the setting of antique reliefs in the Villa Medici illustrated by Venturini about 1680, for which see F. Haskell and N. Penny, 1981, *Taste and the Antique*, pp. 24–5.

[18] R. Berliner, 1958–9, Zeichnungen von Carlo und Filippo Marchionni, *Münchner Jahrbuch der Bildenden Kunst*, IX–X, pp. 298–308. For the later setting of reliefs in sculpture galleries see J. Kenworthy-Browne, 1980, Private Skulpturengalerien in England 1730–1830, in the exhibition catalogue *Glyptothek München 1830–1980*, Munich.

[19] *The Architecture of A. Palladio*, II, London, 1715, pl. 28.

[20] T. Friedman, 1975, The English Appreciation of Italian Decorations, *Burlington Magazine*, CXVII, pp. 841–7.

[21] Vol. III, pl. 34.

[22] G. Beard, 1975, *Decorative Plasterwork in Great Britain*.

[23] The iconographical programme of the Stone Hall is discussed by J. Burke, 1976, *English Art 1714–1800*, pp. 32–3.

[24] Plate 93 (kindly pointed out to me by Kate Eustace).

[25] M. E. Trallaut, 1949, *De Antwerpse "Meester-Constebeldhouwer" Michiel Van der Voort der Oude*, Brussels, pp. 268–73, figs. 123–5.

[26] Rogers, *op. cit.*, p. 228.

[27] N. Pevsner and D. Lloyd, 1967, *Buildings of England, Hampshire*, p. 227 (kindly brought to my attention by Anthony Radcliffe).

[28] Webb, *op. cit.*, pp. 129–30.

[29] 14 February 1767, lots 43–4.

Rysbrack's Reputation and Critical Fortunes

M. J. H. Liversidge

In 1778 Charles Rogers confidently asserted that "It would be superfluous to raise a Monument over him whose Memory will be preserved, so long as Marble shall last, by the many noble Monuments that he has erected over others".[1] By then, however, changing fashion had already dictated that Rysbrack's fame would soon be extinguished and his name all but forgotten in the wake of the new and rapidly prevailing taste in England for the severe refinements of the neo-classical style. Before looking at his consistently high contemporary reputation it may be appropriate first to consider why this should have been so.

The fact that no obituary notice had appeared when he died in 1770 is in itself an indication that his reputation was diminishing,[2] and the harsh opinion of his work expressed before the Royal Academy in 1805 by John Flaxman, England's greatest living sculptor and the acknowledged heir to the purest classical tradition, must have contributed decisively to his almost total critical eclipse. All that Flaxman could find to say of Rysbrack was that he was "a mere workman, too insipid to give pleasure, and too dull to offend greatly".[3]

To be appreciated properly, Flaxman's disparaging comment must be considered in the context of the neo-classicism that had succeeded the styles exemplified by Rysbrack and his contemporaries earlier in the eighteenth century, as well as in relation to the entrenched academic attitudes that would have been familiar to the audience he was addressing. The occasion was a memorial tribute to another Royal Academician, the sculptor Thomas Banks (1735–1805), who had distilled his style from classical sources and had thereby "corrected the grosser impurities and successfully stemmed the torrent of false taste"[4] that had previously afflicted English sculpture. According to Flaxman, "Before his time only one English sculptor (Mr Nollekens)[5] had formed his taste on the antique, and introduced a purer style of art; since then, sculpture has been gradually emerging from its state of barbarity, simple emblems have supplied the place of epigrammatical concepts, and imitations of the fine heads and beautiful outlines of the antique statues have succeeded to lifeless blocks, or caricature copies of common nature."[6] Although Rysbrack's work amply demonstrates his own familiarity with classical prototypes, the generally eclectic manner in which he adapted his sources and his tendency sometimes to preserve in the composition of a piece or in his handling of details certain residual baroque elements, were evidently unacceptable to later eighteenth-century artists and critics whose views on sculpture were more pedantically inclined. Their attitudes are summarised in the *Lectures* Flaxman delivered annually as Professor of Sculpture to the Royal Academy between 1810 and 1826, but the more austerely classicising virtues preferred by the successors to Rysbrack and his contemporaries Roubiliac and Scheemakers, had been defined rather earlier by Sir Joshua Reynolds in his tenth *Discourse* devoted to sculpture, in which he particularly emphasised that "The grave and austere character of Sculpture requires the utmost degree of formality in composition; picturesque contrasts have here no place; . . . the character of Sculpture makes it her duty to afford delight of a different, and perhaps, of a higher kind; . . . the delight resulting from the contemplation of perfect beauty: and this, which is in truth an

fig. 20   Andrea Soldi's portrait of Michael Rysbrack with the terracotta statue of Hercules, 1753, Cat. No. 97. Yale Center
for British Art, Paul Mellon Collection.

intellectual pleasure, is in many respects incompatible with what is merely addressed to the senses."[7] As elsewhere in his *Discourses*, Reynolds stressed the necessity of imitating accurately the superior nobility and ideal beauty of antique models, and when it is remembered how enormous was the influence that his pronouncements exerted on contemporary standards of taste, it is not in the least surprising that Rysbrack's accomplishments should have been so completely overshadowed and neglected so soon after his death.

Paradoxically, however, Rysbrack's work was favourably commented upon by earlier eighteenth-century critics precisely because it appeared to them that in some of his most celebrated sculptures he had in fact revived the elevating spirit of antiquity. In this connection the opinion recorded by George Vertue in 1744 of the clay model for a figure of Hercules (Cat. No. 72) that Rysbrack had just completed and from which he later carved the great marble statue in the Pantheon at Stourhead, is worth noting: it was, he considered "an excellent Model for truth correctnes & excellentcy of stile . . . truely comparable to the ancient statue of Hercules."[8] Vertue relates how Rysbrack chose to imitate in his own version of the subject the canon of the celebrated 'Farnese Hercules' and how, to perfect his treatment of the anatomy, he had observed another well-known classical precedent, by selecting the various parts of his figure from the most truly formed features of several different models, following the example set by Apelles when he painted his picture of Helen of Troy "and as it is sd of the Antient Greek statuarys". The classical appearance of the resulting figure was what most impressed Vertue, as it did again when he saw the enlarged marble version in 1752: "the noble statue of Hercules finisht now . . . is a Master peece of Art – not to be paralelld scarcely by any artist hearetofore for the Greatness & nobleness of the style – the Antient Greek or Roman study and tastes – of rare merrit & excellent Skill will be to him a monument of lasting Fame to posterity."[9] Vertue's opinion was shared by Horace Walpole who wrote of the 'Hercules' shortly after the sculptor's death that it was "his *chef-d'oeuvre* . . . an exquisite summary of his skill, knowledge, and judgement".[10] Walpole judged Rysbrack to have been "the best sculptor that has appeared in these islands since Le Soeur",[11] responsible for reviving the art, and possessing abilities that "taught the age to depend on statuary for its best ornaments". Of all Rysbrack's works the 'Hercules' received perhaps the most sustained critical appreciation. The descriptions of Stourhead which appear in the literature of the picturesque tour later in the eighteenth century and early in the nineteenth invariably draw the visitor's attention to its merits, as Richard Warner does in his 1801 *Excursions from Bath* where he refers to the "noble statue of Hercules" which "for ease, majesty, and anatomical correctness, can hardly be surpassed; indeed he seems to have caught in this specimen of this art, the fine fancy and ideas of the ancient sculptors whom he studied".[12] Despite its classicising appearance, however, the 'Hercules' retains a distinctively eighteenth-century elegance of attitude and form which, to later critics grown accustomed to the sterner Hellenising tendencies of sculptural style in the age of the Greek Revival, must have seemed dated, and the discrepancy between Rysbrack's eclectic manner and the authentic spirit of antiquity became even more evident after the Elgin Marbles were brought to England from the Parthenon and went on exhibition in London for the first time in 1806.

Contemporary references to Rysbrack's work afford a clear picture of the reputation he enjoyed during his lifetime, from shortly after his arrival in England in about 1720 until he died in 1770. Although the public exhibition of Roubiliac's innovative statue of the composer George

Frederick Handel in Vauxhall Gardens in 1738, and the installation in Westminster Abbey of the equally novel monument by Scheemakers commemorating Shakespeare in 1740, affected his business and enhanced his two principal rivals' careers at his expense, Rysbrack never lacked for commissions throughout the period of nearly fifty years during which he worked in England – in itself a measure of his success and of the recognition that he received. For much of this time the invaluable 'Notebooks', in which, over the years, George Vertue compiled *inter alia* his detailed record of London's art world, provide a reliable source from which to form an accurate impression of Rysbrack's critical reception, and these are supplemented by occasional published references which supply further evidence of the qualities for which his work was appreciated.

Rysbrack first came to George Vertue's notice in October 1720 as a promising artist whose "moddels in Clay are very excellent & shows him to be a great Master *tho' young* (about 26 years old)".[13] It did not take long for Rysbrack to establish himself as one of London's leading statuaries, and Vertue's further references to him document his early successes as a sculptor of monuments, decorative reliefs, statues and portrait heads, sometimes adding a note on their critical reception. Thus, the marble relief Rysbrack carved as a chimney-piece for the East India Company's London office (fig. 15) is described in 1729 as being "admird by all Artists & lovers of Art",[14] while in 1733 the equestrian statue of William III done for Bristol is "much approvd on. and by the Criticks skilfull in that Art thought to be the best statue ever made in England".[15] The frequency with which Rysbrack's name is mentioned is in itself a measure of his reputation, and although Vertue notes how later on in the 1740s his fortunes were affected by the competition from Scheemakers and Roubiliac it is clear from the 'Notebooks' and other sources that his work was well received and generally attracted attention. Particularly celebrated examples of Rysbrack's skill included the Westminster Abbey monument to Sir Isaac Newton executed to a design of William Kent's; it is described by Vertue in 1731 as "a noble and Elegant work . . . much to his Reputation. tho the design or drawing of it on paper was poor enough, yet for that only Mr Kent is honourd with his name on it . . . which if it had been deliverd to any other Sculptor besides Rysbrack, he might have been glad to have his name omitted".[16] The interest shown in it may be gathered from a nearly contemporary published account of the Abbey which mentions how the monument "has pretty much divided publick opinion; some extolling it as one of the most perfect pieces both in design and execution, and others again depreciating it, as no way remarkable for either . . . the statue of Sir Isaac has something in it exceedingly venerable, bold, and majestick; it commands attention, and expresses importance."[17] From the 1730s generally, there seems to have been a common consensus among the critics that Rysbrack was the master of his profession in England, a position that he established for himself with the notable success of his monument to the Duke of Marlborough at Blenheim (1732) and the equestrian statue of William III for Bristol (1731–6). These were the subject of a critical essay in an issue of *The Free Briton* in which the writer particularly approved of Rysbrack's ability to convey the heroic qualities of his subjects: "It is a Felicity, we have Reason to be proud of, that the *two* greatest *Men*, whom the modern Times have known . . . have lately had RYSBRACK to give them Life and Likeness in *Brass* and *Marble* . . . No Hand can give the *Expression of a Hero* to any Figure, unless he is blest with Genius to *conceive the* Reality of *Heroism*. There must be the *true Sublime* in the Artist's Imagination, otherwise he will never reach or describe the *Sublime* of such an *elevated character*." Of the 'William III' the writer comments that "The statue MR. RYSBRACK hath formed with infinite Application and Success, is worthy of publick Attention . . . as it is a *Work of Genius*, and will do Honour to this Nation. Methinks I see the Spirit of Antiquity sublimely expressed in every Stroke."[18]

Although Vertue reports that Rysbrack experienced some temporary decline in his business in the 1740s which he attributes to the critical acclaim that attended Roubiliac's 'Handel' and Scheemakers' 'Shakespeare', his reputation always remained high. Inevitably Vertue makes comparisons between them, observing in 1743, for example, how "the great and unproportiond exultation of that statue of Shakespear erected in Westminster Abbey – done by Scheemaker – and so much spoke of in all conversations and in publick print. which has effectually established his Credit & reputation – and at the same time obliterated, in some degree that of Rysbrakes . . . Both are certainly ingenious men. Rysbrake has long been at the top of fortunes wheel here."[19] Their respective merits and contributions to the progress of sculpture in England are summarised by Vertue in a later note set down in 1749: "of all the Arts now practised in England none has shone [in] late years more apparently than that of Sculpture or Statuary workes. – of that kind of artists three or four different masters have established a reputation here equal to any others in foreign Cittys or countryes . . . But for these four artists sculptors now, . . . I can't well tell to whom to give the preferance. indeed Mr. Michael Rysbrake above 25 years ago began & made the greatest progress . . . and from Time to time gave & supported his reputation in Art as a most excellent Sculptor . . . after him Mr. Delvaux. (staid not long.) and Mr. Scheemaker has since made great improvements and many noble works – But the last of them, who had been long struggling for reputation. did some good works . . . Mr. F. L. Rubilliac sculptor has shown the greatness of his Genius in his invention design & execution in Every part equal, if not superior to any others".[20]

Vertue's assertion that England's sculptors were the equals of "any others in foreign Cittys or countryes" may have been prompted by the appearance in 1747 of the Abbé Le Blanc's *Letters on the English and French Nations* in which he commented on the character of the English nation and its culture. In one of his essays Le Blanc briefly referred to the sculpture he had seen while living in England in 1737–8, comparing unfavourably the works of Rysbrack and an earlier baroque carver, Caius Gabriel Cibber (1630–1700), with the achievements of two French sculptors: "if you believe the English, Mr. Gabriel Cibber . . . was another Praxitiles: but does he even deserve to be ranked among the most ordinary sculptors? At present they have one RYSBRACK, a Fleming, whom they likewise hold in high esteem: they have employed him in several monuments of great men, and he has just finished a bust of Milton: but certainly he does not restore life to the dead. Both Mr. Cibber and Mr. Rysbrack appear to me as far below a Puget and a Bouchardon, as Sir Godfrey Kneller was below a Raphael". Le Blanc's severe criticism of the arts generally in England elicited a defence from another Frenchman, André Rouquet, a miniaturist who worked in London for thirty years before moving to Paris in 1752. There he wrote his *L'Etat des Arts en Angleterre* which appeared in 1755 (an English translation, *The Present State of the Arts in England*, was published in London the same year). In his chapter on sculpture Rouquet takes Le Blanc to task for his adverse comments on statuary in England, informing his readers that "there are very able sculptors in England, as well natives as foreigners". The French Roubiliac and Flemish Scheemakers are mentioned approvingly for their monuments in

Westminster Abbey, and Rysbrack receives special attention: "Another Fleming had likewise the honour of being employed in decorating the tomb of Sir Isaac Newton . . . This is he whom Abbé le Blanc very insolently calls *one Rysbrack*; an expression of contempt, denoting an obscure person who deserves to be so, but not at all suitable to an artist whom abilities and good manners have rendered worthy of respect. And yet I will venture to affirm that there is not an academician in France, who would be ashamed to rank with this gentleman as an associate."[21] Rouquet, admittedly, wrote his book in the partisan spirit of an anglophile, but nonetheless his comments are valuable as the opinion of a contemporary artist whose views were formed in a European, not purely English, context.

The most judicious assessment of Rysbrack's abilities to appear later in the eighteenth century is to be found in Horace Walpole's account of the sculptor in his *Anecdotes of Painting in England*. Walpole particularly admired his "deep knowledge of his art and singular industry" and he attributed to his influence a general enhancement in the quality of English monumental sculpture: "as a sculptor capable of furnishing statues was now found, our taste in monuments improved . . . The abilities of Rysbrack taught the age to depend on statuary for its best ornaments."[22] Later writers tend to rely on Walpole's views, though there is a tendency to emphasise the more classicising aspects of his work in conformity with neo-classical tastes as Charles Rogers did in 1778. "His great Abilities were not acquired without great application . . . esteemed . . . by every one who is sensible of true Elegance, & the Beauties of the Antique . . . His stile must be allowed to be perfectly elegant having formed his judgement on the Remains of Antiquity, and the best works of the Modern Masters; this he took particular care not to vitiate by attending to anything that is not left us by the Ancients or produced by the Florentine, Roman or Lombard Schools."[23]

With the passage of time, however, and the emergence of more classically 'correct' sculptors, Rysbrack's reputation gradually faded. It is perhaps symptomatic of his declining critical fortunes that by 1800 in his *Anecdotes of the Arts in England* the Reverend James Dallaway should have wrongly ascribed one of Rysbrack's masterpieces, the 'John Locke' in Christ Church Library, Oxford, to Roubiliac and described it as being "without style or character, neither antique nor modern"; the confusion and judgement are the more puzzling in the light of Dallaway's general remarks on Rysbrack who, he asserts, "in his principal figures was generally happy in his choice of attitudes . . . The attention is seldom diverted from his principal figures to accompaniments, as in many modern instances; and the high finishing of his draperies is admirable."[24] Thereafter, although scattered references to Rysbrack occur in guidebooks to places where his work could be seen, interest in the sculptors of his period generally seems to have been slight, and by the time Allan Cunningham's *Lives of the British Painters, Sculptors and Architects* appeared in 1830 he was apparently not considered worth including. Rysbrack had by then entered the long twilight of relative oblivion from which he only finally emerged in 1954 with the publication of Margaret Webb's scholarly and indispensable monograph, *Michael Rysbrack, Sculptor*, still one of the best critical biographies devoted to a major figure in the English sculptural tradition.

[1] Charles Rogers, 1778, *Prints in Imitation of Drawings*.
[2] His death was formally announced in the *Gentleman's Magazine* but otherwise he received no obituary notice, such as had been published when his rival L. F. Roubiliac died in 1762.
[3] John Flaxman, R.A., 1805, *An Address to the President and Members of the Royal Academy on the Death of Thomas Banks, R.A., Sculptor*.
[4] The comment is from the first lecture delivered by Sir Richard Westmacott, R.A., to the Royal Academy on his succession to the Professorship of Sculpture following Flaxman's death.
[5] Joseph Nollekens, R.A. (1737–1823).
[6] Flaxman, *op. cit.*
[7] Sir Joshua Reynolds, P.R.A., 1780, *Discourse X*.
[8] Vertue, III, pp. 121–2.
[9] *Ibid.*, p. 162.
[10] Horace Walpole, *Anecdotes of Painting in England*. The last volume (IV) containing the account of Rysbrack was published in 1780, although it had been printed in 1771. The most convenient edition is Ralph N. Wornum (ed.), 1888, 3 volumes, (for Rysbrack, III, pp. 33–7).
[11] Hubert Le Sueur (fl. 1610–43), a French sculptor who worked for Charles I.
[12] Richard Warner, 1801, *Excursions from Bath*, p. 111.
[13] Vertue, I, p. 76.
[14] Vertue, III, p. 37.
[15] *Ibid.*, p. 66.
[16] *Ibid.*, p. 50.
[17] James Ralph, 1734, *A Critical Review of the Public Buildings, Statues, and Ornaments, In, and about London and Westminster*, p. 69.
[18] *The Free Briton*, No. 195, 16 August 1733.
[19] Vertue, III, pp. 115–16.
[20] *Ibid.*, pp. 145–6.
[21] André Rouquet, 1755, *The Present State of the Arts in England*, pp. 62–3 (reprinted in facsimile, ed. R. W. Lightbrown, 1970).
[22] Walpole, *op. cit.* (Wornum III, p. 34).
[23] Rogers, *op. cit.*
[24] The Reverend James Dallaway, 1800, *Anecdotes of the Arts in England*, pp. 399–400.

A Technical Examination of Some Terracottas by Michael Rysbrack

Mary Greenacre

Very little has been published on the technique of eighteenth-century terracotta sculpture. For the most part the terracottas themselves must serve as the primary source of information and by understanding the medium, the tools and tooling marks and by the use of X-radiography, some suppositions can be made. Rysbrack has himself made these easier, for his terracottas are entirely his own work, rather than the combined efforts of a studio of apprentices and craftsmen. During the preparation of this exhibition a number of terracottas were examined and conserved at the conservation studios of the Area Museum Council for the South West, and other terracottas were examined *in situ*.

Terracotta has come to refer to an unglazed but fired clay of a particular colour but the word itself means burnt earth, a clay body which has been fired rather than just sun-dried. Because of its particular qualities, clay imposes certain restrictions and disciplines on a sculptor and it is necessary to understand the origins of clay types and the general methods of working terracotta.

Clays are the result of the weathering of feldspathic rocks over many thousands of years, aided by naturally generated acids from the soil and by bacteria associated with the breakdown of organic materials. The product, kaolinite, is made up of crystals which are very small and plate-like in shape. These plateletts are suspended in water which allows them to move over one

fig. 21 Workshop of a sculptor in clay and plaster; from Diderot and d'Alembert's *Encyclopédie*, 1770, VIII, pl. 1.

49

another, thus giving clay its plasticity. Henry Hodges makes a helpful analogy by comparing the plateletts to sheets of glass stacked on top of one another. When the sheets are dry they cannot be moved, yet when wet they slide easily over each other.[1] The greater the volume of water between plates, the greater will be the shrinkage when the water evaporates. During the drying and subsequent firing the crystals merge and become impervious to water. The clays from which terracotta sculpture and all so-called earthenwares are made, are secondary clays. They have been washed down from the original site of weathering and are very finely divided. They also contain many impurities which, to a certain extent, account for the various colours of terracotta.

Secondary clays are very plastic. It is occasionally necessary to alter the properties of the clay by blending in other materials. Such materials are known as 'grog' and are generally of a different chemical type or particle size from the original clay. They increase the porosity of clay or alter the firing temperature. Red earthenware clays fire between 1000 and 1200°C.

The composition of the clay must be suited to the type and scale of the sculpture. It must be 'wedged' before it can be used. Wedging is the process of blending clays to a homogeneous texture and composition while excluding pockets of air from the clay body. Any air trapped within a sculpture during modelling will expand and may cause an object to be damaged or even to shatter, unless a means of escape is provided. This expansion of hot air is further complicated by the generation of a certain amount of steam from the clay during firing and this, too, must be able to escape. During wedging the sculptor must also be careful not to allow any impurities or foreign bodies to be incorporated into the clay. Such impurities could cause drag marks on the surface of the clay while it is being worked or cause the surface to spall during firing. This is also known as blowing-out.

While clay is able to support a considerable weight, especially if carefully and slowly built up, it is usual for a sculptor to give additional strength to an object while it is being modelled by providing an armature round which the clay is formed. The armature is then either removed once the clay has hardened and is self-supporting, or allowed to remain if it is of a material which is inert and unaffected either by the clay body or the subsequent firing.

Clay must be evenly applied to an armature. No one part of a sculpture should be denser than another for it is important that clay dries evenly to avoid cracking. A sculpture should have a firm centre of gravity and be balanced so that the downward thrust of the weight of the clay is supported at the centre of the form.

It is important while building up a figure, to compact each addition of clay firmly to the existing model. An inherent weakness of any freely built object is that clay adheres rather poorly to itself and a great deal of physical pressure is necessary to make clay additions stick. Even then planes of weakness inevitably exist where clay has been added to clay. This is why the applied handles to clay cups break off so easily. If a solidly built object is subjected to physical stress, either by dropping it, knocking it or even heating it, it will break preferentially along these planes of weakness. It is occasionally difficult to distinguish whether or not a clay object has been kiln-damaged or fractured along a plane of weakness at a later date.

If a figure has been formed in such a way that air is unavoidably trapped within the shape, as will happen if a piece is removed for hollowing out and then replaced, allowance must be made to permit hot air and steam to escape during firing. This can be done by allowing holes as part of the design or by filling in any visually obtrusive holes after the object has been fired.

After the initial construction and modelling of a terracotta, it is allowed to dry. The wet clay passes through a period when the first part of the water evaporates, though the clay is still slightly damp. This is the 'green' or 'leather-hard' stage and the surface can still be worked and much of the finer detail is attained at this time. In warm climates the final air-drying can be done out of doors but in northern climates the drying must either be done in the summer months or with the assistance of drying ovens or, at least, of prolonged storage in heated rooms.

A technically perfect piece can be damaged or destroyed if the firing is not also perfect. A careful sequence of temperature elevations must be made and the temperature held at each of these stages before raising it to the next level. Finally the temperature must reach the maturing or sintering point of the particular clay body and then be allowed to cool very slowly. The ultimate colour of a fired terracotta depends on the impurities in the clay itself, the maximum temperature and length of firing and the amount of oxygen present in the kiln during firing and cooling. Variations in any of these factors will produce an uneven and perhaps unsatisfactory result.[2]

RYSBRACK'S TECHNIQUE

With the exception of the statue of Van Dyck (Cat. No. 58) the clay types of all the terracottas examined were remarkably similar. The clay was very fine-grained with little or no grog on the surface. Where the terracotta has been well fired, the colour was generally a warm, light pink-orange, though dark wine colour and even *terraverte* were observed on pieces which had been badly fired, notably the '4th Duke of Beaufort' (Cat. No. 63). The clay of the bust of Edward Colston, which had been severely damaged, allowing the internal construction to be examined, was homogeneous throughout (Cat. No. 6). X-rays showed that the clay had been well prepared.[3] Very few pockets of air were contained within the clay but a slight variation in the clay's density allowed one to distinguish between the handful-sized lumps of clay added as the sculpture was built up.

The busts and figures were built upon a central column of clay. The busts also had secondary cores added as supports for the shoulders and in the case of the 'Colston' these additional columns were 'S'-shaped. The bottom of the 'S' curled into the base of the column while the top arch of the 'S' supported the shoulders. The supporting column of the '4th Duke of Beaufort' is square in section and the X-ray shows it to be beautifully wedged, with no pockets of air. The column can be seen at the back of the bust, neatly trimmed and finished while the areas to either side show finger marks where the clay has been scooped out to lighten the construction. The whole of Queen Elizabeth I's (Cat. No. 51) ruff is very finely finished but beneath it at the back, the clay has been similarly removed. Most of Rysbrack's later busts are constructed in this way (fig. 22).

The X-rays of the busts of Edward Colston and the 4th Duke of Beaufort show shadows in the centre of the central column of clay. These shadows are uneven in width and the damage of the 'Colston' confirmed that they are caused by the space left by the armature. At the centre of the bases of the busts of Colston and of the 2nd and 4th Dukes of Beaufort there is a hole through which the armature was presumably removed and which served as the main escape for air and

fig. 22   4th Duke of Beaufort, Cat. No. 63.

fig. 23   X-ray of 'William III on horseback', Cat. No. 25.

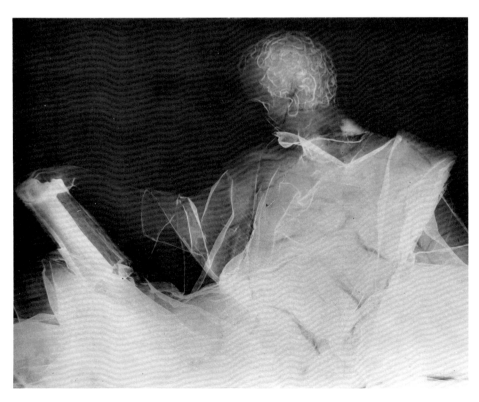

fig. 24   X-ray of 'The Philosopher', Cat. No. 37.

steam during firing. X-rays do not give any indication of an armature in the solidly built figures of Rubens or The Philosopher (Cat. Nos. 57 & 37) although the figure of Rubens has a hole in its base, which also shows wheel or turning marks.

Once the clay columns had settled and gained some strength the actual modelling of the figure could start. Handfuls of clay would have been applied around the core, starting at the bottom and working upwards and the bases of the busts show inevitable small cracks in concentric circles around the core.

The X-rays show the clay being added by the handful to the column of the busts. This is the most practical method of adding clay on such a large scale. On the two smaller figures of The Philosopher and of Rubens a slightly different technique seems to have been used, particularly on the recumbent 'Philosopher' (fig. 24). X-rays reveal the careful application of relatively small amounts of clay one to another. This is most apparent at the head where wedge-shaped pieces of clay were built on top of one another to completely eliminate the formation of any air pockets. The X-ray of the 'Rubens' shows similar small additions of clay towards the top of the figure.[4]

X-ray also tells us that Rysbrack first modelled 'The Philosopher' in the nude, afterwards applying the drapery to the naked figure. Indeed the base upon which 'The Philosopher' rests had to be extended by Rysbrack to allow for some of the folds of cloth behind the plinth against which the figure rests. We can see that Edward Colston's hair was added after the head had been fully formed. The very high relief of the robes of the Beaufort busts may also have been applied, for a small break in the clothing of the '2nd Duke of Beaufort' showed details of modelling underneath.

At the end of the initial modelling the busts and figures underwent further treatment to prepare them for firing. Very large masses of clay shrink considerably during drying and firing and it is necessary to reduce the clay, wherever possible, to a thickness of not more than about 5 cm. The X-rays of the busts reveal that the heads have been hollowed out. The clay surface of the '2nd Duke of Beaufort' shows at the sinister side of the top of the head a distinct cut line where the head might have been trepanned to allow the interior to be scooped out. The spaces left by the armatures reach into these voids. The areas at the back on either side of the central column would have been removed at this time. The smaller solid figures of Rubens and The Philosopher appear not to have been reduced at all.

Once the modelling of the terracotta was complete it would have been allowed to dry to the 'leather-hard' state. At this time the work on the surface would have been subtractive, finishing the smooth areas with a fine-toothed comb and incising and emphasising the detail to improve the appearance of the object before allowing it to dry completely (fig. 25).

Rysbrack was careful to allow his terracottas to dry thoroughly, explaining in one letter to Sir Edward Littleton "The Reason of not sending Sir Francis Bacon is; that it must be Dried first, and afterwards Burned which Cannot be Done till summer, it not Being half Dry Yet."[5] The letter is dated 12 February 1756.

M. I. Webb points out that this bust had actually been completed the month before and yet had still not been sent to be fired by 31 July. It was not delivered until June 1757. Busts which Rysbrack sent to be fired at the same time as the 'Francis Bacon' had actually been completed earlier and it seems that "eighteen months to two years was not considered an unreasonable time for the making of a terracotta bust".[6] Rysbrack may have kept the completed terracottas to dry

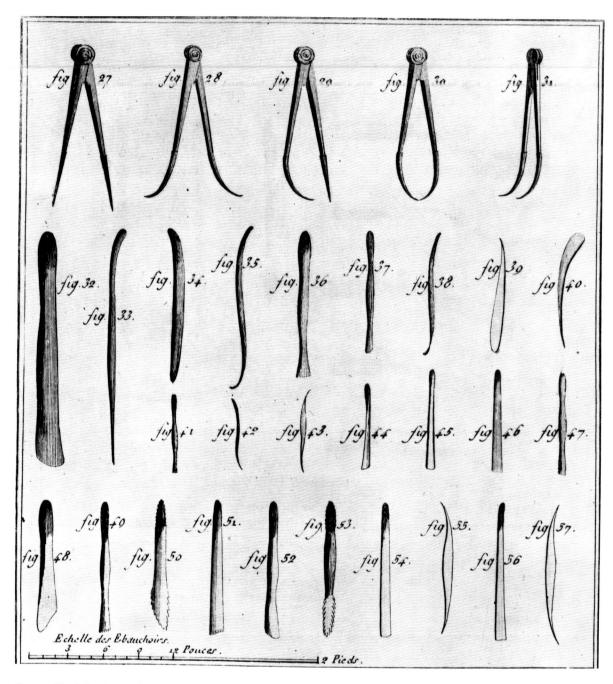

fig 25   Tools for clay sculpture, from Diderot and d'Alembert's *Encyclopédie*, 1770, VIII, pl. 3.

rather than sending them to drying ovens, for he mentions keeping work in the studio and the pieces were often admired by his patrons and visitors.[7] When the terracottas were sufficiently dry they were packed and sent "to be Burnt". It is not clear whether this firing took place under Rysbrack's supervision but it seems likely that Rysbrack did not oversee this crucial aspect of the work. The firing itself seems to have taken some time. In a letter dated 25 October 1757 Rysbrack says, "The Busts are Gone to be Baked, and I expect them every Day, as soon as they are Done I shall give myself the Pleasure to let you know."[8] However, another ten weeks passed before Rysbrack could report on 7 January 1758, "I have recovered my Health very Much since I wrote last, and should have wrote to have acquainted You of the Busts being baked, but I did Not receive them till the Beginning of this Week".[9]

Even after the terracottas had been fired Rysbrack was not yet finished with them. It seems to have been generally accepted that some cracking during firing was inevitable.[10] Rysbrack describes a terracotta of the Pope after Bernini saying the head "is Painted with a thin Red Paint. In regard to Getting off the Paint it would entirely spoil them as there are Small Cracks unavoidably Caused by the Burning, which Are obliged to be stopped with Plaster of Paris; which the paint Strengthens and Makes the whole of one Colour."[11]

The size and extent of fire-cracking vary enormously in the terracottas. Some of the figures appear perfect, for instance the small 'Philosopher' and the 'Rubens', whose only damages seem to be a result of bad handling. The busts of Queen Elizabeth and of Queen Caroline (Kensington Palace) have cracks only where the clay has been removed on either side of the central core at the back. The figure of the 4th Duke of Beaufort has a large crack on the neck but none other of any significant size. The '2nd Duke', however, like the bust of Sir Hans Sloane at the British Museum, has extensive cracking. The three busts which were examined at the studio have one peculiar feature in common which is worth mentioning. Each has a rhomboidal *lacuna* below the sinister ear with a fissure below it which extends to varying lengths down the front of the figure. It is possible that these *lacunae* were intended to allow the steam and hot gases to leave the large void which was made when the head was hollowed. The long cracks down the backs of the busts may be due to the slight imbalance of the form caused by turning the head slightly to one side.

As we have seen, once the cracks were filled Rysback gave the terracotta a surface coating. In an earlier letter to Sir Edward he had written: "Sir with Respect to the Varnish on Milton. You said you did not like the Shining which was on it, for which reason I painted it over with Oil of Turpentine only mixt with Colour to take that off".[12] By painting terracottas Rysbrack was following a tradition which goes back to ancient Greek polychrome figurines.

It is particularly difficult to assess the surface finish of the completed terracottas. The pieces which were examined at Bristol had all, to a lesser or greater extent, been restored at some time in the past. It was not possible to confirm the presence of an original surface.[13] An appendix to the catalogue to the important exhibition 'La sculpture au siècle de Rubens' (Brussels: Musée d'Art Ancien, 1977) makes the point that the cleaning of the sculptures "had uncovered many original surfaces of different types (unadulterated terracotta, terracotta with gesso, terracotta painted white or grey and polychromed terracotta) or surfaces which were the result of subsequent alterations (over-painting with casin, over-painting with oil- or water-based colours imitating terracotta, or with white paint to imitate stone, and occasionally, retouching disguising previous restorations)." The article goes on to state how little is known of this aspect of the finish of terracottas and makes a plea for more work to be done. The clues Rysbrack gives us in his letters, the red of the Bernini and the turpentine and colour of the 'Milton', are enticing but unhelpful. The problem is also complicated by the fact that recently it has become fashionable to expose the surface of the terracotta and some pieces may have been stripped of traces of their original coating. The figure of Rubens was restored in Birmingham in 1958 and is now an uneven colour where some of the restoration has rubbed off. The '2nd' and '4th Dukes of Beaufort' and the small child 'Thomas, 3rd Earl of Coventry', were treated at the beginning of this century and surviving correspondence records that they were previously "coated with stone coloured paint which was removed by Messrs. Bucciani".[14] The bust of Edward Colston had seven layers of paint on it and the small figure of The Philosopher four. The bust of Queen Elizabeth I has only a thin red coating while the companion pieces in terracotta in the Library of Windsor Castle are covered with a thick and disfiguring brown distemper paint.

Once finished, the terracottas were carefully crated in tow and shavings and dispatched to the purchaser.[15] However, Rysbrack was still not necessarily free of his creation. A letter of 7 April 1761, says, "Sir, I am sorry for the accident which has happed to the Model, of the horn of the Cow. The Horn is broke likewise of ye Marble Basso Relievo at the Foundling hospital, but it looks the more antique as Doctor Mead said of it. the accident may be repaired, by modelling the horn in Clay, and making a Mould upon it, and Cast it in Plaster of Paris, fix it on, and Paint it of the same colour as the Model is."[16] Again on 30 November 1765, "I am heartily sorry that any Misfortune has happened to the Plinth of ye Goat, (because it is one of the best things I ever Modelled) and it was packed up as carefully as Possible, but I am much pleased to hear the Damage is not in any of the tender and Principal Parts of the Goat. I know a Friend of Mine Mr. Trubshaw who lives near Your Honour and has worked for me some Years who will mend it." Later in the same letter Rysbrack anxiously adds: "Sir, I desire you will not be Uneasy about the Goat, because when Mr. Trubshaw has mended it, it will be just the same as it was before if it be only painted with a thin Coat of the same Colour."[17]

Occasionally Rysbrack was asked to make reproductions of his busts and certainly on one occasion he produced multiples of his work (see Cat. No. 57). However, Rysbrack did not actually do the casting himself but employed a Mr Vannini to make the moulds and perhaps the copies as well. "According to Your Desire, I have Enquired of Mr Vannini, the Caster in Plaster of Paris. (Whom I Employ when I want) what the Expence will be, of a Mould off of your Honour's Bust, and each Cast out of it: it being a thing Entirely out of my way."[18] In his next letter Rysbrack tells Sir Edward Littleton that "Mr. Vannini assures me that Making the Mould on Your Bust will not Detriment it, the Mould when Made will be Good to Cast 15 or 20 Casts out of it".[19] By this description it would seem that Vannini was making piece moulds rather than using waste moulds or gelatine casting, both of which were processes known at that time. It is not clear, however, whether the bust was intended as a slip-cast or a press moulding.[20]

The small figure of Van Dyck (Cat. No. 58) is hollow and is probably press-moulded. Its clay is of a distinctly different type from that of the solid figures, being very heavily filled with quartz sand, while the sand particles all lie exactly flush with the surface. This type of filled clay is commonly used for pressings or for hard-fired piece moulds. The interior, which is quite visible from below, shows two lines which start at the base of the plinth and run up inside the figure. The clay on the inside shows finger-prints and marks pushed into the clay rather than

fig. 26   Incised signature on 'Rubens', Cat. No. 57.

fig. 27   Press-moulded signature on 'Van Dyck', Cat. No. 58.

drawn along and out of it as in the backs of the hollowed-out busts. Furthermore, the 'Van Dyck' is slightly smaller than the solidly modelled companion figure of Rubens. If the 'Van Dyck' was press-moulded from a mould made from a solid terracotta figure which was the same size as the 'Rubens', one would expect the moulded figure to be smaller. Shrinkage of approximately 10% occurs during firing and this is, in fact, the relative difference between the two figures.[21]

When Rysbrack retired, the contents of his studio were sold over five days. No moulds were included in the sales, although there were seventy-two plasters. The majority of these plasters were specified as antiques or after the work of other sculptors.[22] One, however, was "A cast of an Equestrian Statue of King William, which was made for the City of Bristol".[23] A plaster-of-Paris equestrian statue of William III was examined and conserved in the studio for this exhibition (Cat. No. 25). It is in remarkably good condition considering the fragility of the material and the composition. The damages were mainly to the extended limbs of the figure and the horse. The figure has been oil-gilded at some time in the past. A small sample of the surface was removed from the edge of one of the damages. This sample showed that the figure has three layers of gilding laid over yellow bole and glue or oil.[24] The base plaster-of-Paris appears to have been impregnated with a resinous material and under the gold and over this surface coating is a layer of dark green pigment.[25] It might be that the original appearance of this cast was dark to indicate the final surface of the cast bronze of the full-size statue.

X-rays were taken of this figure and they showed the hollow construction and even thickness of slip moulding (fig. 23). The sculpture seems to have been cast in three moulds and joined together. The horse's head is one piece, the legs and torso of the horse, including the legs and lower body of the figure, make a second piece and the upper body, arms and head of the figure, the third piece. An armature is visible in the dexter arm of the figure and each of the four legs of the horse. This armature extends at one point through the hollow-cast base and can be seen to be of iron and rectangular in section. The X-ray emphasises the beautiful shape and construction of this surviving plaster cast.

Few of the terracottas examined carried signatures. The 'Rubens' carries a clear incised signature (fig. 26) while the 'Van Dyck', in keeping with the method of manufacture, has its signature moulded (fig. 27). Only one other of the pieces examined carried a signature, the bust of the 2nd Duke of Beaufort. This is inscribed into a coating of plaster-of-Paris which entirely covered the back of the central core of the figure. The plaster seems to have been put on to cover the fire crack which extends from the nape of the neck of the Duke down the entire length of the back. The plaster was covered with the red, water-soluble paint layer which was applied in 1908. It was not possible to discover whether this signature was inscribed in the plaster because the plaster was covering an existing signature or whether the previous restorer had taken the liberty of naming the piece. It is more likely that it is the former. No other type of signature has been found on the terracottas which came to the conservation studio.

It is apparent that Michael Rysbrack followed the Flemish methods of modelling and worked mainly with solid clay sculptures, handling the material with confidence and considerable skill. It would seem that from earliest times it was accepted that a certain amount of damage would inevitably occur to terracottas during firing and this reflects the lack of precise control of the kiln conditions at that time. Damages were corrected after firing. Care was taken, however, within the context and design of the sculptures, that firing defects were kept to a minimum. Large masses of clay were reduced if possible by hollowing out or fining down. The smaller figures were well thought out, making use of the overall design to eliminate the need for armatures during the building. The extended dexter arm of 'The Philosopher' depends entirely on the book upon which it rests for support. The very careful construction of these solid figures ensured their withstanding the firing intact. Rysbrack distinguished between the damage caused by burning, about which he was certainly very realistic, and that caused by bad handling. His letters show that he was upset when damages to figures were reported and anxious to have such damages made good: "I hope by this time the Surgeon have cured the Skin of the Goat and that it is done to Your satisfaction, and that it will not be perceived When painted, we are surgeons sometimes and heal Legs and Arms as well as they."[26]

[1] Henry Hodges, 1964, *Artifacts, an introduction to early technology*, p. 21.

[2] See Hodges for a complete description of the firing sequence. Thelma Frazier Winter, 1973, *The Art and Craft of Ceramic Sculpture*, also gives a clear and useful account of the processes involved in the working and firing of clay.

[3] The X-rays were carried out at the Department of Diagnostic Radiography, University of Bristol, by Miss Thea Ovenden. The author is very grateful to Miss Ovenden, and Dr B. P. Edwards who arranged for the X-rays to be made, for the helpful suggestions on the interpretation of the results. X-radiography of all types of clay bodies will affect the thermoluminescent dates of the clay and this should be taken into consideration before any X-rays are taken. It is necessary to keep a careful record of the amount and exposure time of X-rays. X-radiography proved a useful tool for the examination of the terracottas. It revealed details of the construction which would not otherwise have been known. However, not enough pieces have been X-rayed to establish whether or not this could be a means of authenticating Rysbrack's terracottas. It would be useful to make a comparative study of terracottas by thoroughly investigating the methods of other eighteenth-century sculptors.

[4] Using modern forensic methods many terracottas could be effectively 'finger-printed' as a means of attribution.

[5] Webb, 1954, p. 195: Letter II.

[6] *Ibid.*, p. 193.

[7] *Ibid.*, p. 202: Letter XIII.

[8] *Ibid.*, p. 198: Letter VII.

[9] *Ibid.*, p. 198: Letter VIII.

[10] S. J. Fleming, December 1980, Rediscovery of a Verrocchio Madonna and Child. *Museum of Applied Science Center of Archaeology Journal*, 1, No. 5, pp. 149–50. The examination of a terracotta relief is described and includes a description of repairs made to damages which might have occurred during or shortly after firing.

[11] Webb, 1954, p. 200: Letter XI.

[12] *Ibid.*, p. 197: Letter VI.

[13] J. Larson, 1980, The Conservation of terracotta sculpture, *The Conservator*, Vol. 4, pp. 38–45.

[14] Badminton House Muniment Room: letter from Lionel Cust to the Duchess of Beaufort, December 1908.

[15] Webb, 1954, p. 208: Letter XXIII.

[16] *Ibid.*, p. 205: Letter XVIII.

[17] *Ibid.*, p. 207: Letter XXI.

[18] *Ibid.*, p. 199: Letter IX.

[19] *Ibid.*, p. 199: Letter X.

[20] Very good descriptions of casting techniques are in the following publications: J. L. Wasserman, 1969, *Daumier, a critical and comparative study*; John W. Mills, 1976, *Technique of Sculpture*; Thelma Frazier Winter, 1973, *The Art and Craft of Ceramic Sculpture*; John Larson, 1981, Carrier-Belleuse, a technical study of his terracotta sculpture, *French Sculpture*, Bruton Gallery, Somerset (exhibition catalogue).

[21] It is not possible to say with absolute certainty that this mould was made in Rysbrack's time. It would be nice to think that this piece was a pull of the mould perhaps for Rysbrack himself. However, the frequent reproduction of famous pieces by Henry Cheere and others prevents an accurate attribution.

[22] M. I. Webb, 1956 (19 April), Roubiliac Busts at Wilton, *Country Life*, CXIX, pp. 804–5. Mrs Webb makes a very interesting comparison of the techniques of Rysbrack and Roubiliac – one working in the Flemish manner and the other the French. Mrs Webb, after examining a considerable number of busts by both artists feels that Roubiliac modelled his heads in clay and had them cast either by slip moulding or press moulding or even plaster slip casts. Rysbrack on the other hand is credited with modelling his busts direct. Roubiliac's sale from his studio included 202 lots of plasters excluding antiques and 58 lots of moulds.

[23] Webb, 1954, p. 189.

[24] The gilding was as many as five layers thick in areas where damages seem to have been frequent.

[25] The sample was examined with a polarising-light microscope and exhibited characteristics similar to copper resinate.

[26] Webb, 1954, p. 208: Letter XXII.

Catalogue

GAWEN HAMILTON *circa* 1697–1737

1   A "Conversation of Virtuosis . . . at the Kings Armes"   1735

Oil on canvas, 34½ × 43 in, 877 × 112 mm
Inscribed: *Vertue G; Hyssing; Dahl; Thomas Aht; Gibbs Mr.; J. Gouppy; Robinson; Bridgeman/Gar; Barren; Woolet; Rysbrac St.; Kent;*
Provenance: 1904, purchased from Miss Elizabeth Montague, great-granddaughter of Mathew Robinson
Literature: Webb, 1954, *Michael Rysbrack, Sculptor*, pp. 57–69; Burke, 1976, *English Art 1714–1800*, pp. 110–11, pl. 29B; Kerslake, 1977, *Early Georgian Portraits*, pp. 340–2, pl. 951; Sutton, 1981, The age of Sir Robert Walpole, *Apollo* CXIV p. 335, fig. 21; Waterhouse, 1981, *Dictionary of 18th Century Painters*, p. 157, (illus.)
Lent by the National Portrait Gallery, London (NPG 1384)

The title is taken from Vertue's description of the painting which he recorded when it was still unfinished in 1734, and of which he made a sketch, with a key to the sitters.[1] It is unlikely to represent the meeting of a specific club,[2] though all those present were variously members of the Society of Virtuosi of St. Luke, or the Rose and Crown Club. Indeed from Vertue's vivid "account of the Facitious Humors" of the latter in 1724 it was a much less formal, more convivial gathering.[3] Michael Rysbrack, the only sculptor in the group, was a member of both these artists' societies and the steward of St. Luke's in 1735, and the painting is a tangible reminder of the clubbable nature of the man and his popularity amongst other artists.[4]

The sitters subscribed to the painting which was raffled when finished for the benefit of the artist. Vertue notes that Goupy won it, and apparently sold it to the Prince of Wales.[5] The sitters are from left to right:

GEORGE VERTUE (1683–1756), the engraver and antiquary, whose notebooks provide an invaluable picture of the arts at this time; a notable partisan of Rysbrack. He was Secretary of the Rose and Crown Club, and by his own admission "a lover of the Must of Antiquity".[6]

HANS HYSING (1678–1753) a Swedish portrait painter who settled in London in 1700, had worked under Dahl, and painted both Gibbs and Wootton.

MICHAEL DAHL (1659?–1743) another Swede, who had settled in London in 1689 and became the best-patronised portrait painter after Kneller.

WILLIAM THOMAS (fl. 1722–1732), Steward to the Earl of Oxford.

JAMES GIBBS (1682–1754) the architect (see Cat. No. 10) whose chief patron was the Earl of Oxford.

JOSEPH GOUPY (*circa* 1680–1763) a painter who Vertue tells us was "eminent in painting in Water Colours"; he also advised Frederick, Prince of Wales, on the purchase of works of art.[7]

MATHEW ROBINSON (*circa* 1694–1778) a gentleman dilettante, and accomplished amateur artist, particularly of landscape.

CHARLES BRIDGEMAN (died 1738) gardener to the King; landscape architect and designer of the gardens at Stowe, Buckinghamshire, in which Gibbs and Rysbrack were both involved at the time.

BERNARD BARON (1696–1762) a French engraver who settled in London about 1722. He engraved the portrait of Gibbs after Hogarth, the frontispiece to *Biblioteca Radcliviana*, and Gibbs' own bookplate, probably based on a missing relief portrait medallion by Rysbrack.[8]

JOHN WOOTTON (*circa* 1676–1764) landscape painter, who specialised in sporting paintings. He had been a pupil of Jan Wyck and often collaborated with Kent on interior schemes, such as the Hall at Badminton for the 3rd Duke of Beaufort. His nickname in the Club was Pasquin.[9] Seven paintings by him and a portrait by Hysing of him, were included in one of Rysbrack's sales.[10] He was a witness in July 1747 to Rysbrack's agreement with Henry Hoare for the statue of Hercules.[11]

MICHAEL RYSBRACK (1694–1770), the only sculptor present; he modelled the heads of six of the thirteen virtuosi gathered here.[12]

GAWEN HAMILTON (1698–1737) the author of this painting, and like Gibbs a Scotsman. He was one of Hogarth's chief rivals in conversation pieces, which perhaps explains the absence of Hogarth from such a distinguished group, particularly if, as Vertue relates, the cause of their being gathered together was the promotion of "the Interest of Mr. Hamilton".[13]

WILLIAM KENT (1685–1748) architect, decorative painter and designer, and a member of the Burlington House set. Rysbrack worked with him on the redecoration of Kensington Palace very soon after his arrival in England. The north front of Badminton House, some of the interiors, notably the Hall, and Worcester Lodge, were designed by Kent for the 3rd Duke of Beaufort.

1

1 Vertue, III, pp. 71–2.
2 Kerslake, 1977, p. 342.
3 Vertue, VI, frontispiece and pp. 32–7.
4 A painting in the Ashmolean Museum, Oxford, entitled 'A Group of Artists', is very close in composition. It purports to include Rysbrack, but the likeness is not there.
5 Vertue, III, pp. 71–2.
6 Vertue, VI, p. 33.
7 Vertue, III, p. 138; Sutton, 1981, p. 332.

8 Vertue, III, p. 13.
9 Vertue, VI, p. 34.
10 Langford and Son sale catalogue, 14 February 1767.
11 W.R.O. Stourhead 383.4.
12 Gibbs, Kent, Dahl, Thomas, Goupy and Wootton. None, save the Gibbs, are now known. Vertue, III, pp. 56–7.
13 Vertue, III, pp. 71–2. Hogarth was a member of the Rose and Crown Club, Vertue, VI, p. 35.

JOHN VANDERBANK 1694–1739

2 Michael Rysbrack   1728

Oil on canvas, 49½×39½ in, 1257×990 mm
Provenance: 1839, Sir William Beechey Sale; Sir Robert Peel; 1917, purchased through Leggatt's, Peel Heirlooms Sale, lot 89
Literature: Webb, 1954, p. 56, frontispiece; Kerslake, 1977, *Early Georgian Portraits*, pp. 238–9, pl. 703; London: NPG, 1978, *Report of the Trustees*, pp. 14–15, figs. 2, 3
Lent by the National Portrait Gallery, London (NPG 1802)

2

Until 1978 this painting was only tentatively attributed to Vanderbank, and it was assumed that the mezzotint by Faber (Cat. No. 3) was after another version of this portrait. Restoration revealed the antique bust on the left, and eliminated the possibility of there being two differing portraits. The bust on the right does not appear in the mezzotint and was probably added at the time that the original bust on the left was painted out.[1]

John Vanderbank was born in London, the son of the Flemish-born tapestry weaver Peter Vanderbank. He worked under Kneller and in 1720 founded, with Lewis Cheron, the second English Academy in St. Martin's Lane. He assayed history painting and illustration; his version of Don Quixote was chosen in preference to Hogarth's for Lord Carteret's edition of Cervantes, published in 1738.[2] However, it was in portrait painting that, according to Vertue's account, he would have excelled, but for his dissolute life. Like Rysbrack, he lived on the Harley estate, in Holles Street near Cavendish Square. There he and his wife clearly lived above their means, and there he died "of ailments perhaps occasion'd by his irregular living (of women and wine)".[3]

Michael Rysbrack *SCULPTOR*.

---

[1] A letter from John Sequier, 18 July 1839, records that Sequier had bought that morning at Sir William Beechey's sale for £2 "not only an original but an exceeding good work by the Master, and quite perfect although very dirty" (Fitzwilliam, Peel MSS, 2–1949, No. 75). John Sequier was a picture restorer and brother of William Sequier, first Keeper of the National Gallery (Sparrow, 1960a, p. 9fn.12).
[2] London: Iveagh Bequest, Kenwood, 1968, *The French Taste in England*, Cat. Nos. 7a and b.
[3] Vertue, III, pp. 97–8.

JOHN FABER *circa* 1695–1756, after
JOHN VANDERBANK

3   Michael Rysbrack, Sculptor   1734

Mezzotint, platemark 14×10 ins, 357×254 mm
Inscribed within the plate: *J: Vanderbank pinxt.*
1728 J: Faber fecit 1734 Michael Rysbrack, Sculptor
Antuerpiae Natus Sold by J Faber at ye. Goldenhead ye.
Southside of Bloomsbury Square
Literature: Walpole, 1798, *Works*, III, p. 477;
Chilcott, 1840?, *Descriptive History of Bristol,*
Ancient and Modern, p. 263; Chancellor, 1911, *The*
Lives of British Sculptors (illus. opp. p. 99); Kers-
lake, 1977, *Early Georgian Portraits*, pl. 701
Lent by Dr Charles Avery

This print shows Cat. No. 2 before a very
dramatic overpainting which changed the entire
balance of the painting, a balance which modern
restoration has only in part returned.

It has been remarked that the bust on which
Rysbrack leans is quite unlike any known work by
him.[1] It is clearly derived from the 'Venus de
Medici'. Considered throughout the seventeenth
and eighteenth centuries "one of the half-dozen
finest antique statues to have survived",[2] the
full-length statue had become one, if not the main,
attraction of the Tribuna in the Uffizi, Florence.
Jonathan Richardson the younger had spent ten
hours "considering the beauties of the statues"
there.[3] It was eminently desirable and innumer-
able copies were made for English collectors avid
for the antique, though the Duke of Marlborough
was the last to be permitted to acquire a cast from
the original, because of the fear that the taking of
moulds would damage it.[4]

It is suggested here that Rysbrack is represented with a bust after the antique, not merely
"to represent the antique and to stress his knowledge of classical antiquity",[5] but as an example of
his own high achievement in the classical tradition that was so important to the patrons and
artists of the time. It was certainly with this
intention that Andrea Soldi painted him twenty-
five years later, standing proudly before his own
'Hercules' after the 'Farnese Hercules' (fig. 20).
Nor would it be unique. Faber's companion
mezzotint shows Laurent Delvaux with his bust
of Caracalla after the antique.[6]

Rysbrack would have been familiar with the
'Venus de Medici', perhaps from the bronze by
Soldani at Blenheim, but certainly from the plates
in Perrier and Sandrart.[7] Rysbrack's desire to be
accepted as an artist in the classical tradition was
gratified by none other than Horace Walpole,
arguably the greatest aesthete and arbiter of taste
in the eighteenth century. "What Horace Walpole required was the best sculptor in the Italian
classical tradition who was working in England"[8]
and he found him in Rysbrack, who had never
been to Italy. Rysbrack was employed to restore
antique statues that had arrived damaged from
Rome, and to complete the monument to Walpole's mother in Westminster Abbey.

That the bust is not known today, is not
surprising. Its very classicism has probably rele-
gated it to the scores of 'antique' busts in English
country houses. There is a plaster cast of a bust
identical to the bust here, set into the chimney in
the Library at Lydiard Tregoze, Swindon. At
Houghton, where Rysbrack was working for Sir
Robert Walpole at the time Vanderbank painted
his portrait, there is a very similar bust described
as "antique", set into the chimney-piece in the
Saloon.[9]

[1] Webb, 1954, p. 58.
[2] Haskell and Penny, 1981, pp. 56–7, and pp. 325–8,
   fig. 173.
[3] J. & J. Richardson, 1722.
[4] Haskell and Penny, 1981, pp. 56–7.
[5] Webb, 1954, p. 61.
[6] Avery, 1980, pp. 150–70, fig. 21.
[7] Perrier, 1638, pls. 81 and 83. Sandrart, 1680. (See Cat.
   Nos. 73 and 75.)
[8] Webb, 1954, p. 48.
[9] Hussey, 1955, pp. 72–86, fig. 113.

JONATHAN RICHARDSON
the elder 1665–1745

4 Portrait study of Michael Rysbrack

Pencil, $7\frac{5}{8} \times 5\frac{5}{8}$ in, 194×143 mm
Inscribed front and back in ink: *Rysbrac the statuary; by old Mr. Richardson. J. Cranck.*
Provenance: 1942, purchased
Literature: Kerslake, 1977, *Early Georgian Portraits*, pp. 238–9, pl. 700
Lent by the Victoria and Albert Museum, London (EI-1942)

Jonathan Richardson the elder was a portrait painter, connoisseur and writer on the theory and practice of art. He had trained under John Riley, and married his master's niece.[1] His own daughter married the painter Thomas Hudson, to whom Joshua Reynolds was later to be apprenticed. His writings were enormously influential[2] and were not to be superseded until Reynolds' own *Discourses*. In 1722 he published, in collaboration with his son, *An Account of statues, bas-reliefs, drawings and pictures in Italy* which became an essential guidebook for anyone making the Grand Tour. He received the rare distinction for an English author, of having his *Collected Works* translated into French in 1728.

Vertue provides the most vivid obituary of him:

> Tuesday May. 28. 1745. died Mr Jonathan Richardson Senior a portrait painter. of famous reputation in his Art & of the first class in his Time. he was a man of Quick & lively spirits. diligent studious and of loud elocution. lov'd excercise & walking much in his latter days. growing feeble-some years before his death he had a paralitick fitt, that weakened his right hand for which he went to the Bath he usd in a Coach to go from Queens Square (at his house) to St. Jamess park to walk for an hour or two. with his son or his daughter. (so daily almost-and return back to his dinner- this he did to his last. the day he dyd. as soon as he returnd home sat down in his chair. and made his exit. ano Ætat. 80 . . .

> this was the last of the Eminent old painters. that had been cotemporyes in Reputation- Kneller Dahl. Jarvis & Richardson for portrait painting-in England many years-.[3]

His collection of Old Master drawings was renowned and at the sale in February 1747 "there appeard an unexpected ardor in the purchasers and they sold all very well and some to extraordinary prices".[4]

James Cranke (1707–1780), whose signed inscription is on both sides of this drawing, was a Lancashire portrait painter, who also produced copies after the Old Masters.[5]

[1] Vertue, III, p. 67.
[2] 1715, *Theory of Painting*; 1719, *An Essay on . . . Criticism as it relates to Painting*.
[3] Vertue, III, p. 125.
[4] *Ibid.*, p. 134.
[5] Waterhouse, 1981. A portrait of Rysbrack in the Victoria and Albert Museum (P41–1910) is tentatively attributed to Richardson; but it is possibly the portrait mentioned by Vertue (III, p. 162) as begun by Isaac Whood and finished by Joseph van Acken in 1752.

Rysbrac the statuary; by old   m.ʳ Richardson .   I. Cranch

4

JONATHAN RICHARDSON
the elder

5 Edward Colston   1702

Oil on canvas, 50×40 in, 1270×1016 mm
Provenance: 1702, purchased by the Mayor and
Corporation
Literature: Latimer, 1893, *Annals of Bristol*, p. 46;
Waterhouse, 1981, *Dictionary of 18th Century Pain-
ters*, p. 130 (illus.)
Lent by the Lord Mayor and Corporation of the
City of Bristol

This portrait of the Bristol-born philanthropist Edward Colston (1636–1721), is one of
Richardson's earliest portraits. Latimer records
that Colston was requested by the corporation to
sit for his portrait to a London artist "who
executed the picture still in the Council House.
(The cost, including the frame and the case in
which it was forwarded, was £17.11s)".[1] The
Corporation Audit Book for 1702 records payment of £23.8.6 to Alderman Robert Yate "for
Mr. Edward Colston's picture and other
disbursements".[2] It was engraved by George
Vertue in 1722, the year after Colston's death,
and the engraving included in Horace Walpole's
list of Vertue's works under Class 9 "Founders,
Benefactors etc".[3]
    There was another version of this portrait in
Bristol which belonged to the Merchant
Venturers.[4] Mathews in his Bristol guide of 1794
records a half-length painting of Colston "said to
have been a strong resemblance; from this picture
Rysbrack modelled a likeness of his face for his
statue in All Saint's Church".[5] This assertion is
repeated by the Reverend John Evans, while
Chilcott describes a portrait of "the distinguished
philanthropist, Edward Colston, Esq. painted by
Richardson" in the Saloon of the Merchant
Venturers' Hall.[6]
    Evidence in the Merchant Venturers' Book
of Proceedings suggests that Rysbrack worked
from the missing Merchants' version of the
portrait by Richardson.[7] On 17 October 1728 it
was voted and ordered "That our standing
committee do wait upon Mr Francis Colston now
he is in this City . . . and that at the same tyme Mr
Colstone be desired to return the picture of the
late Benefactor Mr Colstone which [crossed out]
was lent him sometime ago". On 15 April 1730 he
still had not returned the painting.

5

[1] Latimer, 1893, p. 46.
[2] B.R.O. No. 70, folio 61.
[3] The City of Bristol Museum and Art Gallery (M3002);
Walpole, 1762, *Anecdotes of Painting in England*, List of
Vertue's Works p. 10 (bound in with Vol. III).
[4] Vertue (IV, p. 52) records a half-length 'Edward
Colston' by Kneller, probably the one of 1693, that
hangs today in the Administrator's Office, St.
Bartholomew's Hospital, London. Dr Friedman points
out that on 16 April 1723, the day Gibbs was elected a
governor, a limner named Partington was ordered to
clean and mend Colston's portrait (St. Bartholomew's
Hospital, *Journal*, Ha 1/10, p. 83).
[5] Mathews, 1794, p. 82.
[6] Evans, *circa* 1823, *The New Guide, or Picture of Bristol with
Historical and Biographical Notices*, p. 65; Chilcott, 1840?,
p. 231.
[7] Society of Merchant Venturers, Books of Proceedings:
A.C.R.L., Microfilm. It is no longer in the Merchants'
Hall. At Colston's School, Stapleton, there is a copy on
which the inscription on the frame reads "painted by
H. S. Parkman, from an original portrait in the
possession of the Society of Merchant Venturers and
presented by him to Colston's Hospital. A.D. 1863".
This copy, now darkened with age, appears to be
identical in composition and detail to Cat. No. 5.
Another portrait in the School Dining Room, said to be
of Colston, in a fine seventeenth-century frame, looks in
comparison with the portraits now in the Merchants'
Hall, more like Thomas than Edward.

MICHAEL RYSBRACK

6   Edward Colston   *circa* 1726

Terracotta, 23 in, 570 mm
Provenance: previously unrecorded
The City of Bristol Museum and Art Gallery
(K4753)

In 1977, this bust, covered in layers of paint, was removed from the façade of Colston Villas, Armoury Square, Bristol. It was brought to the museum for advice about conservation and was identified as the work of Rysbrack.

The development of the site of the City Armoury began in 1837 when it was sold by the Corporation of the Poor. By 1848 only three houses had been erected, with three more planned.[1] Two of the later houses took their name from the bust placed in the niche between them. Of its previous history in Bristol, however, nothing is known. Nor is it included in Vertue's list of 1732.[2]

The vivid character of the bust has led to speculation that it might have been modelled from the life, or from a death mask.[3] Colston died at the great age of eighty-five, the year after Rysbrack's arrival in London. The bust is not that of an old man but of one in the prime of life, and it was almost certainly made in preparation for the monument in All Saints', Bristol, completed in 1728 or 1729. As discussed above (Cat. No. 5), Rysbrack modelled his portrait on Richardson's painting of Colston.

Edward Colston was born in Temple Parish, Bristol in 1636. The son of a merchant and Sheriff of Bristol, he was apprenticed to a mercer in London in 1665. He worked sometime in Spain and continued in the Spanish trade of oil and fruit. While remaining in London, he conducted business in Bristol until 1689, when he retired to Mortlake in Surrey. He was Tory MP for Bristol from 1710 to 1713. Accused of being behind the anti-Hanoverian riots on the accession of George I in 1714, he is the subject of a telling if biased picture given by "A Gentleman who attended the commission" for the trial of the rioters:

> They have among them a sort of Club, who call themselves the Loyal Society, and have under that Name sent up several foolish Addresses in favour of Arbitrary Power, Hereditary Right and Sacheverel, they are very officious on all High Church Festivals, and make more Noise, drink More Beer, and swear more oaths than, half the rest of their Fellow Citizens. These Wretches, 'tis thought, fomented the late Riot, which they durst not do, if they were not satisfy'd of the peaceable and dutiful Disposition of their Opponents, for four in five of the Sober, Honest, Thriving part of the Magistrates and citizens of Bristol, are Whigs. And the Tories cou'd never have carry'd any Point here, but by the Interest of a very great Tory, and 'till lately Nonjuror, Mr C .——— who has shewn how far he prefers good works to purity of Life, by laying out some Thousands of Pounds in building Hospitals here, while himself liv'd very much at his Ease with a Tory, tho' of a different Sex at M – ke.[4]

On his retirement Colston began the great work of charity which so distinguished him, and which still plays a part in the life of Bristol. Colston's charity was, like his politics, motivated by a desire to re-establish the Church of England in Bristol which had become a centre of Dissent and Nonconformism. All his benefactions had the strictest conditions attached to them concerning the religious practice and beliefs of their inmates and staff.

In 1690 the foundation of Colston's almshouses on St. Michael's Hill was the most munificent in the city. In 1706 the Merchant Venturers agreed to administer Colston's gift of a great new boys' school, which was to be bigger and better than the old city schools, Queen Elizabeth's and the Grammar School. The City Corporation had earlier refused the benefaction because of the conditions, which allowed of no "tincture of Whiggism".[5]

[1] B.R.O. 27821 (i).
[2] Vertue, III, pp. 56–7.
[3] Little, 1955, p. 106.
[4] Quoted by Pryce, 1861, p. 422.
[5] Latimer, 1893, p. 47.

ANONYMOUS

7 Heraldic Escutcheon

Wood, painted and gilded, 39×32½ in, 990×825 mm
Emblazoned with the coat of arms of Edward Colston
Inscribed on the back: *J. Baylis J. Davis J. Miles June the 25th 1803 Chas K* [?] *Septr. 11th 1812* [?] *1821 Bennett*
Provenance: 1921, Red Lodge Collection
The City of Bristol Museum and Art Gallery (NX 400)

Traditionally carried on poles in the funeral processions of the great, the number of escutcheons was dictated in theory, by the social status of the deceased. According to Latimer "The great funerals took place at or about midnight, the coffin being borne along the streets with all the pomp of escutcheons, sconces, waxlights, flambeaux, plumes, pennons and mutes".[1] They were occasions of great ostentation, Bristolians apparently being particularly prone to this form of extravagance.

Edward Colston had died in 1721 at Mortlake in Surrey, but his remains were brought back to Bristol for interment in the ancestral vault in All Saints', and Latimer's description of the funeral progress cannot be bettered:

> The funeral procession, which was a week or ten days upon the road, consisted of a hearse with six horses, covered with plumes and velvet, and attended by eight horsemen in black cloaks, bearing banners; and three mourning coaches with six horses to each. At the resting places on the way, a room was hung with black, garnished with silver shields and escutcheons, while upwards of fifty wax candles in silver candlesticks and sconces were placed around the coffin, covered with a silver-edged velvet pall. The gloomy cavalcade reached Lawford's Gate on the night of the 27th October, where it was met by the boys of deceased's schools in St. Augustine's and Temple, the almspeople in the hospital on St. Michael's Hill, and the old sailors maintained at Colston's charge in the Merchants' Almshouse. (The thirty old people received new clothes for the occasion.) The procession, accompanied by torches, with the schoolboys singing psalms, made its way to the church amidst continuous torrents of rain, and the interment took place about midnight, in the presence of as many persons as could crush into the building. The bells of the various parish churches tolled for sixteen hours on the day appointed for the funeral.[2]

Latimer, when describing the funeral in 1729 of another Bristolian, Cornelius Stevens of Queen Square, whose hearse was covered in heraldic escutcheons, quotes the London *Weekly Journal*'s report that "the mob, as was its custom, tore off the glittering panoply". Two of Colston's escutcheons had survived the two hundred years until 1921, because they probably became part of the regalia of the charitable societies that administered his will, and were carried in the annual procession commemorating the great benefactor's birthday on 13 November.

[1] Latimer, 1893, pp. 8–9.
[2] *Ibid.*, p. 129.

7

JAMES GIBBS 1682–1754

8 **"A Monument now making to the Memory of Edward Colston, Esq; to be erected at Bristol. The Figures are by Mr. Rysbrack".**
From *A Book of Architecture* by James Gibbs, 1728

Engraving, plate size 14×9¾ in, 378×248 mm
Inscribed within the plate with a scale in inches and: *p 113 Jacobo Gibbs. Architecto. I. Harris. sculp.*
On the back in ink: *Somerset No 5343*
The City of Bristol Museum and Art Gallery (M1646)

The title is taken from Gibbs' introduction to his *Book of Architecture* (p. xxiii), published in 1728 (see Cat. No. 11).

G. SCOTIN

9 **"THE MONUMENT OF THE LATEWORTHY, GREAT, GOOD, PIOUS AND CHARITABLE Edward Colston Esqr."** 1751

Engraving, plate size 23½×18½ in, 597 ×461 mm
Signed within the plate: *G. Scotin sculp.*
Inscribed within the plate with the title and: *Printed, and Publish'd according to Act of Parliament 1751.*
The City of Bristol Museum and Art Gallery (Mb 423)

Scotin's engraving is much closer in detail to the monument than the engraving in Gibbs' *Book of Architecture* (Cat. No. 8) where the *putti* and the decoration above the pediment are different. The egg-and-dart motif, which appears in the engraving along the edge of the table top, is missing in the finished monument. It is possible that Scotin, who was a fellow member of the Rose and Crown Club,[1] based his engraving upon a missing drawing by Rysbrack.

[1] Vertue, VI, p. 35.

THE MONUMENT OF THE LATEWORTHY, GREAT, GOOD, PIOUS, AND CHARITABLE Edward Colston Esq'.

8   9

10

MICHAEL RYSBRACK

10   James Gibbs   1726

Marble, 20 in, 510 mm
Inscribed on the back: *Iac: Gibbs Arch: Ml. Rysbrack Sculp: 1726*
Provenance: 1885, presented to St. Martin-in-the-Fields by William Boore
Literature: Webb, 1954, p. 53, fig. 10, and p. 216; Little, 1955, *The Life and Work of James Gibbs*, pl. 29; Whinney, 1964, *Sculpture in Britain 1530–1830*, pl. 59B; Kerslake, 1977, *Early Georgian Portraits*, pl. 262
Exhibited: Liverpool: Walker Art Gallery, 1958, 'Painting and Sculpture in England 1700–1750', Cat. No. 49. London: Iveagh Bequest, Kenwood, 1959, '18th Century Portrait Busts', Cat. No. 28
Lent by the Vicar and Churchwardens of St. Martin-in-the-Fields, London

James Gibbs (1682–1754) was the outstanding architect of the early eighteenth century. Rysbrack knew him very well, for it was to Gibbs that Rysbrack was recommended on first coming to England in October 1720,[1] and for whom he did much work. On Vertue's account it appears to have been a not altogether happy working relationship. Gibbs apparently employed Rysbrack "for his own advantage not for Encouragement"; Vertue speaks of "extravagant exactions" on Rysbrack's labour, and of his poor reward, and he sums it up as "an unreasonable gripeing usage to a most Ingenious Artist. (in his way) far more merrit than Gibbs ever will be. Mr [Master] of."[2]

James Gibbs was born in Aberdeen. He went to Rome originally to study for the priesthood, but took up architecture and studied under Carlo Fontana. On his return he settled in London and became the leading architect of the time. Vertue, who was not apparently very fond of Gibbs, says grudgingly "he has fortund very well here, by his industry and great business of publick & private works".[3]

His work includes St. Mary-le-Strand (1714–17), St. Martin-in-the-Fields (1721–6), parts of the Senate House and King's College, Cambridge, and the Radcliffe Camera, Oxford, which was opened in 1749. He was both the architect and a governor of St. Bartholomew's Hospital. He was resident architect to Lord Oxford, working both at Wimpole in Cambridgeshire, and overseeing the development of the Harley Estates in London, on which he owned three houses. He lived in Henrietta Street and was one of Rysbrack's neighbours.

Vertue refers to three portraits of Gibbs by Rysbrack. He records a "Modeld" bust, probably of terracotta, a marble bust, and a "basso relievo. with a wigg on."[4] The terracotta and the *basso-relievo* are missing, but two marble busts of James Gibbs by Rysbrack are known today. Besides the present work, there is one in a niche in the Radcliffe Camera.[5] It, too, is signed and dated 1726, but it is *al antica*, and therefore without a wig. It is probably the one described by Vertue as "Mr. *Jacomo* or James. Gibbs Architect . . . his head a Modeld by Mr. Rysbrack extreamly like him a bald head. Cutt in Marble from that".[6] An engraving in *Biblioteca Radcliviana* (pl. XI) shows the niche with a bust *al antica* in situ, and it is possible that Gibbs intended it to be his own, and that it has been there since the building was completed.[7]

One aspect of the collaboration between the architect and the sculptor has not been remarked on before. It is quite clear that Rysbrack frequently drew in the figures on Gibbs' architectural drawings. The effigy on the Buckingham monument in Gibbs' *Book of Architecture*, pl. 116, is more than coincidentally like the effigy in the Rysbrack design, Cat. No. 44. In two Gibbs designs for the entrance to the interior of the Radcliffe Camera, the figure of Dr Radcliffe overlaps the architectural drawings.[8] It is in Rysbrack's characteristic brown ink and wash, and the shading has a subtlety notably absent from Gibbs' rendered designs, as in Cat. No. 14. The first design is reversed ready for engraving.[9]

A marble bust of Gibbs was in Horace Walpole's collection at Strawberry Hill in the Star Chamber and was sold in a sale on 13 May 1842 (lot 99). "A fine bust of Jac. Gibbs by Rysbrack" was lot 88 in a Christie's sale on 27 March 1783.[10]

[1] Vertue, I, p. 76.
[2] Vertue, III, p. 17.
[3] Vertue, III, p. 133.
[4] Vertue, III, p. 13.
[5] Lane Poole, 1912, No. 685, pl. XXXV.
[6] Vertue, III, p. 13.
[7] The equivalent niche on the opposite side was not to be filled until 1789 with the terracotta bust of the builder of the Radcliffe Camera (Webb, 1954, p. 180).
[8] Ashmolean, Oxford: Gibbs Collection, I, 111b and III, 82. In the introduction to *Biblioteca Radcliviana*, published in 1747, Gibbs states "Mr Michael Rysbrack to be Sculptor, to cut the Doctor's Figure in Marble".
[9] Gibbs, 1747, pl. XII; ledgers R and S, Messrs C. Hoare & Co., confirm the payment of £220 to Rysbrack by the Trustees of Dr John Radcliffe as stated in the

agreement of March 1744, published by Webb, 1954, p. 168, but the dates of payment, 13 April 1745, £100, and 10 September 1746, £120, suggest that the statue was begun later and finished sooner than was thought. The ledgers record payments of £605 to James Gibbs by the Trustees between 1742 and 1748.

[10] Gunnis, 1953, p. 335.

JAMES GIBBS

11   "A Book of Architecture, containing Designs of Buildings and Ornaments, London"   1728

Open at plate 123.
Inscribed in the plate with a scale and: *Jacobo Gibbs Architecto E. Kirkall sculp:*
Lent by Bryan Little

In his introduction Gibbs describes this plate as "Three Monuments: The middle one is *Sir John Bridgman's* set up at *Ashton* in *Warwickshire*, and the others for two ladies." The left-hand design is the pattern from which the monument to Mary Edwards (1736), wife of Walter Edwards, in St.

James's, Bristol, is taken. This monument is not signed, and has not previously been attributed to Rysbrack.[1]

It has been suggested that Michael Sidnell was responsible for its execution.[2] Sidnell, "freemason and stone cutter", was a member of St. James's Vestry,[3] and his name occurs regularly in the audits of the corporation. He worked on Redland Chapel and was responsible for erecting Colston's monument in All Saints', which he boldly signed. Sidnell was also among the subscribers to the *Book of Architecture*. His signed monument to Thomas and Jane Edwards (1733), also in St. James's, is clearly inspired by Rysbrack's monument to Andrew Innys (1726) in St. John's (figs. 30 and 29). It lacks the assurance of the Innys monument and its detail, particularly the cherubs' heads, is poor in comparison (fig. 28).

There are numerous examples of Rysbrack adapting this design by Gibbs (see Cat. Nos. 12 and 33) but the monument to Mary Edwards is the closest. It has the solidity and balance typical of Rysbrack's wall tablets; there is nothing mean or skimped in the interpretation of the original design. It has all the style of a metropolitan piece.

11

75

Certain technical details are typical of Rysbrack's work, particularly the pounced background of the Vitruvian scrolling along the base of the tablet, which is identical to that on the Tynte monument at Goathurst (fig. 36).

The name Edwards occurs frequently in the city's records; members of the family were important within Bristol, in the county and in London. Thomas Edwards, senior (1644–1727) is described in 1690 as an "attorney at law".[4] He acted for the Astry family of Henbury and for the Smyths of Ashton Court. Arabella Astry, Countess of Suffolk, left him £400 in her will.[5] He was a guardian and governor of the Bristol Corporation of the Poor, a witness to the Colston Settlements, and the principal executor of Colston's will.[6] He and his second wife Jane, the sister of Henry Walter, Mayor of Bristol in 1715 (see Cat. No. 12, fig. 32) were benefactors of the parishes of St. James and St. John.[7] Four of his sons, Thomas, Walter, Joseph and William, followed him into the law.[8]

It is not clear from documents of 1711, which describe Thomas Edwards as of "The Middle Temple, London" and "the Six Clerkes Office in Chancery Lane" which generation is referred to; the latter shows, incidentally, that Andrew Innys was an associate.[9] A document of 1737 referring to Thomas Edwards, junior, as "of the Middle Temple, London Esq" shows that he and his wife had an interest in land at Westerleigh that was being developed for coal.[10] He married Mary, daughter of Alderman Sir William Hayman, and Edward Colston's niece. He stood as Tory candidate for Bristol on Colston's retirement and was returned in the election of 1714.[11] The following year, in the general election occasioned by the death of Queen Anne, amidst chicanery on both sides the vote was scrutinised and Edwards was disallowed. He petitioned against the ruling in 1715, 1717 and 1718 to no avail.[12] He, too, was an executor of Colston's will under which his wife inherited.[13]

His brother Walter Edwards who commissioned the monument in St. James's to his wife, Mary, signed a letter of 1730 from Chancery Lane;[14] in 1735 he is described as "of the Parish of St. Dunstan in the West, London"[15] and in 1738 he wrote to Henry Woolnough, a Bristol lawyer married to John Elbridge's niece and heiress Rebecca, from his house in Lincolns Inn Fields.[16] In a letter dated 25 July 1738 he writes to Woolnough "most other people being upon going out of Town . . . I intend for my brother Freemans in Gloucestershire next week from whence I shall

come down to Bristol towards the latter end of August".[17] Walter Edwards had married Mary the daughter of Richard Freeman of Batsford Park in Gloucestershire.[18] Two Freemans are recorded in the list of subscribers to the *Book of Architecture*. Walter's son Thomas took the name of Freeman and inherited Batsford but also had "a good estate" at Redland.[19] Walter Edwards died in 1752 and left money at interest in his will for the repair of two monuments in St. James's; one to the memory of his father and mother, Thomas and Jane Edwards by Sidnell, the other to his wife, Mary Edwards, by Rysbrack.[20]

This volume of the *Book of Architecture* is inscribed on the flyleaf *Margaret Cavendishe-Harley Febr. 1731–2*. Lady Margaret Cavendish-Holles-Harley was the daughter of Gibbs' patron the Earl of Oxford. Rysbrack did the bust of her, now at Welbeck Abbey, Nottinghamshire, in 1723, when she was eight.[21]

---

1 Barrett (1789) records the monument and its inscription, Pevsner (1958a) does not mention it. Gunnis notes the possibility on the Conway Library photograph of it.
2 Little, 1955, p. 107.
3 B.R.O. P/St.J./V./4.
4 B.R.O. AC/WO 10 (1) a.
5 B.R.O. AC/AS 4 (34) i.
6 Bristol Record Society, III, 1932; A.C.R.L., 'Colston Settlements,' L36.3.
7 B.R.O. P/St.J/Ch. W./1c); Barrett, 1789, p. 491.
8 B.R.O. AC/AS (6); AC/AS 4 (34) a and c; 41 16 (5).
9 B.R.O. AC/WO 10 (3); 30631 (14) a and b.
10 B.R.O. AC/AS 70/2; 4204.2.
11 Beavan, 1899, p. 165; Latimer, 1893, p. 102.
12 Latimer, 1893, p. 108.
13 Of the two daughters of this marriage one married Francis, Lord Middleton, the other Alexander Ready who subsequently took the name Colston: Wilkins, 1920; C. Hoare and Co., Ledger Accounts.
14 B.R.O. AC/WO 3(1).
15 B.R.O. 08022 (11).
16 B.R.O. AC/WO 13 (20) g.
17 B.R.O. AC/WO 13 (15) a.
18 Appendix No. 7; Batsford Park was engraved by Kip for Atkyns' *Ancient and Present State of Glostershire*, 1712, pl. 14.
19 Rudder, 1779, p. 802.
20 Manchee, 1831, I, p. 451.
21 Webb, 1954, fig. 35.

fig. 28 Detail from the monument to Andrew Innys, 1726, St. John's, Bristol.

fig. 29 Monument to Andrew Innys, 1726, St. John's, Bristol.

fig. 30 The monument to Thomas and Jane Edwards by Michael Sidnell, 1733, St. James's, Bristol.

fig. 31 The monument to Mary Edwards (died 1736), St. James's, Bristol.

fig. 32 The monument to Henry Walter (died 1737), by F. Curtis of Bristol. The Lord Mayor's Chapel, Bristol.

MICHAEL RYSBRACK

12 Sketch incorporating designs for a pair of monuments either side of an altarpiece, one with a profile elevation, possibly for St. James's, Bristol

Pen and ink and brown wash, 16×18 in, 406×479 mm
Inscribed with a scale
Provenance: 1864, purchased from Miss Helen Oaks of Bath
Lent by the Victoria and Albert Museum, London (4248)

The design for a monument on the left-hand side of this drawing is very close to the Gibbs design used for the monument to Mary Edwards (died 1736) in St. James's, Bristol (Cat. No. 11), while the design on the right has close affinities with another Bristol monument, that to Henry Walter (died 1737) in the Lord Mayor's Chapel.[1] That neither corresponds exactly to either executed monument is not surprising for Rysbrack often produced an alternative to a Gibbs design.

The designs themselves have the precision characteristic of his working drafts, but the hasty allusion to an altarpiece is unique among the drawings that have survived. The altarpiece indicated in the centre is of a late-seventeenth-, early-eighteenth-century type depicting Jehovah,

12

Moses and Elijah supporting tables of the Law. An altarpiece in St. James's was replaced by another, painted by Nicholas Mead, in 1753–4.[2] The subject of the earlier one is not known, that of the second was the Transfiguration.[3] A change of fashion in theology as well as aesthetics may have dictated the change. At St. Mary Redcliffe, Hogarth's triptych of 1755–6 replaced an earlier one of 1709.[4]

The scheme was not carried out, however. The monument to Mary Edwards is now in the south aisle of St. James's (fig. 31) while the Henry Walter monument was executed and perhaps designed by F. Curtis and placed in the Mayor's Chapel (fig. 32).[5]

[1] Henry Walter, Mayor of Bristol in 1715, was the uncle of Mary Edwards' husband, Walter Edwards.
[2] B.R.O. P/St.J./V./20/6.
[3] A watercolour by Thomas Manning is in the Braikenridge Collection at the City of Bristol Museum and Art Gallery (M2823).
[4] Liversidge, 1980, p. 8.
[5] Gunnis, 1953, p. 119. Curtis' monument is closely related to the monument to William Colston (died 1701) in All Saints', Bristol, erected by Edward Colston. The William Colston monument is in the style of the workshop of Grinling Gibbons (Stewart, 1963, pp. 125–6). Curtis simplified and updated the composition, with reference to Gibbs.

JAMES GIBBS

13a Design for the monument to Sir Edward Seymour, Bt, Maiden Bradley, Wiltshire   1728–30

Pen and ink and grey wash, $13\frac{5}{8} \times 11$ in, 346×280 mm
Literature: Little, 1955, *The Life and Work of James Gibbs*, p. 106, pl. 17

Design for a monument

Pencil, pen and ink and grey wash, $13\frac{3}{4} \times 10\frac{5}{16}$ in, 349×262 mm
Lent by the Visitors of the Ashmolean Museum, Oxford (Gibbs III 52b and a)

Until recently Cat. No. 13 was thought to be an alternative design for the Colston monument (Cat. No. 8).[1] However, the contract between Francis Seymour, subscriber to *A Book of Architecture* and Walter Lee, Marylebone mason, dated 11 June 1728, specifies a marble tomb "according to the draught or design drawn thereof by James Gibbs Esqr. . . The Figures and all the rest of the Carving about the said Monument shall be carved and finished by Michael Rysbraelk, Statuary" at a cost of £500, and Lee received £400 by 9 October 1729.[2] The *Grub-Street Journal* reported on 29 January 1731 that Francis Seymour "in just veneration for the memory of his illustrious Grandfather, and in due Obedience to the last Will and Testament of Lieutenant General William Seymour, Second Son of the deceased . . . hath caused the monument to be erected. 1730'.[3]

Sir Richard Colt Hoare in his *History of Modern Wiltshire, the Hundred of Mere* said that it was the only tomb worthy of notice in the parish church at Maiden Bradley, but qualified this by adding that "Like the material of which it is formed, it is a heavy performance."[4]

Sir Edward Seymour (1633–1708) was MP first for Gloucester and later for Devonshire, Totnes and Exeter, and Speaker of the House of Commons in 1673.

[1] Little, 1955, p. 106.
[2] P.R.O., Chancery Masters Exhibits, C107/126. Referred to in Gunnis, 1953, p. 335.
[3] No. 56, p. 56. I am grateful to Dr Terry Friedman for these two references.
[4] Hoare, 1822, pp. 109–10.

80

13

fig. 33 The monument to Sir Edward Seymour, Bt, 1728–30, Maiden Bradley, Wiltshire

14

JAMES GIBBS

14 Design for the monument to Sir Ambrose Crowley (*circa* 1659–1713) **and his wife Mary** (died 1727)**, Mitcham, Surrey**

Pen and ink and wash, $7\frac{3}{4} \times 4\frac{1}{2}$ in, 197 × 114 mm
Provenance: 1866, purchased from B. Quaritch
Literature: Physick, 1969, *Designs for English Sculpture, 1680–1860*, pp. 76–7, fig. 44
Lent by the Victoria and Albert Museum, London (4910.52)

81

15

MICHAEL RYSBRACK

15　John Cossins　　　　1734

Marble, 24½ in, 622 mm
Provenance: 1762, removed from Redland Court to Redland Chapel
Literature: Roper, 1931, *Effigies of Gloucestershire*, p. 181; Webb, 1954, p. 213; Wilson, 1976, Rysbrack in Bristol, *Apollo*, CIII, p. 24; Gomme, Jenner and Little, 1979, *Bristol, an architectural history*, fig. 107
Lent by the Diocese of Bristol

"The marble bust of John Cossins Esqr. Founder of this Chapel and of Martha his wife were this day removed from Redland Court their late dwelling House into the chapel and placed in two Niches prepared for them according to their request in their life time. Those busts where carved in 1734 by Michael Rysbrack of London". This brief account, written almost certainly by John Innys, is contained in the contemporary 'Chronological Account of the Most Material Occurences relating to Redland Chapel'.[1] Unlike the other two busts by Rysbrack (Cat. Nos. 19 and 20) in the chapel, the identity and artist of the busts of John and Martha Cossins were not forgotten and are repeated in numerous local guides and topographical histories.[2] Roper in 1931 believed them to have been executed "from life for the drawing room of the court."[3] Cossins had bought Redland Court in 1732 and its rebuilding was not completed until 1735.

Cossins (1682–1759) was born and brought up in London in the parish of St. Gregory on the south-west side of St. Paul's churchyard.[4] His father was a grocer, and a member of the Bowyers' Company to which John was admitted in 1705. In 1714 he married Martha Innys, daughter of a Bristol lawyer. His brothers-in-law, John and William Innys, were near neighbours (Cat. Nos. 19 and 20).

In 1732, at the age of 50, Cossins purchased the manor at Redland from his wife's uncle Gregory Martin. Since 1712 the manor had been mortgaged to Martin Innys and to his wife's father, Andrew Innys.[5] Cossins proceeded to take down the old Manor House and Redland Court was completed within three years in 1735. In 1740 work on Redland Chapel was begun.

John Cossins appears to have taken no part in the public life of Bristol. Although he was appointed a High Sheriff for Gloucestershire, he was represented in this office by his brother-in-law John Innys. He may well have been involved in the founding of the Bristol Infirmary to which he left one hundred pounds in his will.[6] He also left money to the three hospitals of "St Bartholomew, Bethlehem, and Christ, in London", of all three of which he had been a governor.

[1] B.R.O. P/RG/R/3b, being a transcript of the original 'Redland Burial Lists' which has disappeared, quoted by Wilkins, 1924, pp. 30–1.
[2] Rudder, 1779, p. 803, "well executed in marble by Rysbrack"; Shiercliff, Mathews and Chilcott, etc.
[3] Roper, 1931, p. 181.
[4] Except where stated, information on the Cossins family is drawn from the inscriptions on the reverse of the Vanderbank portraits (Cat. Nos. 17 and 18); Wilkins, 1924; and 'A Chronological Account . . . Redland Chapel', (B.R.O. P/RG/R/3b).
[5] Charlton and Milton, 1951, pp. 36–7.
[6] B.R.O. 8015.10 (copy) 23 December 1756.

MICHAEL RYSBRACK

16　Martha Cossins　　　　1734

Marble, 24 in, 610 mm
Provenance: 1762, removed from Redland Court to Redland Chapel
Literature: as Cat. No. 15
Lent by the Diocese of Bristol

The St. John's Parish Registers record Martha's baptism on 22 October 1688.[1] The youngest daughter of the fourteen children of Andrew Innys (fig. 29, Appendix No. 5), she married John Cossins on 5 October 1714. It was her uncle Gregory Martin who had mortgaged Redland to her father and elder brother Martin, and from whom her husband purchased it in 1732. She clearly took an active part in the building projects at Redland and we find her laying the four corner stones of the houses built to augment the income of the chapel, on 25 April 1758. She was her husband's heiress and executrix and after his death continued his patronage. She maintained the fabric of the building, put in new seating and commissioned the font. Martha Cossins died on 11 February 1762, and "was interred in the Chapel Vault on the 18th which Vault is full up and Closed up not to be opened up anymore".[2] She left Redland first to her brother Jeremy, and then to John, after which it was to go to Jeremy's son-in-law, Slade Baker.[3]

[1] B.R.O. P/St. JB/R/1b).
[2] B.R.O. P/RG/R/3b).
[3] B.R.O. 8015(11).

JOHN VANDERBANK

17 John Cossins

Oil on canvas, $29\frac{1}{4} \times 24\frac{1}{2}$ in, 743×615 mm
Inscribed on paper pasted on back, probably in John Innys' hand: *John Cossins of Redland Court Esqr. Son of Roger Cossins of London by Martha one of the five Daughters and Co-Heiresses of Francis Saville of London Esqr. He was born in London Feb. 20. 1682 Married Martha the Youngest Daughter of Andrew Innys of Bristol Gent. Feb. 5. 1714 Bought the Mannor of Redland Court Jul. 18. 1732 Rebuilt the Mansion House wch. was finished July 14. 1735 paid his Fine for Sheriffe of London and Middlesex June 23. 1737 Built the Chapel at Redland Wch. was opened Oct. 5. 1743. was appointed High Sheriffe for the County of Gloucester Feb. 25 1755. Was sworn into that office March 10 1755; but was represented by his Brother in Law John Innys. He departed this Life at Redland Court April 19. 1759. Aged 77. And was interred in the Vault under the Communion Table Post Funera Virtus. J. Vanderbank p.*
Provenance: John Cossins; Redland Chapel; 1948, on permanent loan to Redland High School
Literature: Charlton and Milton, 1951, *Redland, 800–1800*, (illus.)
Lent by the Diocese of Bristol

The attribution to John Vanderbank derives from the inscription on the reverse and has not been questioned, but the over-restored nature of this portrait and particularly of its pair (Cat. No. 18) reduces their interest to that of documents. The portraits could date from 1714, the year of the sitters' marriage but this is several years before the earliest of Vanderbank's signed and dated portraits.[1]

The altarpiece in Redland Chapel is also attributed to Vanderbank.[2] It is a copy after Annibale Carracci's 'Entombment', which was then at Houghton and which was subsequently sold to Catherine the Great, and later destroyed in a fire at the Hermitage. Shiercliff in his *Bristol and Hotwell Guide* of 1793 gives it not to John Vanderbank, but to his younger brother, Moses. Described as a history painter, Moses Vanderbank (fl. 1720–1745) has only one other recorded commission, the altarpieces of 1745 for the church at Adel, Leeds.[3] If the copy after Carracci was specifically commissioned for Redland Chapel, it is certainly likely that Moses was the artist, as his brother died in 1739, a year before work on the chapel was begun.

[1] Waterhouse, 1981.
[2] Wilkins, 1924, p. 27 fn, records a note in John Innys' hand on the front page of the Chapel Minute Book.
[3] Croft-Murray, 1970, II, p. 289.

17

JOHN VANDERBANK

18 Martha Cossins

Oil on canvas, $29\frac{1}{4} \times 24$ in, 743×610 mm

Inscription pasted on the back, probably in John Innys' hand: *Mrs Martha Cossins Wife of John Cossins Esq. of Redland Court and youngest Daughter of Andrew Innys, Bristol, Gent,* [illegible] *Daughter of* [illegible] *Martin of Bristol* [illegible] *of Redland Court She was born* [illegible] *16 1688 Departed this life* [illegible] *1762 Aged 74. Vanderbank p.*

Provenance: John Cossins; Redland Chapel; 1948, on permanent loan to Redland High School

Literature: as Cat. No. 17

Lent by the Diocese of Bristol

MICHAEL RYSBRACK

19 William Innys   *circa* 1734

Marble, $26\frac{1}{2}$ in, 673 mm

Provenance: unrecorded before 1924

Literature: Wilkins, 1924, *Redland Chapel and Redland*, p. 26; Roper, 1931, *Effigies of Gloucestershire*, p. 181; Gomme, Jenner and Little, 1979, *Bristol, an architectural history*, p. 139

Lent by the Diocese of Bristol

This bust and that of John Innys (Cat. No. 20) are set above the doorways to the right and left of the entrance vestibule of Redland Chapel, at a point where the eye is naturally carried forward towards the altar. It is perhaps not surprising that they have been so long ignored.

There is no documentary evidence for the sitter or artist of either of these busts, nor is there any record of the date at which they were transferred to Redland Chapel. Wilkins, in his account of Redland, published in 1924, makes the earliest reference to them and remarks that they are "probably John Innys and his wife".[1] John Innys died a bachelor and the subjects are indubitably men. Roper suggests that they are possibly Jeremy and John Innys.[2] There is still, however, no attribution as to artist. Pevsner first tentatively attributes them to Rysbrack, but hazards nothing as to the sitters.[3] Jenner, in a footnote, tacitly accepts the attribution to Rysbrack but proposes John Strahan (see Cat. No. 32) and John Innys as the likely sitters.[4]

There is a distinct likeness in the features of the two busts, despite the obvious difference in the age of the sitters. It is not inconceivable that the elder of them is Jeremy Innys, the tobacco merchant, a trustee of Redland Chapel and, very briefly, owner of Redland Court.[5] He, too, had London connections, going there on parliamentary business on behalf of the Merchant Venturers.[6] But it is much more probable that, as a pair, they represent the booksellers and publishers William and John Innys, the former of whom was eminent in the trade. As brothers-in-law of John Cossins and his neighbours in the West End of St. Paul's for more than thirty years, they were later to make their home with him at Redland. It seems likely that all four busts were sculpted in 1734, the documented date for Rysbrack's busts of John and Martha Cossins.

The two busts are *en négligé*, that is to say they are in informal or indoor dress, even more so than John and Martha Cossins, for Mr Cossins wears a wig while Mrs Cossins' appearance verges on the classical, a convention of portrait painting at the time. Rysbrack did incorporate busts *en négligé* in designs for monuments, such as those to Sir Godfrey Kneller in Westminster Abbey or Sir Richard Newdigate (Cat. No. 34), but like Coysevox's bust of Matthew Prior in Westminster Abbey these two busts were almost certainly originally intended for a domestic setting.

The baptism of William Innys "Son of Andrew Innys and Elizabeth" is recorded in the Parish Register of St. John the Baptist, Bristol, on 5 January 1685.[7] An elder brother of the same name had died within twenty-four hours of birth in April 1677.[8] In 1702 he was apprenticed to Benjamin Walford, bookseller of the West End, St. Paul's Churchyard, London, and freed on 6 June 1709. In 1710 he took over Walford's business and in the same year, his brother John was bound to him as apprentice. They became partners in 1720 on John's receiving his freedom.[9] That year they brought out an eight-page miscellaneous catalogue of books which they had published, that included Clarendon's *History of Rebellion* in six volumes, Stype's *Life of Archbishop Whitgift* and La Neve's *Monumenta Anglicana* in five volumes. They were also the 'agents' for many of Sir Isaac Newton's works. William Innys had become "one of the leading booksellers in London".[10] In 1732 he took his apprentice, Richard Manby, into partnership[11] and it was this partnership that undertook the second edition of Gibbs' *A Book of Architecture* and, in collaboration with others, brought it out in 1739. During this time, too, Innys was caught up in the publication of Ludolf Kuster's *Suidas Lexicon*, a most unsuccessful publishing venture.[12] William Innys was one of the Upper and Under Wardens

of the Stationers' Company in 1739, 1740, 1743 and 1744, and he was Master in 1747 and 1748.[13]

He was still actively engaged in publishing in 1756, the year of his death, bringing out Totton's *Two Sermons* in association with Joseph Richardson. But he moved to Bristol soon after, for his will, dated 13 September 1756, begins "I William Innys of London Bookseller but now Resident at my brother-in-law's John Cossins of Redland Court . . ."[14] He left money to Christ's Hospital of which he had been a governor, and £20 for mourning for his partner Joseph Richardson and his wife. He died at Redland on 1 December 1756 and was interred in the vault of St. John the Baptist, Bristol, on 7 December. He had been one of the original trustees named in the deed of endowment for Redland Chapel in 1749.[15]

[1] Wilkins, 1924, p. 26.
[2] Roper, 1931, p. 187.
[3] Pevsner, 1958a, p. 471.
[4] Gomme, Jenner and Little, 1979, p. 139 fn. 6.
[5] B.R.O. 8015 (11); Jeremy Innys succeeded his sister Martha, who had died in 1762, and died in 1765.
[6] Society of Merchant Venturers, 'Books of Proceedings': A.C.R.L., Microfilm.
[7] B.R.O. P/St. JB/R/1b).
[8] B.R.O. P/St. JB/R/1a).
[9] McKenzie, 1978.
[10] Plomer, 1922.
[11] McKenzie, 1978.
[12] Roberts, 1956.
[13] McKenzie, 1978.
[14] B.R.O. 8015 (22).
[15] B.R.O. P/RG/R3b.

MICHAEL RYSBRACK

20 John Innys *circa* 1734

Marble, 25½ in, 648 mm
Provenance: unrecorded before 1924
Literature: as Cat. No. 19
Lent by the Diocese of Bristol

The youngest and last of the Innys family, John Innys is directly or indirectly the source of almost all our information about Redland and the Cossins–Innys family.

Born in 1695, "John Sonn of Andrew and Elizabeth Enis" was baptised on 16 July of that year.[1] He was apprenticed to his brother, William, as a bookseller in London in 1709. In 1720, on gaining his freedom, he joined his brother in partnership. John is recorded as taking on an apprentice in 1727 and at about this time he set up in business on his own.[2] Almost nothing is known of his business though he was still in London in 1749 as the deed of endowment for Redland Chapel described him as "of London, Stationer".[3] The first notice of his having retired to Redland comes in the inscription on the flyleaf of his copy of Camden's *Britannia* which reads "John Innys/1754/Redland Glouc."[4] The following year he represented John Cossins as High Sheriff of Gloucestershire.

John Innys pursued the interests of a man of leisure. In 1767 he was visited by Sir Joseph Banks, who was very dismissive and thought his garden "very trifling, scarce one good Plant in the whole Collection. Mr Innis values himself cheifly upon officinal Plants, consequently is well stored with nettles, Docks etc".[5]

That he had an orderly turn of mind is clear from his *System of Cosmography*, a topographical collection which he described in a letter in 1749 as "the amusement of my leisure hours for above thirty years".[6] The one hundred and thirteen volumes are now at Holkham in Norfolk. The three volumes of 'Biographical Memoranda' are painstakingly neat alphabetical lists of the world's great men, their dates of birth and their deaths.[7] It is not surprising, therefore, to find that on 3 November 1757 an entry in his own 'Chronological Account of . . . Redland Chapel' reads "Ordered that all the writings be fairly copied into a Book and properly attested and that Mr. John Innys be desired to take care of the same."[8] John Innys died on 27 October 1778.

[1] B.R.O. P/St. JB/R/1b).
[2] McKenzie, 1978.
[3] B.R.O. P/RG/R/3b); Wilkins, 1924, p. 32.
[4] B.R.O. 08482 (2).
[5] Perceval, (ed.), 1898, p. 25.
[6] *Ibid.*; Perceval points out that there is a copy of this letter in Vertue's letterbook (1743–6) in the British Museum. Wilkins, 1924, p. 89.
[7] Innys, A.C.R.L., 10921–3.
[8] B.R.O. P/RG/R/3b): Wilkins, 1924, p. 36.

89

JOHN JACOB DE WILSTAR

21 "Ye GARDEN FRONT of REDLAND-COURT being the Seat of JOHN COSSINS Esq. 1735"

Pen and ink and watercolour, $14\frac{1}{8} \times 26$ in, 356×660 mm
Inscribed with title and scale in feet and:*Delin I.I. de Wilstar Inventet & Executed by I. Strahan Archit.*
Lent by the British Library (K.Top. XIII 773b)

Redland Court is one of the few works that may be firmly attributed to John Strahan, about whom very little is known of either his origins or his training. He was working in Bristol by 1726 when the stone gallery and organ of St. Mary Redcliffe were put up to his design.[1] The following year he was in Bath working in Kingsmead and Beaufort Square. In 1729 he was paid two guineas among the disbursements for pulling down and rebuilding Redcliffe Gate.[2] Redland Court was begun in 1732 and completed three years later.[3] Several other houses have been attributed to Strahan on stylistic grounds, most convincingly Frampton Court, Gloucestershire, built for Richard Clutterbuck in 1731.[4]

It seems very likely that Strahan was responsible for the design of Redland Chapel, which he did not live to see completed (see Cat. No. 22). John Wood in his *Description of Bath* published in 1742 notes that Strahan is dead.[5]

With such scant biographical information it is all the more remarkable that "John Straughan Surveyor of Bristol" should be among those listed by Vertue in 1732 as having been "Modelld from the life" by Rysbrack.[6] This bust, recorded as missing[7] or as one of the busts at Redland Chapel[8] may yet be the one recently discovered in the Lord Mayor's Chapel (see Cat. No. 32).

John Jacob de Wilstar was a property surveyor and valuer much employed by the Corporation of Bristol.[9]

[1] Ison, 1952, pp. 45–6.
[2] B.R.O. 04026 (99) folio 84.
[3] Inscription on Vanderbank's portrait of John Cossins, Cat. No. 17.
[4] Hussey, 1955, pp. 33, 127–30; Colvin, 1978, pp. 787–8. Clutterbuck was an official of the Bristol Custom House, and almost certainly acquainted with the Elbridge-Cossins circle.
[5] Quoted by Ison, 1952, pp. 52–3.
[6] Vertue, III, pp. 56–7.
[7] Webb, 1954, p. 225.
[8] Gomme, Jenner and Little, 1979, p. 139 fn. 6.
[9] Ison, 1952, p. 38.

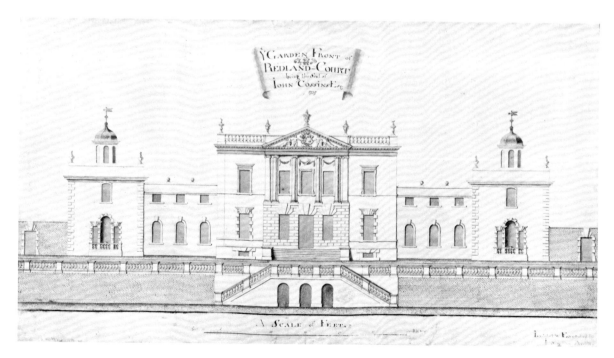

WILLIAM HALFPENNY died 1755

22 Redland Chapel, Bristol

Pen and ink and grey wash, $11\frac{1}{2} \times 24\frac{1}{2}$ in, 294×615 mm
Signed and dated: *William Halfpenny Architect Delin 1742*
Inscribed in pencil: *Nr what Redland Court 1 mile N. of Bristol yrs* [?] *see Grimm's*
Literature: Colvin, 1978, *A Biographical Dictionary of British Architects 1600–1840*, p. 378; Ison, 1978 (reprint), *Georgian Buildings of Bristol*, foreword; Gomme, Jenner and Little, 1979, *Bristol, an architectural history*, p. 135 fn. 4
Lent by the British Library (K. Top CXXIV supp. cat. f 37)

"All the original drawings were this day sent to the Chapel and locked up in one of the Chests in the Vestry" reads the entry for 23 November 1757 in John Innys' 'Chronological Account of . . . Redland Chapel'.[1] This drawing and Cat. Nos. 24a, b and c may well have been among them, but there must once have been others which would have helped to clarify the vexed question of the identity of the architect of Redland Chapel.[2]

Halfpenny's drawing of the chapel is dated 1742, two years after the first stone was laid on 1 July 1740.[3] His inscription on the drawing is misleading, perhaps with a certain calculated opportunism. The chapel was almost certainly designed by John Strahan, the architect of Redland Court, whose death prevented him from supervising the building of the chapel.[4]

Halfpenny and John Cossins signed a contract for the completion of the chapel in May 1742 and it is receipted in December of the same year.[5] It is clear that the contract was for an overseer of workmen and that it concerned the completion of the structure of the chapel and the more basic interior decoration rather than the excellent furnishings and carved decoration which were very largely designed and carried out under Thomas Paty's direction between 1743 and 1747.[6] Halfpenny himself worked for Paty on the chapel in 1747 earning two shillings and fourpence an hour.[7]

William Halfpenny, like Strahan, is an ill-documented figure. His earliest known works were the unexecuted designs of 1723 for Holy Trinity Church, Leeds, one of which he illustrated in his *Art of Sound Building*, 1725. But he was not the architect of the church.[8] By 1730, the probable date of publication of his *Perspective Made Easy*, he was in Bristol, for among the plates that illustrate it, are views of the Hotwells, Queen Square (fig. 6) and the Drawbridge. It has been suggested that he worked for Strahan on his arrival in Bristol.[9] In 1739 he presented plans for the new Exchange,[10] and a little later for a scheme to enlarge the Infirmary. The Coopers' Hall in King Street, now the façade of the Bristol Old Vic Theatre, is the only surviving building generally

William Halfpenny Architect Delin 1742

accepted as being designed by Halfpenny. He was the author of numerous architectural pattern books, and died in 1755.

[1] Wilkins, 1924, p. 37.
[2] Rudder, 1779, makes no attribution; Shiercliff, 1789 and 1793, states that Halfpenny was the architect; Ison, 1952, pp. 37–8, 54, 61 argues at length for Halfpenny; Gomme, Jenner and Little, 1979, pp. 135–9, using the same documents, argues for Strahan.
[3] Redland Chapel Trust Papers: 'Account of . . . Redland Chapel'.
[4] Ison, 1952, p. 46.
[5] Redland Chapel Trust Papers, quoted by Ison, 1952, p. 55.
[6] Redland Chapel Trust Papers and Cat. No. 24a.
[7] Redland Chapel Trust Papers. Divine service was first held in the chapel on 5 October 1743.
[8] Colvin, 1978, p. 378.
[9] Ison, 1952, p. 37.
[10] B.R.O. 04713.

ANONYMOUS, BRITISH SCHOOL

23 The Interior of Redland Chapel, Bristol
circa 1750

Pen and ink and wash, 20½×26 in, 521×679 mm
Inscribed within the design: *TO JOHN COSSINS ESQUIRE This Draught is Humbly*
Inscrib'd by your most Obedient and Oblig'd Humble Servant. James Stewart Junior.
Exalted Cossins here thy worth we view,
Here, thou Gods glory and thy own dost show:
So neat a Temple, fraught with every Grace,
Jehovah, makes, no doubt, his dwelling place.

From this fair Altar may thy Incense rise,
And gain a Seat for thee above the Skies:
May that great God, for whom you've rais'd this Throne,
As a reward, exalt thee near his own.

Inscribed on the back in John Innys' hand: *Redland Chapel near Redland Court in the Parish of Westbury-on-Trym, Gloucestershire. One Mile North from Bristol and iii Miles North from London.*
Lent by the British Library (K. Top XIII 95a)

James Stewart "Junior" was the son of another school master of the same name.[1] He described himself as writing master and accountant. His *History of the Famous City and Port of Bristol* was begun in 1733 after meeting one of the Buck brothers on Brandon Hill. He intended "to take original drawings of the inside and outside of every public building in the city".[2] Stewart may have looked to John Cossins as a possible patron for the publication of his *History*, the first volume of which was complete by 1753. He died in 1755 and nothing came of the scheme, but, though never published, his drawings are the earliest important group of Bristol views.

Despite the dedication, however, Stewart cannot be the author of this particular drawing, for it has a sophistication wholly lacking in the many drawings by him in the Bodleian Library, Oxford.[3]

[1] I am grateful to Jonathan Barry of St. John's College, Oxford for information about Stewart and for bringing the Gough MSS. to my attention.
[2] Bodley MSS. Gough 'Somerset 2' folio XIV.
[3] Bodley MSS. Gough 'Somerset 8' folio XIV.

23

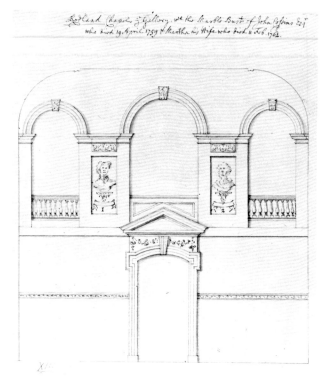

Redland Chapel ye Gallery, wth the Marble Busts of John Cossins Esqr who died 19 April 1759 & Martha his Wife who died 11 Feb 1762.

24a

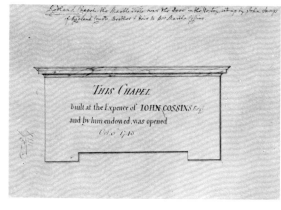

Redland Chapel, the Marble Table over the Door in the Vestry, set up by John Innys of Redland Court, Brother & Heir to Mrs Martha Cossins.

THIS CHAPEL
built at the Expence of IOHN COSSINS Esq:
and by him endowed, was opened
Octr 5 1743

24c

Redland Chapel   the Monuments in the Vestry, erected at ye Expence of John Innys of Redland Court, Brother & Executor to Mrs Martha Cossins.

94

24b

24a Design for the incorporation of two busts in the Gallery wall in Redland Chapel

Pencil, pen and ink and sepia wash, $10\frac{7}{10} \times 9\frac{9}{10}$ in, 270×251 mm
Inscribed in ink in John Innys' hand: *Redland Chapel, ye Gallery, wth the Marble Bust of John Cossins Esqr who died 19 April 1759 & Martha his Wife who died 11 Feb. 1762.*
Lent by the British Library (K. Top. XIII 95b)

Thomas Paty worked at Redland Chapel from 1740 when building work began, and continued to supply the Cossins family with furnishings such as the font, after the chapel's completion.[1] John Innys continued the patronage. The inscription is no evidence for the date of the drawing, which may have been part of John Cossins' original proposals for the interior (see Cat. No. 22). Although the busts were to be placed in the positions shown here they are now in arched niches within the rectangular panels, with no decorative detail.[2]

Thomas Paty was a mason, carver and architect. In a long working life he was responsible, among other things, for the ornament of Redland Chapel, the Exchange, the Royal Fort and Arno's Court, all of it, whether in wood, stone or plaster, of an exceptionally high order, of such a high order, indeed, that Dening was prompted to attribute some of the details at Redland to Rysbrack.[3] John Innys called him "one of the best carvers in England . . . by whom all the rest of ye ornaments . . . were designed & carved."[4] Paty became the leading architect, statuary and contract mason of Bristol. It was no doubt in this last capacity that Henry Hoare employed him to dismantle and pack both the High Cross and St. Peter's Pump for carriage to Stourhead.[5]

[1] Redland Chapel Trust Papers: bill dated October 1755, carving and gilding of font £6 16s, and marble basin 14s.
[2] Gomme, Jenner and Little, 1979, fig. 107.
[3] Dening, 1923, p. 87.
[4] Redland Chapel Trust Papers: John Innys' short MS. 'Account of . . . Redland Chapel'; many bills and receipts to Paty survive amongst the papers; the earliest is dated 1740 and in 1743 the price of carving the ornaments of the chancel and pulpit in lime-wood was £106.
[5] W.R.O. Stourhead papers 383.907: Thomas Tyndall to Henry Hoare, 7 August 1766; 383.6, 14 March 1768.

24b Design for the monument to John and Martha Cossins and other members of their family, in Redland Chapel

Pencil, pen and ink and watercolour with later additions, $10\frac{1}{4} \times 12\frac{1}{4}$ in, 258×311 mm
Inscribed in ink in John Innys' hand: *Redland Chapel, The Monument in the Vestry, erected at ye Expense of John Innys of Redland Court Brother Heir & Executor to Mrs Martha Cossins.*
Lent by the British Library (K. Top XIII 95d)

The 'Chronological Account of . . . Redland Chapel' records that on 15 July 1762 "The Monument in the Chapel Vestry to the memory of the Founder John Cossins Esqr. and of Martha his wife an of Mr and Mrs Marissal and of Anne Innys was this day finished it was designed and Executed by Mr Thomas Paty of Bristol."[1]
The date of Martha Cossins' death was apparently initially left blank on Paty's drawing. This would suggest that the design was commissioned by Mrs Cossins before her death on 11 February 1762.

[1] B.R.O. P/RG/3b); quoted by Wilkins, 1924, p. 41.

24c Design for the founder's memorial plaque in Redland Chapel

Pen and ink and wash, $7\frac{3}{4} \times 10\frac{1}{4}$ in, 197×261 mm
Inscribed in ink in John Innys' hand: *Redland Chapel, the Marble Table over the Door in the Vestry, set up by John Innys of Redland Court, Brother & Heir to Mrs Martha Cossins.*
Lent by the British Library (K. Top XIII 95c)

This memorial is recorded as being set up on 16 July 1762.[1]

[1] B.R.O. P/RG/3b).

Cat. No. 25 Before conservation.

MICHAEL RYSBRACK

25 A model of the statue of William III in Queen Square, Bristol

Plaster and gold leaf, $27\frac{1}{4}$ in, 692 mm (including base)
Provenance: unknown
Literature: Shepherd, 1927, *Catalogue of the Wilberforce House Collection*, No. 103
Lent by Kingston upon Hull, City Museums and Art Galleries

This cast is first recorded on display in the Wilberforce House Museum in 1927. It was then described as the "Model of the equestrian Statue of King William III, in the Market Place."[1] Until now its relationship to Hull's 'William III' by Rysbrack's rival, Peter Scheemakers has not been questioned. But the model is clearly far closer to Rysbrack's Bristol statue. It is the gilding of both the model and the Hull statue that has led to the confusion. Paint samples suggest that this model has always been gilded, though an identical cast in a private collection had a bronzed finish until very recently, but was gilded because it, too, was thought to relate to the Scheemakers.[2]

There are several references in eighteenth-century sale catalogues to such plaster casts. The most notable is that in one of Rysbrack's own sales at Langfords', on 18 April 1767, when lot 89 was described as "A CAST of an EQUESTRIAN STATUE of King WILLIAM, *which was made for the City of* Bristol, by Mr. RYSBRACK". It was sold for £50. Again, at one of the sales of the collection at Twickenham of the painter and connoisseur Thomas Hudson (25 February 1785), one of the lots was a plaster cast, "King William on Horseback by Rysbrack".[3]

There are other references to equestrian statues of King William that may have been plaster. At the sale of Joseph van Acken's possessions on 11 February 1751, "King William on Horseback" was one of several lots by Rysbrack.[4] Van Acken (see Cat. No. 57) was Thomas Hudson's drapery painter[5] and it is possible that Hudson bought his cast at this sale; the description of both is identical. Yet another reference to an equestrian statue of William III occurs in the catalogue of Peter Vanina's sale on 3 and 4 April 1770.[6] Rysbrack, in a letter to Sir Edward Littleton dated 21 January 1758, mentions "Mr. Vannini, the Caster of Plaster of Paris. (Whom I Employ when I want) . . . it being a thing Entirely

out of my way."[7]

For a full account of the commissioning of the statue of William III, for Queen Square, Bristol, see the essay on the subject in this catalogue.

[1] Shepherd, 1927, No. 103.
[2] Collection of G. K. Beaulah, Hessle.
[3] Gunnis, 1953, p. 336.
[4] Gunnis, 1953, p. 335.
[5] London: Iveagh Bequest, Kenwood, 1979, *Thomas Hudson 1701–1779*.
[6] Gunnis, 1953, p. 408; Christie's 3 and 4 April 1770.
[7] Webb, 1954, Appendix 1, p. 199.

MICHAEL RYSBRACK

26 Study of a Horse's Head

Pen and ink, red chalk and brown wash, $6\frac{1}{4} \times 4\frac{3}{4}$ in, 159 × 121·mm
Signed: *Rysbrack, Inventor*
Provenance: L. G. Duke, C.B.E.: sold lot 71, Christie's, 8 June 1976; 1977, purchased by the Felton Bequest, for the National Gallery of Victoria
Exhibited: Bristol: City Art Gallery, 1952, 'Exhibition of Stuart Drawings', No. 52
Lent by the National Gallery of Victoria, Melbourne, Australia

There are various lots that refer specifically to drawings of horses in the sales of Rysbrack's collection. On 16 February 1764 Mr Langford sold lot 48, "Sixteen of horses by *Wyck*" and lot 49 "Six by Mr. *Rysbrack*". The reference to Wyck is illuminating but other references are not so clear; in 1774 Mr Christie sold lot 3 on 8 February as "12 modern metzotintos, 20 ditto small horses, &c" and the following day lot 20 "2 books, the dock-yard and horses coloured".[1]

[1] There is a study of a horse's head at the Yale Center for British Art, U.S.A., that has been attributed to Rysbrack, but in technique it is quite unlike this or any other work by him (I.R. 383/66).

Rysbrack, Inventor.

26

FRANCOIS PERRIER 1590–1650

27 Marcus Aurelius

From Perrier's *Segmenta nobilium signorum et statuarii*, Paris, 1638
Engravings
(a) Plate size, $9\frac{3}{10} \times 6$ in, 237×151 mm
Inscribed in the plate with monogram *F P B* and *11*
(b) Plate size, $8\frac{1}{10} \times 5\frac{9}{10}$ in, 206×150 mm
Inscribed in the plate with monogram *F P B* and *12*
Lent by B. Weinreb Ltd, London

The 'Marcus Aurelius' was the most important statue to survive, unburied, from antiquity, and was engraved more than any other such work.[1] It was long thought to represent Emperor Constantine, whose conversion after the battle of the Milvian Bridge in A.D. 312 established Christianity as the religion of the Empire. This misattribution almost certainly accounts for the survival of the bronze equestrian after the collapse of the Western Empire. Its inclusion by the Farnese Pope Paul III in Michelangelo's scheme on the Capitol in 1538, represents a union of an old Christian symbol with the new understanding and passionate interest in the antique. Since then it has become a symbol of Rome itself.[2] Other equestrian statues before Rysbrack's had been inspired by it, notably Donatello's 'Gattamelata' at Padua, Verrocchio's 'Colleoni' in Venice and the many representations of Louis XIV, and Louis XV on horseback (see Cat. No. 28). Rysbrack owned Perrier's extraordinarily influential book of engravings for a copy was included as lot 58 in his sale on 18 February 1764.[3] Perrier was the first to restrict his engravings to only the finest of antique sculpture, a hundred prints of less than a hundred statues.[4] Though every engraver showed the 'Marcus

27a

27b

99

Aurelius' in a different attitude, Perrier was one of the few to show it from the rear, thereby heightening the three-dimensional quality and making it of the greatest use as a reference to a sculptor.

[1] Haskell and Penny, 1981, pp. 252–5; the groups of 'Alexander and Bucephalus' were probably as important.
[2] Oxford: Ashmolean Museum, 1981, *The Most Beautiful Statues*, Cat. No. 49.
[3] Langford and Son sale catalogue.
[4] Haskell and Penny, 1981, p. 21. See Cat. Nos. 73 and 75.

CHEVALLIER after R. CHARPENTIER

28 "Galerie de Girardon" 1710

Open at plate VI
Lent by the Warburg Institute, University of London

François Girardon was born at Troyes in 1628, the son of a metal founder. Under the patronage of Chancellor Séquier he was sent to Rome in 1648. On his return to France he soon became a 'Sculpteur du Roi' and acted as a superintendent for sculpture in the royal schemes for Versailles and elsewhere. He died in 1715.[1]

His collection of antique and modern sculpture was a very important one. It was displayed in his studio in the Louvre, and to preserve it for posterity he had the main objects engraved by Chevallier, after drawings by René Charpentier, in a fictitious architectural setting invented by Oppenord.[2]

This plate, from the thirteen of the *Galerie de Girardon* shows in particular a reduced model of Girardon's equestrian statue of Louis XIV, commissioned in 1685. The statue was intended for the Place Vendôme, then known as the Place Louis-le-Grand. The statue was cast in bronze in one piece in 1692 by J.-B. Keller, and unveiled on 13 August 1699, on a pedestal later decorated by G. Coustou.[3]

There were numerous bronze reductions, and Rysbrack owned a "PLAISTER . . . One of *Lewis* XIV, on horseback by *Girardon*."[4] The most striking difference between the two equestrian monuments is the absence of a full-bottomed wig in the later of the two. Plates from the *Galerie de Girardon* were included in one of Rysbrack's sales.[5]

[1] Souchal, 1981, II, p. 14.
[2] Landais, 1961.
[3] Souchal, 1981, II, p. 55.
[4] Langford and Son sale catalogue, 18 April 1767, lot 59. The wax model for Girardon's 'Louis XIV' is now at Yale University Art Gallery (1959.56).
[5] Langford and Son, 21 February 1764, lot 23.

Vue de plusieurs Morceaux des ouvrages faits par le S. Girardon placez dans le milieu de sa Gallerie aus quels il a fait adjouter les Architectures dessinées par le S. Oppenort.

100

29

JAN WYCK *circa* 1640–1700

29 William III, the Landing at Brixham, Torbay, on 5 November 1688

Oil on canvas, 62×52 in, 1570×1321 mm
Signed and dated: *J. Wijck Ao 1688*
Provenance: 1939, presented by Sir James Caird
Literature: Archibald, 1954, *Portraits at the National Maritime Museum*, pl. XIX; *History Today*, September 1959, p. 583
Lent by the National Maritime Museum, London

William, Prince of Orange (1650–1702) achieved fame in England for his defence of the Netherlands against the depredations of the French under Louis XIV. The son of Charles I's daughter Mary, he had married in 1677, Mary, the daughter of the future James II by his first wife. When James converted to Catholicism these factors were behind the invitation to William to usurp the throne. He landed in Torbay near Brixham in Devon, from an armada of fifty ships, and marched with 14,000 troops on Exeter and Bristol. The date of the landing, 5 November, encouraged a revival of annual celebration and the burning of papal effigies. From 1688 until his death in 1702 he was continually on the battle-field both in the Netherlands against the French and in northern Ireland. While he was never personally popular, his reign became symbolic of the revolutionary Act of Settlement of 1701, the Protestant succession and resistance to French domination in Europe.

Jan Wyck painted a number of battle-pieces showing the King at the Battle of the Boyne (a signed example is at Blenheim Palace), and at the Siege of Namur in 1697.[1] William III is not thought to have owned a white charger, but the artist probably saw it as a symbol of Kingship.[2]

Although Rysbrack did not use this painting as a source for his equestrian statue in Queen Square, Bristol, he did own "sixteen [drawings] of horses by *Wyck*".[3] The painting differs from the statue in that the King wears contemporary not classical dress, and the horse in *en levada*, a pose which had a great tradition in equestrian por-traits, and echoes Rubens' now destroyed portrait of the Duke of Buckingham.[4] For sculptors the *levada* was a considerable feat. Bernini succeeded in the marble 'Constantine the Great' in the Basilica of St. Peter's, Rome, but the casting of such a composition in bronze was rarely attempt-ed; one of the best-known examples is Falconet's equestrian statue of Peter I, in Leningrad.

A more likely contemporary source was Kneller's portrait of 'William III Landing at Margate' in 1701 after the peace of Ryswick. This painting hangs in the First Presence Chamber at Hampton Court. Here the King wears imperial military dress, and, like Louis XIV in his eques-trian portraits, the curious anomaly of a wig. Rysbrack's friend Vanderbank had 'quoted' directly from this for an equestrian portrait of George I on the staircase of No. 11 Bedford Row, sometime after 1714.[5]

[1] Piper, 1963, p. 379.
[2] Archibald, 1954, pl. XIX.
[3] Langford and Son sale catalogue, 16 February 1764, lot 48.
[4] Strong, 1972, p. 54, fig. 24.
[5] Croft-Murray, 1962, p. 260, fig. 122.

G. VALCK (1651/2–1726), after KNELLER

30 William III

Engraving, plate mark $22\frac{1}{4} \times 16\frac{1}{4}$ in, 565×413 mm
Inscribed within the plate: *IE. MAINT IEN-DRAY. VOX POPULI VOX DEI GULIELMUS III Dei Gratia Angliae Scotiae Franciae & Hiberniae Rex Fidei Defensor &c G. Kneller ad vivum pinxit. G. Valck Excudit*
Provenance: 1873, purchased
Lent by the Victoria and Albert Museum, London (25810.1)

WILLIAM FAITHORNE 1616–1691

31 William III, altered from the portrait of Cromwell

Engraving, cut margins, $22\frac{1}{2} \times 17$ in, 571×432 mm
Inscribed within the plate: *The EMBLEME of ENGLANDS Distractions As also of her attained, and further expected Freedome, & Happines*
Provenance: 1872, purchased
Literature: Fagan, 1888, *A Descriptive Catalogue of the Engraved Works of W. Faithorne*, p. 31, 3rd state
Lent by the Victoria and Albert Museum, London (25488)

This engraving was originally published in 1658, as an allegorical representation of Oliver Cromwell, and was later altered to William III. The symbolism emphasises the connection with church and state: Cromwell and then William III as upholders of the true religion, freed from the tyranny of Rome (the Whore of Babylon) and foreign domination, and of the constitution embodied in Magna Carta, and the return to stability and peace. William III's invasion of England was the subject of numerous etchings and engravings of popular political propaganda, both in England and the Netherlands.[1]

[1] Mendez, 1981, No. 22.

30

31

MICHAEL RYSBRACK

32   Henry Blaake

Marble, 24 in, 625 mm
Signed, under sinister shoulder: *Ml. Rysbrack Sculpt:*
Literature: Roper, 1931, *Effigies of Gloucestershire,* p. 82
The Lord Mayor's Chapel, Bristol

This previously unattributed bust comes from above the wall tablet dedicated to Henry Blaake in the Lord Mayor's Chapel, Bristol. Henry Blaake died in 1731 and the wall tablet was put up by his daughter in 1747. There is nothing about the design to suggest that the two were integral, and the damage done to the shoulders suggests rather that the bust was a later addition to the somewhat mean tablet.

What little is known about Henry Blaake or Blake is to be found in Common Council Proceedings. He is first mentioned on 22 March 1711 when Nathaniel Wade, Steward of the Sheriffs Court and Deputy Town Clerk resigned. In the election to replace him as Steward, Henry Blake was elected "by a Greater Majority".[1] On 11 August 1714 "Henry Blaake Esqe. Steward of Ye, Sherriffes Court" was among those taking the oath of allegiance to George I, and on 27 October of that year "Mr Steward Blaake" was in London on legal business for the council.[2]. In 1720 he surrendered the office of Steward "with all its profits and advantages" and petitioned for the office of Town Clerk. He was elected, after a decision that "no practising Attorney in any court should be Clerke to the Town Clerke". He was sent to London in 1721 to solicit a bill to allow for the building of the Exchange. The following year he was presented with the rare honour of the Freedom of the city. One of his last official acts was to write a letter to the president of St. John's College, Oxford about an exhibition for one of Bristol's Grammar School boys, and a copy of the letter signed by him, is in the Proceedings for 19 June 1731. In July "Mr Mayor acquainted the house that the reason of his rallying them together at this time was to elect a Town Clerk in the Room of Henry Blaake Esq, deceased".[3] He was seventy-two when he died.

Henry Blaake is a peculiarly anonymous personality; much more is known about his predecessor John Romsey and his successor William Cann. Unlike them he seems to have played little part in the life of the city. His name does not appear in property transactions, in the affairs of the important charitable organisations, in politics or commerce. As a practising lawyer he was probably more often in London than in Bristol,[4] and the council's decision not to appoint a practising lawyer as deputy to the Town Clerk must reflect this. It is probably safe to assume that he frequented the London houses of other Bristol families, the Edwardses, lawyers like himself, and the Innys brothers, sons of a Bristol lawyer (see Cat. Nos. 19 and 20).

The bust, in sharp contrast to the Innys busts (Cat. Nos. 19 and 20) is strictly classical, suggesting a patrician sitter. This fact encouraged the questioning of the identification of Blaake as the sitter. However, the number of busts *al antica* of members of what today would be described as the professional classes is surprisingly high at this time.[5] If the bust was presented to the city, perhaps in acknowledgement of the Freedom bestowed on the sitter, senatorial dress would have been more appropriate than contemporary informal dress.

It has been impossible to ascertain at what point the bust was added to the wall tablet in the Mayor's Chapel. One possibility is the time of the chapel's restoration in the 1820s, under the direction of the City Chamberlain, Thomas Garrard. He was also responsible for the supervision of the rebuilding of the Council House, and a noted antiquarian.[6] Further evidence for the 1820s being a *terminus postquem* is found in an entry in the Accessions Register of the Bristol Institution for 7 February 1828. It reads "504. Alderman A. Hilhouse. Bristol. A cast from the bust of Mr. Blake Chamberlain of Bristol by M. Rysbrack."[7] It is also recorded in the general committee minutes.[8] The incorrect title of Chamberlain may only be a personal misconception of Garrard's.

32 Detail of signature during conservation.

32 Before conservation.

Recent cleaning of the bust revealed traces of a resin of the kind used in the taking of casts.

If it is not Henry Blaake then there remains the possibility of the other recorded but unidentified bust with Bristol connections. Vertue lists a bust of "John Straughan Surveyor of Bristol" in 1732, but Vertue himself may have been mistaken.[9]

[1] B.R.O., C.C.P. 1702–22, folios 283–4.
[2] *Ibid.*, folios 353 and 364.
[3] B.R.O., C.C.P. 1722–1738, folios 245–6.
[4] Ralph, [1973] p. 16 "the town clerk was absent from the City for most of the time, being a barrister who invariably practised in London".
[5] For example: Rysbrack's 'Richard Chauncy', in St. James's, Edgcote, Northants; Henry Cheere's 'Lord Chief Justice Raymond' (*circa* 1730), Thomas Adye's 'Paul Joddrell, Solicitor General' (*circa* 1740), both in the Victoria and Albert Museum.
[6] B.R.O. General Committee Books 1737–1835, 04282 (2) 1799–1819; 04282 (3), 1819–35.
[7] The City of Bristol Museum and Art Gallery.
[8] B.R.O. 32079 (9).
[9] Vertue, III, p. 57.

MICHAEL RYSBRACK

33 A finished design for a monument, possibly that to John Wyndham, Alvediston, Dorset

Pen, ink and watercolour, $14\frac{3}{4} \times 10\frac{1}{4}$ in, 375 × 261 mm
Profile elevation, inscribed with a scale and on the back in ink: *The Height 10ft. 8 in/Width 6.3/Projection 1.5* and in pencil: *Colonl. Cottr. number No (3)*
Provenance: 1882, purchased
Lent by the Victoria and Albert Museum, London (8933.49)

The design is derived from Gibbs' *Book of Architecture* pl. 113 (Cat. No. 11). There is another very similar design in the Department of Prints and Drawings at the Victoria and Albert Museum, for the signed monument to Charlotte and Mary Pochin at Barkby in Leicestershire, dated 1747.[1] An earlier use of this type of tablet is the Tynte monument of 1742 at Goathurst, Somerset, though there the urn has been replaced by a portrait bust (fig. 36). That the scrolled ornament on the Wyndham monument does not support the urn plinth as it does in this design (fig. 34) may be either the result of missing ornament, like the swags in the design, or a misinterpretation of the design by the mason who set up the monument.

The monument to John Wyndham of Norrington at Alvediston, is signed *M. Rysbrack Fecit* and dated June 1746. It was commissioned by his son Thomas, Lord Wyndham (1681–1745), Lord Chancellor of Ireland who was raised to the peerage in 1731, but who died before its completion. His own very fine monument in Salisbury Cathedral, signed by Rysbrack, must date from about the same time.

[1] V.A.M. 4230: Physick, 1969, pp. 96–7, fig. 63.

33

fig. 34 The monument to John Wyndham and Alice, his wife, 1746, at Alvediston, Dorset.

fig. 35 Detail of the Wyndham monument, Alvediston, Dorset.

MICHAEL RYSBRACK

34 A design for the monument to Sir Richard Newdigate, St. Mary's, Harefield, Middlesex 1732

Pencil, pen and ink and brown wash, $10\frac{5}{16} \times 10\frac{1}{4}$ in, 262×261 mm
Inscribed with a scale and on the back in pencil: *Ed. Stanton. plan for 2nd Sir R. Newdigate muniment at Harefield Ch. Sir Richard 2nd Bt. 1709–10. Ch. of St. Mary*
Literature: Webb, 1954, pp. 76–9
Lent by the British Architectural Library, R.I.B.A. (L5/2)

fig. 36 The monument to the Reverend Sir John Tynte, Bt, at St. Edward's, Goathurst, Somerset.

The inscription on the back is incorrect. The design is for the monument to the 3rd Sir Richard Newdigate who died in 1727. Rysbrack's bill for £132 for "the monument and bustow of Sir Richard Newdigate", is dated 1732.[1] The monument, as executed, is not quite so simple and includes the Vitruvian-scroll ornament along the base of the inscription tablet common to other Rysbrack monuments of the type. It is included here as an illustration of the combination of wall tablet and portrait bust found in the monument to the Reverend Sir John Tynte at Goathurst in Somerset for which no design survives (fig. 96).

[1] Gunnis, 1953, p. 335.

108

34

MICHAEL RYSBRACK

35 The finished design for the monument to the Reverend Thomas Busby and Ann, his wife, Addington, Buckinghamshire 1753

Pencil, pen and ink and watercolour, $15 \times 10\frac{1}{4}$ in, 381×260 mm
Laid on card; profile elevation, inscribed with a scale and on the back with measurements
Provenance: 1864, purchased from Miss Helen Oakes of Bath
Literature: Physick, 1969, *Designs for English Sculpture 1680–1860*, pp. 86–7, fig. 55
Lent by the Victoria and Albert Museum, London (4235)

The monument, signed and dated 1753, follows this design exactly. It includes two motifs, the cherub holding a hooped serpent symbolic of eternity, and the broken column, which has both a biblical and a classical significance, but which more particularly signifies the extinction of an ancient line. Rysbrack would appear to be innovative in the use of this particular motif.[1] He used it first on Sir Chaloner Ogle's monument (*circa* 1751) in Twickenham Parish Church and then on the monument to John Sympson in Canterbury Cathedral in 1752.

The inscription on the monument states that it was commissioned by the two daughters, "only issue" of the Reverend Thomas Busby (died 1725) and his wife Ann (died 1745).[2] The elder daughter Ann married Sir Charles Kemeys Tynte in 1737 or 8 and her unmarried sister Jane lived with them.[3] Lady Tynte was still presenting to the living of Addington in 1792.[4]

The monument to his brother, the Reverend Sir John Tynte, in St. Edward's, Goathurst, was commissioned by Sir Charles Kemeys Tynte in 1742. It is not signed but it is from a design that is a marriage of Cat. Nos. 33 and 34. It is described in Collinson's *History of Somersetshire* and recorded in Pevsner, where it is attributed to Rysbrack.[5] John Tynte, Rector of Goathurst, had succeeded his brother Halsewell in about 1733 and lived a retired life. He died in 1740 and was succeeded by his younger brother Charles, MP for Bridgwater.

The Tyntes were a leading West Country family. The baronetcy was created in 1673 for loyalty to the monarchy and successive Tyntes were MPs for Bridgwater, which was clearly a pocket borough. With the exception of the Reverend John Tynte they cannot be described as provincial squirearchy. His elder brother Halsewell was a subscriber to the *Book of Architecture*. Had he lived he might well have rebuilt Halswell House, Goathurst, to a Gibbs design. Plate 37 shows a design for a house "for a Person of Quality in *Somersetshire* . . . The Principal Front commands a fine Prospect of the Severne"; this could describe the site of the existing house, built by his grandfather in 1689. Charles Kemeys Tynte kept a town house in Hill Street, London, was painted by Hogarth, banked with Hoare's, collected paintings, and devoted much time and interest to laying out the gardens at Halswell.[6] The inventory of his wife's plate was made by the silversmith Paul de Lamerie in 1747.[7] She it was who, in 1785, commissioned the monument at Goathurst to Sir Charles from Joseph Nollekens, then the leading sculptor.

It is perhaps worth noting the names which arise in miscellaneous correspondence, and which occur elsewhere in this exhibition: Andrew Innys who acted for the first Sir Halsewell Tynte,[8] Thomas Edwards in 1720, the Seymours of Maiden Bradley in 1740 and Mr Wyndham, MP for Ilchester, in 1736.[9]

[1] Kemp, 1980, p. 180.
[2] Physick, 1969, p. 87.
[3] S.R.O. Halsewell Tynte papers, Boxes 54 and 59. These papers are unscheduled and unless otherwise stated, reference will be made only to the contents of Boxes 54 and 59.
[4] S.R.O. Halsewell Tynte, Box 54.
[5] Collinson, 1791, I, p. 83. Pevsner, 1958b, p. 185.
[6] S.R.O. Halsewell Tynte, Boxes 54 and 59.
[7] S.R.O. Halsewell Tynte, Box 59.
[8] B.R.O. 6608 (10).
[9] S.R.O. Halsewell Tynte, Box 54. Copplestone Warre Bampfylde of Hestercombe jointly commemorated his admiration and friendship for both Henry Hoare and Sir Charles K. Tynte by an inscription on an urn in 1786. Woodbridge, 1970, p. 60 fn. 49.

35

III

MICHAEL RYSBRACK

36 A finished design for the monument to John Methuen and Sir Paul Methuen, K.B., Westminster Abbey 1758

Pencil, pen and ink and watercolour, $12\frac{7}{16} \times 8\frac{3}{8}$ in, 316 × 212 mm
Laid on card; inscribed with a scale and on the back in pencil: *Wm Baker Bath Abbey and Walcot*[1]
Provenance: 1866, purchased from B. Quaritch
Lent by the Victoria and Albert Museum, London (4910.15)

The monument in the south choir aisle is signed *Michl. Rysbrack Fecit.* As executed (fig. 37) it is less successful than this design.[2] Two factors may have affected the final appearance: the dark veined-marble base has been replaced by a stepped arrangement in a "White and Vein'd Marble" which is described in the contract dated 23 February 1758 as "an Addition",[3] and may have been at the instigation of the client, as were the cherubs on the Methuen monument at Bradford-on-Avon. The other factor may have been the restrictions imposed by the Abbey, for the marble background does not continue to the full height of the pyramid in the executed design.[4]

John Methuen (*circa* 1650–1706) was the eldest son of Paul Methuen, a cloth merchant of Bradford-on-Avon. He was a lawyer, a master in chancery and MP for Devizes in 1690. In 1697 he became Lord Chancellor of Ireland, a post he retained until sent as Ambassador Extraordinary to Portugal where he concluded the commercial treaty of 1703 known as the 'Methuen' or 'Port Wine Treaty'. He died at Lisbon in 1706 and was buried in Westminster Abbey. His son Paul (1672–1757) entered the diplomatic service in 1690 and later became Ambassador to Portugal and to Spain and Morocco. Comptroller of the Household in 1720, he was invested and installed as one of the original Knight Companions of the Bath in 1725. He collected paintings when he retired in 1730. The monument to their memory was commissioned by Paul Methuen of Corsham Court in Wiltshire, a great-nephew of John and cousin, godson and heir of Paul. He had bought Corsham in 1745 specifically to house the latter's magnificent collection of paintings, and built a gallery for that purpose.[5] It is interesting to note that the chimney-piece and the posthumous bust of Sir Paul Methuen which dominate the Picture Gallery are by Rysbrack's rival Peter Scheemakers, and were completed in 1763.[6]

Paul Methuen of Corsham had earlier commissioned Rysbrack to design and execute a monument to his grandfather Anthony, the younger brother of John, his own father Thomas and their wives Gertrude and Ann. The monument is in Holy Trinity Church, Bradford-on-Avon (fig. 38 and Appendix No. 1). The drawing does not survive but the strictly architectural design derives from those in Gibbs' *Book of Architecture* (pls. 113 and 114) for the Colston monument at Bristol (Cat. No. 8) and the Cavendish monument at Bolsover in Derbyshire. Rysbrack had used a similar formula for the monument to Sir Charles Pye at Clifton Campville in Staffordshire, in 1737.

The contract signed between Paul Methuen and Michael Rysbrack on 2 July 1744, particularised in greater detail than the later one of 1758. Written in Rysbrack's hand, it is full of idiosyncracies of spelling that belie the sculptor's twenty-four-year residence in England.[7] He was to be paid £270 and the monument was to be set up by "the Letter Endt of may next". However, a note in another hand records "Two Marble Boys added charged at 60£ more than above Contract".[8] The cherubs on the pediment were

fig. 37 Monument to John Methuen and Sir Paul Methuen, K.B., Westminster Abbey.

an afterthought, which perhaps explains the delay, for the monument was only set up and outstanding debts settled in 1746.[9]

[1] The monument in Bath Abbey to William Baker (1770) is quite unlike this design and there is nothing in Walcot Church, Bath that relates to it in any way.

[2] There are two related designs in the Department of Prints and Drawings at the Victoria and Albert Museum, both of them preliminary, which differ only in detail (V.A.M. D1043–1887 and 4238).

[3] W.R.O. Methuen papers Box 49, 5086 (see Appendix No. 2 for a full transcript).

[4] Smith in *Nollekens and his Times* (p. 136) describes such an imposition placed by the Dean on Flaxman's monument to the Earl of Mansfield. Roubiliac is said to have wept when he saw how his work, the monument to Field Marshal Wade, had been treated (Ackermann, 1812, *The History of the Abbey Church of St. Peter's Westminster*, II, p. 37, quoted by Physick, 1969, p.21 fn. 2).

[5] Hussey, 1955, pp. 228–9, fig. 420.

[6] *Ibid.*, fig. 421; Whinney, 1964, p. 119; W.R.O. Methuen papers Box 49, 5050.

[7] See Appendix No. 1 for a full transcript.

[8] W.R.O. Methuen papers Box 49, 3641.

[9] W.R.O. Methuen papers Box 49, 1660.

fig. 38 Methuen monument, Holy Trinity Church, Bradford-on-Avon.

fig. 39 Detail of the Methuen monument, Holy Trinity, Bradford-on-Avon.

MICHAEL RYSBRACK

37 Model for a reclining figure in classical dress

Terracotta, $11\frac{1}{4} \times 20\frac{1}{2} \times 6\frac{1}{4}$ in, $286 \times 521 \times 159$ mm
Provenance: 1766, purchased by Charles Rogers; 1784, William Cotton, by descent; 1853, presented to Plymouth Public Library
Literature: Physick, 1969, *Designs for English Sculpture 1680–1860*, p. 81
Lent by the City Museum and Art Gallery, Plymouth

In his accounts and inventory, Charles Rogers twice records the purchase of this model for which he paid £4.12.6.[1] Under "Bronzes, Models, Plasters etc" the entry reads "25 Jany. 1766. A Model of a Philosopher lying down and reading by M. Rysbrack"; the wording is the same under "Prints etc". It was probably lot 40, "A figure laying, and holding a book", sold at Langfords' on 25 January 1766.[2]

The model was considered until recently to be for the figure of Sir Isaac Newton for the monument in Westminster Abbey (1731). There is, however, a model for that figure in the Department of Sculpture at the Victoria and Albert Museum.[3] There, even on such a small scale, the unmistakable likeness of Newton is in the characteristically broad face, and the rather long, unkempt hair. It is a likeness caught even in such a hurried sketch as Cat. No. 45. That same likeness is not here in the aquiline features and classically short hair.

The Newton model is worked in a tense, tight manner. The modelling of this figure is broader, and there is an exaggerated elegance which is almost mannered. In this it is nearer in technique to the model for the statue of John Locke at Christ Church, Oxford, which is signed and dated 1755.[4]

The image of a figure *al antica*, reclining in various attitudes, was much used by Rysbrack as Cat. Nos. 40 and 46 demonstrate. The central figure in the Foley design is close in spirit to this model;[5] the closest is that of the effigy on the

37 Before conservation.

Daniel Pulteney monument (1732) in Westminster Abbey Cloisters. This monument was executed by Rysbrack to the design of the Italian architect Leoni, who may have introduced Rysbrack to the image of a reclining figure holding a book, which has its origins in sixteenth-century Italy.[6]

[1] The City Museum and Art Gallery, Plymouth: W.B. 104, 'Memorials and Correspondence of Charles Rogers Esq. F.R.S. and F.S.A.'.
[2] Langford and Son sale catalogue.
[3] V.A.M. A1–1938: Webb, 1954, p. 65, fig. 21.
[4] V.A.M. 33–1867. For a discussion of the technique of Cat. No. 37 see pp. 000.
[5] In the alternative design, not exhibited, the seated figure on the left holds an open book (V.A.M. 4910–1: Physick, 1969, p. 31, fig. 13).
[6] For example, the monument to Matteo Corte (1544–8), Campo Santo, Pisa, designed by Niccolo Tribolo and executed by Antonio Lorenzi: Holderbaum, 1957, fig. 12.

MICHAEL RYSBRACK

38 "The Monument of the Right Honble. the Earl of Exeter, which was made at Rome by Monsieur Moyneau"

Pencil, pen and ink and brown wash, $18 \times 11\frac{7}{8}$ in, 458×303 mm
Two pieces of paper laid on card; inscribed on the mount: *Michl. Rysbrack, Sculptr.* and on the back in ink with the title
Provenance: Charles Rogers; 1784, William Cotton, by descent; 1853, presented to Plymouth Public Library
Exhibited: London: Sotheby's, 1979, 'Old Master and English Drawings and European Bronzes', Cat. No. 40, illus. p. 62
Lent by the City Museum and Art Gallery, Plymouth

This is the only known drawing by Rysbrack of a monument by another sculptor. John, 5th Earl of Exeter (died 1700) commissioned this monument while in Rome on the Grand Tour in 1699.[1] It was designed by a French sculptor, then resident at Rome, Pierre-Etienne Monnot (1675–1733) and finished in 1703. The following year it was set up in St. Martin's, Stamford, Lincolnshire.

George Vertue, in the train of the Earl of Oxford in 1727, records a visit to Burleigh House, near Stamford to see the collections.[2] He remarks in his characteristic shorthand on "the Monument of the Earl of Exeter. & his Lady. by. Monnot. Roma fecit. the Earls head well. the Ladys not so well. the two statues leaning, rather too small. or the other standing statues too large. the statue standing on the left the best."[3]

It is of the greatest significance that Rysbrack should have made this drawing after the monument. He had never been to Italy, but he would have been acquainted from engravings with the classical prototype on which Monnot had probably based his pair of semi-recumbent effigies.[4] The tomb figures of Alexander Severus and Julia Mammaea had been engraved by P. Santi Bartoli and by Montfaucon, and Rysbrack had copies of both the *Gli Antichi Sepolcri* and *L'Antiquité Expliquée*.[5] But in the Exeter monument itself he had an example of the most *avant-garde* piece of classicism, and influential as it was on the work of others, notably James Gibbs (fig. 2)[6] and Peter Scheemakers, Rysbrack was to make its characteristics peculiarly his own.

It should also be remembered that the 5th Earl of Exeter commissioned portrait busts of himself, his wife, and his brother William Cecil, now at Burleigh House, which in their classical quality were far in advance of their time.[7] There is nothing like them in Europe until Rysbrack's '3rd Earl of Nottingham' in 1723 which set the fashion for many others such as Cat. Nos. 32 and 50.

[1] Honour, 1958, pp. 220–1, fig. 4.
[2] Vertue, II, p. 31.
[3] *Ibid.*, p. 34.
[4] Whinney, 1964, p. 253 fn 14.
[5] At the sale of his collection of *Prints, Drawings and Books of Prints* which began on 15 February 1764 and continued for ten days, lot 51 on 21 February was "*Bartoli*'s antichi Sepolcri" and on 25 February lot 55 was "MONTFAUCON'S *Antiquities*, with the Supplement, 15 vol" (Langford and Son sale catalogue).
[6] Gibbs, 1728, pl. 116.
[7] Honour, 1958, figs. 1 and 5.

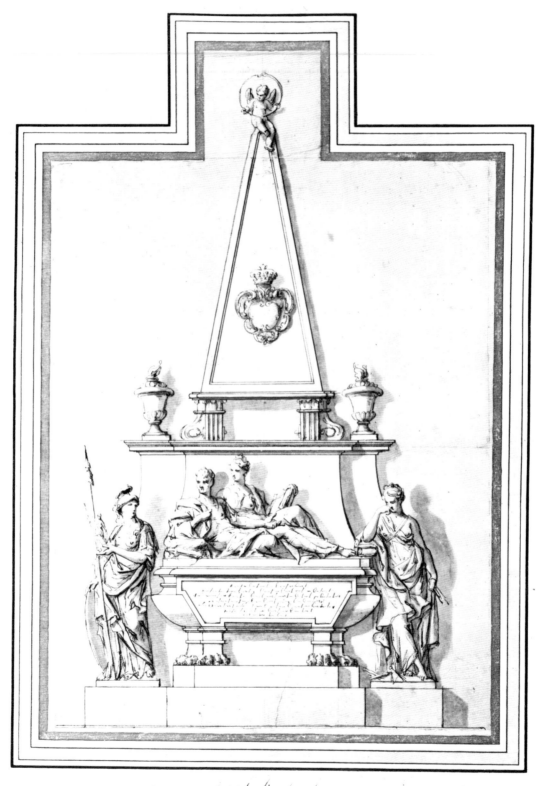

116

38

39

MICHAEL RYSBRACK

39 Design for the monument to Thomas, 1st Baron Foley, St. Michael's, Great Witley, Worcestershire

Pen and ink and brown wash, $11\frac{2}{5} \times 7\frac{3}{5}$ in, 291×194 mm (arched top)
Laid on card
Literature: Gunnis, 1953, *Dictionary of British Sculptors 1660–1851*, p. 335
Lent by the Victoria and Albert Museum, London (E430–1946)

Another design in the Department of Prints and Drawings at the Victoria and Albert Museum differs in the disposition of the figures.[1] The existence of two designs goes some way to allaying Webb's doubts as to whether Rysbrack himself was the designer, for this monument relates closely to the Marlborough monument at Blenheim (1732), which was carved by Rysbrack but designed by Kent.[2]

Neither this drawing nor the design at the Victoria and Albert, corresponds to the final but less successful arrangement of the figures (fig. 40). The unhappy imbalance of scale prompts the suggestion that the monument was not set up as the sculptor had intended. Delays quite often ensued between the completion of the sculptor's work and its installation, usually by a local mason. This happened at Badminton (see Cat. Nos. 62–71), and here at Witley, the church, although consecrated in 1735 was entirely refurnished by Foley's heir, after his purchase in 1747 of the interior decorations of Gibbs' chapel at Cannons.[3]

George Vertue had a high regard for the Foley monument, and included it together with the Marlborough monument, among Rysbrack's "Great and Famous workse" as one of the "standing Monuments to his Fame", and he considered the "seaven statues disposd in a most excellent manner".[4] Vertue may, however, have formed his opinion on seeing only the drawings.

This drawing, cut down and laid on a particularly attractive eighteenth-century mount, is a good example of the esteem in which Rysbrack's drawings were held by his contemporaries.

Thomas Foley (died 1733) was MP for Stafford and Worcester, and was one of twelve Tory peers created in 1712.

[1] V.A.M. 4910–1: Physick, 1969, p. 31, fig. 13.
[2] Webb, 1954, pp. 96–7; Whinney, 1964, p. 90.
[3] Hussey, 1945.
[4] Vertue, III, pp. 115–16.

fig. 40   The monument to Thomas, 1st Baron Foley, St.
Michael's, Great Witley, Worcestershire.

MICHAEL RYSBRACK

40 The finished design for the monument to Sir Watkin Williams Wynn, St. Mabon's, Ruabon 1751

Pen and ink and watercolour, $13\frac{7}{8} \times 9\frac{1}{2}$ in, 352×241 mm

Profile elevation, inscribed with a scale and in ink: *No. 6* and on the back: *This is the Drawing approved of By his Grace the Duke of Beaufort, and Doctor King. The Height 16 ft. 2 in Width 8 ft 10 in Projection 2 ft 10 in*

Provenance: 1946, purchased

Literature: Gunnis, 1953, *Dictionary of British Sculptors 1660–1851*, p. 335; Physick, 1969, *Designs for English Sculpture 1680–1860*, pp. 94–5, fig. 61

Lent by the Victoria and Albert Museum, London (E426-1946)

The monument is signed *M. Rysbrack Sculpt. 1754.* It was commissioned by the widow of the deceased[1] with the advice of the 4th Duke of Beaufort (see Cat. No. 63) and Dr King.[2] It differs from the design only in the removal of the cartouche from the pyramid to be replaced by a pair of cartouches on either side of the inscription table (fig. 41).

Rysbrack's estimate was for £485 and the contract quoted in Physick gives the cost of the marble and individual costings of the components:[3]

Value of marble	£176
Statue	£150
Boy and medal	£50
Ornaments	£33
Masonry	£28
Polishing	£48

Whinney points out that the reclining figure is based on the 'Newton' and that the cherub and medallion derive from the John Gay monument (1732), both in Westminster Abbey.[4] However, both types are so frequently used by Rysbrack and in such a variety of ways that it is difficult to say which is the prototype. The direct inspiration for the reclining figure *al antica*, must be that of the Earl of Exeter in St. Martin's, Stamford (see Cat. No. 38). The cherub leaning on a medallion is closer to that on the Stanhope monument (1731) in Westminster Abbey, which is used again in designs submitted for the Argyll monument (1744–5) (see Cat. Nos. 46–8).

Sir Watkin Williams Wynn (1693?–1749) was MP for Denbighshire from 1716 until his death. In 1729 he introduced a bill to prevent bribery at elections, which was enacted. A portrait of him after Michael Dahl in the National Portrait Gallery records the event with the inscription *An Act for the more effectual preventing Bribery and Corruption in the Election of Members to Serve in Parliament Brought*.[5] The painting was engraved by Vertue in 1742. The leading Tory in north Wales, he was implicated in the Jacobite rising of 1745. He was a close friend of the 3rd and 4th Dukes of Beaufort and appears with the 3rd Duke in two paintings by Wootton at Badminton; a design for a commemorative column to him is among the Beaufort papers.[6] His son married the 4th Duke's daughter, Henrietta.[7] He, like the Beauforts, was an executor of Dr Radcliffe's will, and is included in Gibbs' dedication for the *Biblioteca Radcliviana* in 1747. As a trustee for the building of the Library at Oxford he was among those who contracted with Rysbrack for the statue of the Doctor in 1744.[8]

fig. 41 The monument to Sir Watkin Williams Wynn, 1754, St. Mabon's, Ruabon.

ADSERTORI LIBERTATIS PVBLICAE

40

121

1 Physick, 1969, p. 95.
2 Principal of St. Mary Hall, a fervent Jacobite who had sponsored James Gibbs for the honorary degree of M.A. bestowed at the opening of the Radcliffe Camera in 1749: Little, 1955, p. 136. He also wrote the inscription for the 4th Duke of Beaufort's monument: Roper, 1931, p. 466.
3 Physick, 1969, p. 95.
4 Whinney, 1964, p. 117.
5 NPG 2614: Kerslake, 1977, p. 321.
6 G.R.O. Beaufort papers, Maps 70.
7 Inscription on monument to 4th Duke of Beaufort, Badminton: Roper, 1931, pp. 446–7.
8 Webb, 1954, pp. 167–8.

MICHAEL RYSBRACK

41 A finished design for the monument to Sir Watkin Williams Wynn, St. Mabon's, Ruabon 1751

Pencil, pen and ink and watercolour, $14\frac{3}{4} \times 10\frac{1}{2}$ in, 376×266 mm

Profile elevation, inscribed with a scale and in ink *No. 4* and on the back *The Height 15 feet 10 in Width 7 feet 7 in*

Collector's mark: *CR*

Provenance: Charles Rogers; 1784, William Cotton, by descent; 1853, presented to Plymouth Public Library

Literature: Physick, 1969, *Designs for English Sculpture 1680–1860*, p. 95

Lent by the City Museum and Art Gallery, Plymouth

That this drawing is inscribed *No. 4* and Cat. No. 40 is inscribed *No. 6* is clear evidence of Rysbrack providing his potential clients with a wide choice of designs from which to choose. This service would appear to be peculiar to him; Roubiliac did not draw with any enthusiasm and preferred to submit a model in clay.[1] Rysbrack's highly finished and beautifully coloured designs were for submission to prospective clients, while the pen and ink and brown wash drawings were, it is suggested, for the use of the sculptor himself and the mason who set up the finished monument. The series of drawings for the Beaufort and Argyll schemes clearly demonstrate Rysbrack's method and his meticulous and thorough approach.

[1] Physick, 1969, p. 119.

4²

42 Design for a reclining figure in classical dress, with a cherub leaning on a cartouche

Pen and ink and brown wash, $13\frac{7}{8} \times 10\frac{3}{8}$ in, 352×263 mm
Inscribed in pencil: *Rysbrack*
Provenance: 1864, purchased from Miss Helen Oakes of Bath
Lent by the Victoria and Albert Museum, London (4239)

This and Cat. No. 43 may be preparatory drawings for a model such as Cat. No. 37. They have an easy liveliness not usually associated with Rysbrack's designs for monuments, while the melancholy attitude of the two figures is more expressive than the usual sobriety of his monumental effigies.

The problems of linking an unidentified drawing to a completed monument are well demonstrated by this design. It is very close to the group on the monument to James, 1st Earl Stanhope (1733) in Westminster Abbey, a design for which is in the Department of Prints and Drawings at the British Museum.[1] Here, however, the figure is in classical civilian, rather than military dress, and in this aspect it is closer to the monument to Bennet Sherard, 1st Earl of Harborough (1732) at Stapleford in Leicestershire,[2] which itself relates to the Foley monument (Cat. No. 39).
The cherub leaning on a shield or cartouche appears on the Stanhope monument and in the design for the Argyll monument (Cat. No. 46). It is a cousin of that on the Williams Wynn monument (fig. 41), and both are related to those who lean on medallion portraits of the deceased on the Heathcote monument (1733) in St. Mary's, Edith Weston, Leicestershire, and the Gay monument (1736) in Westminster Abbey. Both of these have their source in Girardon's monument to Bonneau de Tracy, Governor of Tournai (1683), once in the Cathedral but destroyed in the Revolution. It was engraved by Sébastien Le Clerc.[3] Rysbrack owned a volume of Le Clerc's engravings which was sold at his sale on 15 February 1764, lot 54.[4]

[1] B.M. 1859–7–9–99: Physick, 1969, p. 83, figs. 52 and 54.
[2] Whinney, 1964, pl. 66.
[3] Whinney, 1964, pp. 90–1; Souchal, 1981, II, p. 50, fig. 55.
[4] Langford and Son sale catalogue.

43 Design for a reclining figure in classical dress

Pencil, pen and ink and brown wash, $13\frac{1}{4} \times 9\frac{7}{8}$ in, 336×251 mm
Provenance: 1866, purchased from B. Quaritch
Lent by the Victoria and Albert Museum, London (4910.58)

43

Mich.ᵉˡ Rysbrack Sculptᵗ

44

MICHAEL RYSBRACK

44 A preliminary design for a monument

Pencil, pen and ink and brown wash, $17\frac{13}{16}\times13\frac{1}{16}$ in, 452×332 mm
Laid on card; signed: *Michl. Rysbrack Sculptr.*
Provenance: Charles Rogers; 1784, William Cotton, by descent; 1853, presented to Plymouth Public Library
Lent by the City Museum and Art Gallery, Plymouth

    The reclining figure in classical armour is very like that in Gibbs' design for a monument to "His Grace the late Duke of Buckingham", in the *Book of Architecture*, pl. 116 (fig. 2), which itself relates very closely to the monument to the Earl of Exeter by Monnot (see Cat. No. 38). The Buckingham monument (1721) in Westminster Abbey was, however, executed by Plumière, Delvaux and Scheemakers.[1] The entablature with its supporting seraphs' heads was used much later by Rysbrack in the Reade monument at Hatfield in Hertfordshire, which is signed and dated 1760.[2]

[1] Whinney, 1964, p. 79, pls. 54B and 55.
[2] Physick, 1969, pp. 104–7.

MICHAEL RYSBRACK

45 A preliminary design for the monument to Sir Isaac Newton, Westminster Abbey

Red chalk, pen and ink and grey wash, $13\times9\frac{1}{4}$ in, 329×235 mm
Inscribed on the back in pencil (probably copied from former mount): *For Sir Isaac Newton by M. Rysbrack*
Collector's mark: *CR*
Provenance: Charles Rogers; 1784, William Cotton, by descent; 1853, presented to Plymouth Public Library
Exhibited: London: Sotheby's, 1979, 'Old Master and English Drawings and European Bronzes', Cat. No. 58, illus. p. 63
Lent by the City Museum and Art Gallery, Plymouth

    The monument to Sir Isaac Newton (1642–1727), "perhaps the finest of all the post-medieval tombs in the Abbey",[1] was commissioned by John Conduitt who had married the scientist's niece and succeeded him as Master of the Mint. Rysbrack is thought to have taken Newton's death mask for Conduitt,[2] for whom he also executed the very fine bust at present on loan to the Victoria and Albert Museum.[3] The monument was completed in 1731 to a design by William Kent to which Rysbrack had made subtle changes.[4]

    The present drawing shows Rysbrack working out an entirely personal idea, unrelated to Kent's design, and it is evidence of his growing independence.

[1] Whinney, 1964, p. 89.
[2] Webb, 1954, p. 78. There are three plaster casts of the death mask: Portsmouth sale, Sotheby's, 14 July 1936; The Royal Society; Trinity College, Cambridge; and an iron cast, NPG 2081.
[3] This bust appears in Hogarth's 'The Conquest of Mexico'.
[4] V.A.M. E424–1946; B.M. 1859–7–9–100: Physick, 1969, figs. 48 and 49.

45

46

MICHAEL RYSBRACK

46 A finished design for the monument to John Campbell, 2nd Duke of Argyll, K.G., K.T.

Pencil, pen and ink and watercolour, $15\frac{5}{8} \times 10\frac{1}{8}$ in, 398×258 mm
Inscribed with a scale and on the back in ink: *The Height 19 feet 8 ins Width 12 feet 4 ins* and in pencil (possibly copied from former mount): *For John Duke of Argyll by M. Rysbrack*
Provenance: Charles Rogers; 1784, William Cotton, by descent; 1853, presented to Plymouth Public Library
Literature: Physick, 1969, *Designs for English Sculpture 1680–1860*, p. 119
Exhibited: London: Sotheby's, 1979, 'Old Master and English Drawings and European Bronzes', Cat. No. 41, illus. p. 62
Lent by the City Museum and Art Gallery, Plymouth

The commission for the monument in Westminster Abbey to John Campbell, Duke of Argyll (1680–1743) was an important one. Rysbrack had done portrait busts of the Duke and Duchess,[1] and the number of his designs that survive for this commission are an indication of the importance he attached to it. It went, however, to the French sculptor Louis François Roubiliac, who, according to Vertue "had been long struggling for reputation". It was completed in 1749 and acclaimed, so much so that Vertue declared "this monument now out shines for noblenes & skill all those before done, by the best sculptors, this fifty years past".[2]

Rysbrack's designs were probably done about 1744 or 5, for Roubiliac's terracotta model is dated 1745 (fig. 42).[3] There are echoes of Plumière's monument to the Duke of Buckingham (see Cat. No. 44) and to the Stanhope monument (see Cat. No. 42). More remarkable is the similarity of the two competitive schemes, particularly in the allegorical figures, which was probably at the request of the client, the Duke's widow. Here Minerva, or Wisdom, supports the dying Duke, while in Roubiliac's design she looks up from a seat below on the right.[4]

Both have their source in late-seventeenth-century monuments in St. Peter's, Rome: Algardi's 'Leo XI', P. E. Monnot's 'Innocent XI', and the later monument to Gregory XIII by Rusconi. Another red-chalk drawing, also in the Cottonian collection, but not exhibited here (fig. 43) is a straight quotation of Rusconi's 'Minerva', which had been engraved by J. Freij. Gibbs owned this engraving, and Rysbrack probably did too, for several lots in Langfords' sale in 1764 and again at Christie's in 1774, included engravings by J. Freii, Fry, or Frey.[5]

At the Chicago Art Institute, amongst an important group of twelve designs for various monuments, are five unusually free designs closely related to this drawing.[6]

[1] Vertue, III, p. 56.
[2] *Ibid.*, p. 146.
[3] V.A.M. 21–1888.
[4] Physick, 1969, p. 121, fig. 4.
[5] Ashmolean, Oxford: Gibbs Collection, VI, p. 1.
[6] Harris, n.d., p. 190, nos. 1–5.

MICHAEL RYSBRACK

47 A finished design for the monument to John Campbell, 2nd Duke of Argyll, K.G., K.T.

Pencil, pen and ink and watercolour, $15 \times 9\frac{1}{4}$ in, 383×235 mm
On the back is an unfinished design in pencil, pen and ink for a monument with urn and cherub
Inscribed on the back in pencil (possibly copied from former mount): *For John Duke of Argyll. by M. Rysbrack*
Collector's mark: *CR*
Provenance: Charles Rogers; 1784, William Cotton, by descent; 1853, presented to Plymouth Public Library
Literature: Physick, 1969, *Designs for English Sculpture 1680–1860*, p. 119
Lent by the City Museum and Art Gallery, Plymouth

47

MICHAEL RYSBRACK

48 A preliminary design for the monument to John Campbell, 2nd Duke of Argyll, K.G., K.T.

Pencil, red crayon and brown wash, $15\frac{15}{16} \times 10\frac{1}{4}$ in, 405×261 mm

Laid on card: the mount inscribed: *M. Rysbrack*

Provenance: Charles Rogers; 1784, William Cotton, by descent; 1853, presented to Plymouth Public Library

Exhibited: London: Sotheby's, 1979, 'Old Master and English Drawings and European Bronzes', Cat. No. 62, illus. p. 63

Lent by the City Museum and Art Gallery, Plymouth

This drawing is one of several preparatory drawings for the Argyll monument. There are four in a folio volume, bought by Sir John Soane at Nollekens' sale in 1824,[1] and another in the Cottonian collection at Plymouth (fig. 43), all of them in red crayon and wash.

Hope and Fortitude stand sentinel and Fame supports a medallion aloft, as she does in Cat. No. 45. Minerva takes a more active part than is usual for Rysbrack's figures, while Time leans solicitously over the dying Duke.

[1] Soane Museum, London (folios 23, 27, 28, 30).

fig. 42 Terracotta model for the monument to John Campbell, 2nd Duke of Argyll, by Louis François Roubiliac, 1745; Victoria and Albert Museum, London.

fig. 43 Preliminary design for the Argyll monument in Westminster Abbey; Plymouth Art Gallery.

MICHAEL RYSBRACK

49   A finished design for a monument to a woman

Pencil, pen and ink and watercolour, $13\frac{7}{8} \times 10\frac{3}{16}$ in, 352×258 mm
Inscribed with a scale and on the back in ink: *The Height 14 feet 8 in. Width 7 feet 7 in*
Collector's mark: *CR*
Provenance: Charles Rogers; 1784, William Cotton, by descent; 1853, presented to Plymouth Public Library
Lent by the City Museum and Art Gallery, Plymouth

49

The inscription on the bust reads:

Henry St. John
Vifcount Bolingbroke

MICHAEL RYSBRACK

50 Henry St. John, 1st Viscount Bolingbroke 1737

Marble, 26 in, 661 mm
Signed: *Ml. Rysbrack Sculpt*
Inscribed on the socle: *Henry St. John Viscount Bolingbroke Secretary of State to Queen Anne Aged 59 AD 1737*
Provenance: sometime after 1751, Lydiard Tregoz, Swindon
Literature: Hussey, 1948 (19 March), Lydiard Tregoz, Wilts-I, *Country Life*, figs. 2, 9, and 10; Webb, 1954, p. 178, fig. 88, pp. 179 and 212; Webb, 1956 (24 May), Portraits of Bolingbroke, *Country Life*, pp. 1131–2; Kenworthy-Browne, 1980, *National Trust Studies*, pp. 68–71, fig. 6
Lent by the Borough of Thamesdown from Lydiard Mansion

A mercurial figure, politician, man of letters, a friend of Swift, Gay and Pope, a leading exponent of deism, the theological controversy of the day, Henry St. John, Viscount Bolingbroke (1678–1751) was a High Tory who espoused the Jacobite cause. For this he was impeached and attainted in 1714/15. He continued to foment opposition to the Whig administrations of Sir Robert Walpole during the 1720s and 30s.

There are two almost identical busts. If the date, 1737, on the socle of this, the Lydiard Tregoze version, is the date of execution, it is probable that the Petworth version was the one recorded by Vertue in 1732.[1]

The Petworth bust may have been given to Sir William Wyndham by Bolingbroke, in recognition of his close friendship and long and loyal support in the House of Commons. Bolingbroke's *Letters to William Wyndham* were published in 1753.

The contemporary bracket of the Lydiard bust and its extremely cut-away back suggest an architectural setting such as an overdoor or chimney-piece. It was probably intended for Battersea House, Bolingbroke's London residence, for he never went to Lydiard Tregoze. In 1739 he surrendered his reversion of it to his half-brother John, who on the death of their mutual father in 1741 became Viscount St. John. It was John who rebuilt the house at Lydiard Tregoze.

[1] Vertue, III, pp. 56–7; Kenworthy-Browne, 1980, p. 69, pls. 4 and 5.

MICHAEL RYSBRACK

51 Queen Elizabeth I

Terracotta, 27 in, 686 mm
Literature: Webb, 1954, pp. 146 and 215
Lent by Her Majesty The Queen

This is probably from a series of royal portrait busts, of which only three survive, at Windsor Castle (figs. 44 and 45). Webb was hesitant about the attribution of this bust, which had been set into a chimney-piece and painted stone-colour. The bust has since been cleaned, and greater knowledge of Rysbrack's technique makes it clear that it is undoubtedly by him.

Queen Caroline, consort of George II, was, like Prince Albert after her, both an astute and active politician and an imaginative patron of the arts. In August 1733 *The Free Briton* congratulated her on her "*peculiar Affection* to this Country, and to the *Natives of Great Britain*", pointing out that in commissioning busts of Newton, Locke, Clarke and Wollaston by Rysbrack, she had not included "her own *leibnitz*"[1] Vertue records a visit by her to Rysbrack's studio on 10 June 1735, principally to see the equestrian 'William III', but "also the Busts of Marble of Kings & Queens done lately by him to adorn some palace".[2] On 30 June the *Gentleman's Magazine* notes "Her Majesty has ordered Mr. *Risbrack* to make the Bustos in Marble of all the Kings of *England* from *William the Conqueror*, in order to be placed in her New Building in the Gardens at *Richmond*".[3] The scheme was never completed, probably because the Queen's death in 1737 intervened, though eleven terracotta models including this one had been made and found their way into the Royal Collection at Windsor.[4]

A stone version in the Temple of British Worthies at Stowe has been attributed to Rysbrack, and was recorded as such by Vertue in 1732.[5] It may well be a later replacement, however. Another possible version appears with 'Alfred' on a pair of brackets in the background of Hogarth's portrait of Mary Edwards (1742), now in the Frick Collection, New York.

Rysbrack's sources for this portrait bust are likely to have been various. He would have been acquainted with the "Ragged Regiment" of wooden funeral procession effigies in a press at Westminster Abbey, of which the 'Queen Elizabeth' was, according to Vertue, "the truest countenance. of her face".[6] He would also have

51 Reproduced by gracious permission of Her Majesty The Queen.

known Maximilian Colte's marble tomb effigy of 1605, for which the portrait source may well have been a death mask.[7] Both of these were obviously of the Queen in old age, and, as was Rysbrack's habit with posthumous busts, he represents the Queen in the prime of life. He may well have seen the Ditchley portrait when Gibbs was working there, and the portrait at Kensington Palace, where he worked with Kent in the early 1720s.[8]

[1] Webb, 1954, p. 148.
[2] Vertue, III, p. 75.
[3] Webb, 1954, p. 145.
[4] All but 'The Black Prince' and 'Edward VI' were damaged beyond repair when a shelf collapsed in the Orangery at Windsor in 1906: Webb, 1954, p. 146.
[5] Webb, 1954, p. 215; Vertue, III, p. 71.
[6] Vertue, I, pp. 157–8.
[7] Strong, 1963, pp. 152–4, illus. Strong points out that the only other portrait documented as being a direct record of her features is a pencil study by Zuccaro: *op. cit.*, p. 17.
[8] NPG 2561; Vertue (IV, p. 65) records seeing the Kensington Palace portrait in 1734.

fig. 44 The Black Prince, terracotta, Windsor Castle. Reproduced by gracious permission of Her Majesty The Queen.

fig. 45 Edward VI, terracotta, signed and dated 1738, Windsor Castle. Reproduced by gracious permission of Her Majesty The Queen.

GEORGE VERTUE 1684–1756

52   Queen Elizabeth I   1732

Line engraving, 11×7 in, 280×175 mm
Inscribed within the plate: *Vol. VIII. p. 217.
G. Vertue sculp.*
Provenance: Hope Collection
Literature: O'Donoghue, 1910, II, p. 148
Lent by the Visitors of the Ashmolean Museum,
Oxford

Horace Walpole said of Vertue that though
he was a strict Roman Catholic "yet even those
principles could not warp his attachment to his
art, nor prevent his making it subservient to the
glory of his country . . . who has preserved more
monuments of queen Elizabeth? Whatever
related to her story he treated with a patriot
fondness; her heroes were his".[1]

This plate was engraved for Rapin and
Tindal's *History of England.*[2]

[1] Walpole, 1762b, *The Life of George Vertue.* p. 14.
[2] Rapin-Thoyras, P. de. (translated by N. Tindal), 1725–31, *History of England*, III, p. 217.

MICHAEL RYSBRACK

53   Sir Peter Paul Rubens

Marble, 25 in, 635 mm
Provenance: *circa* 1760, Hagley Hall, Worcester-
shire
Literature: Webb, 1954, pp. 111 and 224, fig. 45
Lent by Viscount Cobham

This and Cat. No. 54 are almost certainly
two of "the three busts in marble – he [Rysbrack]
has done. of – Rubens. –Quellin & Vandyke",
recorded by Vertue in 1746. He went on to say
that they were "highly finisht. and masterly
done", and were "standing proofs of his great
skill".[1] There is a display of technical virtuosity,
particularly in the lace collars of all three works,
which is unparalleled in any other marble bust by
Rysbrack.

The terracotta model for this bust, signed
and dated 1743, was sold at Christie's, 2 June
1961, lot 17.[2] It was probably the same as the bust
of Rubens sold as lot 44 under "MODELS in
Terra Cotta", at Rysbrack's sale, 20 April 1765.[3]

[1] Vertue, III, p. 132. The "Quellin" is thought to be
Vertue's mistake for 'Quesnoy' or 'du Quesnoy', known
as 'il Fiammingo': Webb, 1954, p. 111. The marble
version is in the Museo di capodimonte, Naples, De
Ciccio Collection: Watson, 1963, figs. 21 and 24. The
terracotta model, signed and dated 1743, is in the Royal
Ontario Museum, Toronto (958.204/22W.5g): Webb,
1954, fig. 44.
[2] Watson, 1963, fig. 26.
[3] Langford and Son sale catalogue.

52

53

54

MICHAEL RYSBRACK

54 Sir Anthony van Dyck

Marble, 24 in, 610 mm
Provenance: *circa* 1760, Hagley Hall, Worcester-shire
Literature: as Cat. No. 53
Lent by Viscount Cobham

The terracotta model for this bust, signed and dated 1743, is in the collection of the Earl Spencer at Althorp, Northamptonshire.[1]

[1] Webb, 1954, p. 226, and fig. 43.

55

WILLIAM GREENE the younger

55 Sir Peter Paul Rubens, after Michael Rysbrack   1747

Oil on canvas, 28× 17¼ in, 710×438 mm
Signed and dated: *W. Greene Jnr. Pinxit 1747*
Figure inscribed: *Sir Peter Paul Rubens*
Literature: Webb, 1954, p. 110; Waterhouse, 1981, *Dictionary of 18th Century Painters*, p. 150
Exhibited: London: Somerset House (Sabin Galleries Limited), 1979, 'Art Treasures Exhibition'
Private Collection

There was at one time a set of nine monochrome paintings by William Greene after Rysbrack's terracotta figures of Rubens, van Dyck, and Duquesnoy: three of each seen from different angles.[1]

The reason for their execution is conjectural. Monochrome, or *grisaille* paintings were frequently used in the eighteenth century as interior decoration in imitation of sculpture: as mock reliefs in chimney-pieces, overdoors, or in painted niches in halls and on stair wells. Greene may have been taking advantage of the popularity of Rysbrack's figures. The paintings may, however, have been part of their promotion, for artists were, by tradition, very loyal to their fellows, and just such a promotion had been staged for Gawen Hamilton in 1734 (see Cat. No. 1).

William Greene was acquainted with Gibbs and Rysbrack, for he engraved the headpieces of the proclamation for the opening of the Radcliffe Camera.[2]

[1] Photographs, V.A.M., Sculpture Department Photographic Archives. The two paintings of Rubens and van Dyck sold at Sotheby's on 27 August 1955, lot 66, may be Cat. Nos. 55 and 56. Sotheby's (repeated by Waterhouse, 1981) recorded their date as 1765, but this may have been a misreading.
[2] London: Sabin Galleries Limited, 1970, *English Portraits 1500–1830*, Cat. No. 15. It is interesting to note that a painting entitled 'An Oxford Book Auction', in the Bodleian Library, is signed [?]*Greene Junr. Pinx 1747*; the style of the signature almost exactly corresponds to these *grisailles*: Sparrow, 1960b, p. 452; illustrated in Waterhouse, 1981.

WILLIAM GREENE the younger

56 Sir Anthony van Dyck, after Michael Rysbrack 1747

Oil on canvas, 28×17¼ in, 710×438 mm
Signed and dated: *W. Greene Jnr. Pinxit 1747*
Figure inscribed: *Sir Anty. Vandyke*
Literature: as Cat. No. 55
Exhibited: London: Somerset House (Sabin Galleries Limited), 1979, 'Art Treasures Exhibition'
Private Collection

Another of Greene's paintings of the 'van Dyck' is now with Cyril Humphris, London. It came from the collection of Sir George Bellew and was exhibited in 'English Portraits 1500–1830', Sabin Galleries Limited, November–December, 1970, Cat. No. 15. It is signed and dated *W. Green Invt Pixt 1747/9[?]*.

MICHAEL RYSBRACK

57 Sir Peter Paul Rubens 1743

Terracotta: 24½ in, 622 mm
Signed and dated: *Mich: Rysbrack 1743*
Inscribed: *PETRUS PAULUS RUBENS EQUES*
Literature: Webb, 1954, p. 224; Watson, 1963, A Bust of Fiammingo by Rysbrack Rediscovered, *Burlington Magazine*, CV, p. 445; Whinney, 1964, *Sculpture in Britain 1530–1830*, p. 116 and pl. 94B; Whinney, 1971, *English Sculpture 1720–1830*, p. 44
Exhibited: Birmingham: City Museum and Art Gallery, 1953, 'Works of Art from Midland Houses', Cat. No. 187
Lent by the Earl of Harrowby

In 1743 Vertue recorded that Rysbrack had "lately since made three moddels in Clay, being the representation of 3 most excellent Artists. (about 2 foot hi each figure) Rubens. Vandyke & Fiamingo Quenoy all three his Country men. these three modells, for the invention being standing, the gracefullness of the Actions the dispositions of their habit. attitudes. and natural likeness, is most excellent. Q[uestion] if any other Artist living coud do better, and more masterly execute them."[1]

Vertue also tells us that Rysbrack's popularity had been eclipsed by that of Peter Scheemakers, after the completion, in 1740, of the latter's monument to Shakespeare in Westminster Abbey, and that he was feeling "the effect in the decline of Busines".[2] There is no mention of there being a financial motive, rather that he had time on his hands and "these [statuettes] are now the effects of leisure & study."[3]

But the following year the *Daily Advertiser* of Wednesday 4 January 1744, carried an announcement of "Proposals for casting in Plaister of Paris" the three figures "now in the Collection of Mr. Joseph Van Hacken". The price to subscribers would be seven-and-a-half guineas the set, and subscriptions would be taken by "Mess. Claessens and Ven Hagen, at Mr. Rysbrack's in Vere Street, near Oxford Chapel, where the Models may be seen and the Proposals deliver'd and likewise at Mr. John Brindley's, Bookseller to His Royal Highness the Prince of Wales, in New Bond Street."[4] In 1747 Vertue makes a note of the project, commenting that van Aken had "paid for them [the originals] freely".[5] The implication is that Joseph van Aken, the drapery painter, who had come from Antwerp at about the same time as Rysbrack, was a partner in this financial venture. If Rysbrack instigated the

first castings it is quite likely that the work was done by Peter Vannini or Vanina, for there were statuettes of Rubens and van Dyck in Vanina's sale in 1770.[6] It would appear to have been quite an ambitious project and this may explain the existence of the series of paintings by William Greene (see Cat. Nos. 55 and 56). "Original models of Rubens, Van Dyck and Fiammingo" were included in the sale of the collection of Joseph van Aken on 11 February 1751.[7]

Van Aken died in 1749 and it is interesting to note that the first plaster versions by Cheere at York Castle Museum (Kirkleatham) are signed *Cheere F 1749*.[8]

[1] Vertue, III, p. 116.
[2] *Ibid.*
[3] *Ibid.*
[4] British Library: Burney, 387b.
[5] Vertue, III, p. 135.
[6] See Cat. No. 25; Gunnis, 1953, p. 408.
[7] Gunnis, 1953, p. 335.
[8] Leeds: Temple Newsam House, 1974, *The Man at Hyde Park Corner*, Cat. Nos. 67 and 68.

MICHAEL RYSBRACK

58 Sir Anthony van Dyck

Terracotta, 22½ in, 572 mm
Impressed signature and date on plinth: *Mich: Rysbrack 1743*
Inscribed: *ANTONIUS VAN DYCK EQUE*
Provenance: 1957, purchased from Mr H. Ross of Bridgwater, who had acquired it locally
Literature: Watson, 1963, A Bust of Fiammingo by Rysbrack Rediscovered, *Burlington Magazine*, CV, p. 445; Leeds: Temple Newsam House, 1974, *The Man at Hyde Park Corner*, pp. 10–12, Cat. No. 69; Wilson, 1976, Rysbrack in Bristol, *Apollo*, CIII, p. 24, fig. 4; Wilson, n.d. *Sculpture from the City Art Gallery, Bristol*
The City of Bristol Museum and Art Gallery (N5723)

This figure is not one of the original set of three statuettes of Rubens, van Dyck, and 'Il Fiammingo'. For a discussion of the difference in size and manufacture between this statuette and Cat. No. 57 see Mary Greenacre's essay on Rysbrack's technique in this catalogue. The conclusion drawn is that the Bristol 'van Dyck' is a press-moulded piece, perhaps taken as a test for the production of plaster casts.

The financial venture undertaken by Rys-

brack and van Aken, discussed in the entry for Cat. No. 57, certainly succeeded in capturing the popular imagination. If William Greene's *grisailles* were not part of the initial promotion, then they certainly bear eloquent witness to the popularity of this series of figures. The figures were produced in surprising numbers, in a variety of media and over a considerable period of time, only the 'Fiammingo' losing favour.

On van Aken's death in 1749 John Cheere took up the production of plasters, the figures being finished to look like bronze.[1] Another 'Statuary' also in the business of producing plaster casts was Charles Harris (died 1795). An undated catalogue of his stock lists "Fiomingo, Rubens and Vandyke" at two guineas each.[2] The 'van Dyck' was later reproduced by Wood and Caldwell in unglazed stoneware, known as 'jasper' or 'black basalte' ware.[3] The pair of 'Rubens' and 'van Dyck' in bronze, in the Victoria and Albert Museum, are now considered to date from the nineteenth century.[4]

Two other variants of Rysbrack's series of great Flemish artists are worth considering here. The first are the ivory statuettes after the series by Jacob Frans Verscovis, another Fleming, who died in London in 1749. The 'Rubens' and 'van Dyck' were sold at Christie's on 12 May 1970, lot 44. The 'Fiammingo', though slightly different in detail from a statuette said to be terracotta and sold at Christie's on 4 December 1956, is on Horace Walpole's cabinet now in the Victoria and Albert Museum.[5] The second is a terracotta plaque with van Dyck in high relief in the Musées Royaux des Beaux-Arts in Brussels. Formerly attributed to the Flemish sculptor Mathieu van Beveren (1630–1690),[6] Dr Charles Avery recently pointed out that it has close affinities with the Bristol 'van Dyck'. But whether it is by Rysbrack remains open to question.

[1] Leeds: Temple Newsam House, 1974, pp. 10–12.
[2] V.A.M. Library Box 1: 37y. It is possible that the pair of bronze figures of Rubens and van Dyck at Stourhead are by Charles Harris for he was working for Sir Richard Colt Hoare in 1781: W.R.O. Stourhead papers 383.57. 'Van Dyck' was cast without the sinister arm, as was the plaster in the Soane Museum, while Cheere's 'van Dyck' at York Castle Museum (Kirkleatham) retains it.
[3] Leeds: Temple Newsam House, 1974, Cat. No. 70.
[4] V.A.M. A23–1955 and A24–1955: Whinney, 1971, Nos. 8 and 9.
[5] Webb, 1954, fig. 42, p. 112.
[6] Brussels: Musée d'Art Ancien, 1977, *La Sculpture au siècle de Rubens'*, Cat. No. 164.

P. PONTIUS (1603-1658), after
VAN DYCK

59   Sir Peter Paul Rubens

Line engraving, $9\frac{3}{4} \times 6\frac{3}{5}$ in, 248×168 mm
Inscribed within the plate: *D. PETRUS PAULUS
RUBBENS EQUES. REGI CATOLICO IN
SANCTIORE CONSILIO A SECRETIS AEVI
SUI APELLES ANTVERPIAE Ant. van Dyck
pinxit. Paul. Pontius sculpsit. Cum privilegio*
Provenance: Hope Collection
Literature: Walpole, 1762a, *Anecdotes of Painting*,
II, p. 78; Wibiral, 1879, *L'Iconographie d'A. Van
Dyck d'après les recherches de Weber*, 62, 5th state
Lent by the Visitors of the Ashmolean Museum,
Oxford

Rysbrack owned numerous engravings by
van Dyck which appear several times in the sale
catalogues as unspecified: "Eight heads by *Van
dyck*" or "Eleven heads by *Van dyck* Eight ditto
Eight ditto" and so on.[1]

[1] Langford and Son sale catalogue, 15, 17 and 18
February 1764, lot 60, lots 24 and 25, and lots 9, 10, 11.

VORSTERMAN, after VAN DYCK

60   Anthony van Dyck

Line engraving, $9\frac{4}{5} \times 6\frac{1}{10}$ in, 249×155 mm
Inscribed within the plate: *D. ANTONIUS VAN
DYCK EQUES CAROLI REGIS MAGNAE BRI-
TANIAE PICTOR ANTVERPIAE NATUS. Ant
Van Dyck pinxit. Vorsterman sculp. Cum privilegio.*
Provenance: Hope Collection
Literature: Wibiral, 1879, *L'Iconographie d'A. Van
Dyck d'après les recherches de Weber*, 79, 4th state
Lent by the Visitors of the Ashmolean Museum,
Oxford

D. PETRVS PAVLVS RVBBENS EQVES.
REGI CATOLICO IN SANCTIORE CONSILIO A
SECRETIS AEVI SVI APELLES ANTVERPIAE

D. ANTONIVS VAN DYCK EQVES
CAROLI REGIS MAGNAE BRITANIAE PICTOR ANTVERPIAE NATVS.

59   **60**

98

61 Thomas, 3rd Earl of Coventry

Terracotta, 19 in, 482 mm
Signed on the base, under sinister shoulder: *Mich: Rysbrack*
Inscribed on the back: *Thomas Earl of Coventry Aetat Sua X*
Literature: Cust, 1908, A Terra-cotta Bust of Thomas Third Earl of Coventry, by John Michael Rysbrack, *Burlington Magazine*, XIII, p. 362 (illus.); Webb, 1954, pp. 173 and 213
Lent by His Grace the Duke of Beaufort, K.G.

Thomas, Earl of Coventry died while still a minor, in his tenth year on 28 January 1711/12. His mother Anne, Countess of Coventry had been widowed in the previous year. The sister of the 2nd Duke of Beaufort, she returned to live as a member of the Beaufort household, until her death in 1763. She thus outlived the 2nd, 3rd and 4th Dukes. She was the author of *Meditations and Reflections*

It is possible that the commission for this bust came from the Countess of Coventry as a posthumous memorial. It may be as late as the monuments to the 2nd and 3rd Dukes of Beaufort of the 1750s. It compares, however, with earlier works: the busts of William, 1st Earl of Radnor as a boy (paid for in 1739),[1] and John Barnard, signed and dated 1744, now in the Metropolitan Museum, New York. The four designs, (Cat. Nos. 64–7) do suggest an earlier connection between Rysbrack and the Beauforts. There is a portrait of Thomas, Earl of Coventry, by Riley in the East Room at Badminton.

[1] Muniment Room Longford Castle: 'Extracts from the Private Account Book of Jacob, 1st Viscount Folkestone, 1722–1761'.

62 Henry, 2nd Duke of Beaufort 1754

Terracotta, $23\frac{3}{8}$ in, 600 mm
Inscribed[1] on the back: *Mich: Rysbrack 1754*
Literature: Roper, 1931, *Effigies of Gloucestershire*, p. 465; Webb, 1954, p. 211; Webb, 1956 (24 May), Portraits of Bolingbroke, *Country Life*, pp. 1131–2, fig. 3
Lent by His Grace the Duke of Beaufort, K.G.

This posthumous bust is the model for the effigy of the 2nd Duke in Badminton Church. It was probably based on Vertue's engraving, dated 1714, after a portrait of the 2nd Duke by Dahl.[2]

Webb in an article in *Country Life* suggested that this bust had a physical resemblance to Henry St. John, Viscount Bolingbroke (Cat. No. 50), and that it was not, after all, Henry, 2nd Duke of Beaufort. The likeness is superficial however, and the grounds for thinking that the 4th Duke might have commissioned a bust of Bolingbroke are not entirely convincing.

Henry, 2nd Duke of Beaufort (1684–1714) was, it is true, a Jacobite Tory like Bolingbroke. He had been Lord Lieutenant of Bristol, a member, like Edward Colston (Cat. No. 6) of the Loyal Society, and a party to the plot to seize Bristol for the Stuarts. He would have led the western Jacobites in opposition to Walpole and the Hanoverians, had he not died at the height of the disaffection in 1714. His place as leader of the opposition to the Whigs in the West Country, was taken by Bolingbroke's friend Sir William Wyndham, and his sons, the 3rd and 4th Dukes, maintained Jacobite sympathies.

[1] The inscription on the back is probably a modern copy of the original signature; for a discussion of recent and past conservation work see Mary Greenacre's essay on Rysbrack's technique in this catalogue.
[2] O'Donoghue, 1908, I, p. 146.

63 Charles Noel, 4th Duke of Beaufort

Terracotta, $22\frac{7}{8}$ in, 580 mm
Literature: Webb, 1954, p. 211
Lent by His Grace the Duke of Beaufort, K.G.

This bust is the model for the standing figure of the 4th Duke on his monument in Badminton Church. But it is probable that the bust is an *ad vivam* likeness, for the existence of Rysbrack's design (Cat. No. 71) argues the possibility that the 4th Duke, when commissioning the memorial to his father and his brother, had intended that a statue of himself should also be included on the monument as chief mourner.

Charles Noel, 4th Duke of Beaufort (1709–1756) succeeded his brother on his death in 1746. He "distinguished himself in the senate by a steady opposition to unconstitutional and corrupt measures, and endeared himself to mankind by his social virtues."[1] An executor in his brother's place during the final stages of the building of the Radcliffe Camera, Gibbs' *Biblioteca Radcliviana* was dedicated to him, among others. The 4th Duke's personal patronage, besides the commissioning of so handsome a monument as Cat. No. 68, included the two views of Badminton by Canaletto, of about 1748.[2] It was he who approved the choice of design for the monument to Sir Watkin Williams Wynn at Ruabon (see Cat. No. 40).

[1] Rudder, 1779, p. 256.
[2] Constable, 1962, Nos. 409 and 410.

64 A preliminary design for a monument

Pencil and brown wash, $19\frac{1}{8} \times 12\frac{1}{4}$ in, 487×311 mm
Inscribed with a scale, and on the back in ink: *4 in No. Mr Risbrack's Monuments* and, in pencil, with a drawing of a wall tablet with a bust
Lent by His Grace the Duke of Beaufort, K.G.

This and the following three designs are unlike any other surviving drawings by Rysbrack. They represent a transitional stage in his development as an independent designer of monuments. The absence of pen and ink, the lack of confidence in the treatment of the architecture, and the somewhat conventional, not to say old-fashioned, figures reminiscent of the work of the Stantons and John Nost, and of Gibbs' Colston and Seymour monuments (see Cat. Nos. 8, 13a), all suggest an early date. The idiom is indeed very like that of the monument to the 1st Duke of Beaufort, at that time in the Beaufort Chapel at Windsor.[1]

They may well be designs for a monument to the 2nd Duke, who died in 1714, and were perhaps commissioned either by the 3rd Duke in the late 1720s or early 30s or by Anne, Countess of Coventry, the widowed sister of the 2nd Duke.[2] Nothing came of the commission, perhaps because the drawings were too traditional. The 3rd Duke had been on the Grand Tour and had acquired a considerable collection of antique and contemporary works of art while in Rome.[3] It was to be the 4th Duke who initiated the commission for the monument to the 2nd and 3rd Dukes (Cat. No. 68).

[1] Whinney suggested Grinling Gibbons as the designer and sculptor of this monument (Whinney, 1964, pp. 57–8, pl. 39A) but there is a design among the Beaufort papers for the monument to the 1st Duke of Beaufort, probably by John Nost: G.R.O. Beaufort papers, Estate Maps and Plans 72.
[2] Colvin, 1968, argues that James Gibbs did some architectural designs for the 3rd Duke of Beaufort in about 1729 or 30 and that these, also, were not executed.
[3] Michaelis, 1882, p. 61; Sutton, 1981, p. 321.

64

66

6₅

6₇

MICHAEL RYSBRACK

6₅   A preliminary design for a monument

Pencil and brown wash, $19\frac{1}{4} \times 12\frac{1}{2}$ in, 491×316 mm
Inscribed with a scale
Lent by His Grace the Duke of Beaufort, K.G.

66   A preliminary design for a monument

Pencil and brown wash, $19\frac{1}{2} \times 12\frac{3}{8}$ in, 495×315 mm
Lent by His Grace the Duke of Beaufort, K.G.

6₇   A preliminary design for a monument

Pencil and brown wash, $19\frac{5}{16} \times 12\frac{9}{16}$ in, 491×320 mm
Inscribed with a scale
Lent by His Grace the Duke of Beaufort, K.G.

68

68 A finished design for the monument to the 2nd and 3rd Dukes of Beaufort, St. Michael's, Badminton, Gloucestershire

Pencil, pen and ink and watercolour, heightened with body colour, $18\frac{3}{8}\times13\frac{3}{8}$ in, 466×340 mm
Inscribed with a scale and on the back in ink: *The Height 21 Feet 7 in – pts Width 14.11.6*
Lent by His Grace the Duke of Beaufort, K.G.

This is a larger scheme than the one actually carried out. The two figures on either side are absent from the executed design (Cat. No. 70). The figure on the left is the very same as that on the design for the monument to the 4th Duke (Cat. No. 71). This suggests that the scheme was originally commissioned by the 4th Duke after the death of the 3rd Duke in 1746 and that the 4th Duke wished to be included on the monument in the role of chief mourner, or donor.[1] His untimely death before the completion of the scheme meant the adaptation by the sculptor of the figure, perhaps already carved, for a monument to the 4th Duke, probably at the request of his widow and executors. In his executors' accounts for 1756–7, which include an inventory and sale of possessions and outstanding debts, an entry under "London Bills" reads "To Rysbrack Carver . . . 200./ /."[2]

At Rysbrack's sale on 24 January 1766, Mr Langford sold "Two figures of the Dukes of *Beaufort*, Father and Son"; they were lot 60 under "Models". The attitude of the mourning female figure on the right recalls that of the 'Flora' at Stourhead (Cat. No. 74).

The medallion portrait held by the 2nd Duke is of his second wife, Rachel Noel, mother of the 3rd and 4th Dukes. The heavy pall (fig. 46) was used so frequently by Rysbrack, notably on the Marlborough monument at Blenheim and the Foley monument at Great Witley, that Webb was prompted to describe it as a "studio prop".[3] It also appears draped over the plinths behind 'Rubens' and 'van Dyck' (see Cat. Nos. 57 and 58).

[1] Messrs C. Hoare and Co.: Ledger T, folio 47 records the payment of £100 on 10 August 1749 by the Duke of Beaufort to Rysbrack.
[2] Muniment Room Badminton: 'Accounts of Executors of Duke of Beaufort 1756–70', I, Shelf 22, No. 22.
[3] Webb, 1954, pp. 94–5.

69 A finished design for the monument to the 2nd and 3rd Dukes of Beaufort, St. Michael's, Badminton

Pen and ink and watercolour, $13\frac{15}{16}\times13$ in, 354×249 mm
Laid on card; inscribed with a scale and in pencil on the mount in a modern hand: *Study for the monument of Henry, 2nd Duke of Beaufort, (d. 1714) his wife & daughter. Badminton.*
Provenance: 1866, purchased from B. Quaritch
Literature: Physick, 1969, *Designs for English Sculpture 1680–1860*, pp. 98–100, fig. 65
Lent by the Victoria and Albert Museum, London (4910.45)

69

70

MICHAEL RYSBRACK

70 A design for the monument to the 2nd and 3rd Dukes of Beaufort, St. Michael's, Badminton

Pencil, pen and ink and brown wash, $15\frac{3}{16} \times 10\frac{1}{8}$ in, 385×258 mm
Inscribed with a scale and on the back in ink: *The Height 19 Feet 4 in Width 10.4*
Lent by His Grace the Duke of Beaufort, K.G.

This design corresponds almost exactly to the monument as executed (fig. 46), and its very poor condition suggests that it was perhaps the working drawing used by the mason.[1]

The monument is signed *Ml. Rysbrack Fect*, and dated 1754. However, it was not set up until very much later. In 1766 the 2nd Duke's effigy was still in London.[2] From 1769 to 1774 the 4th Duke's widow, who was to be responsible for its erection, was absent in Italy.[3] Rudder in his *New History of Gloucestershire* in 1779 does not record the monument among others in the church.[4] The church was rebuilt by the Patys after a Gibbsian plan, for the 5th Duke, and completed in 1785.[5] It seems likely that the monuments were only then set up.

They are first recorded in Shiercliff's *Bristol and Hotwell Guide* of 1793 as "two superb marble monuments, one erected to the memory of the late Duke, the other to his father: Both of which were sculpted in Italy". This false attribution is repeated with monotonous regularity by the numerous editions of Chilcott's and Mathews' rival *Guides*. The Reverend John Evans, *circa* 1823, says of "Badmington . . . we still recollect having been highly gratified with the graceful dignity of two statues in it, to the honour of members of the family. Of the date of these statues, and of the individuals to whose memory they are consecrated, we have no remembrance, and can only recollect that the statues themselves are said to have been executed in Italy."[6] The explanation of the general misconception as to the origins of the monuments, must lie in the 4th Duchess' long absence in Italy. It underlines the supposition that they had not been set up before her departure, and it is very indicative of the state of the arts in England, and particularly of sculpture, that while the names of the commemorated had been forgotten, their supposed Italian quality should be worthy of comment.

[1] A very similar drawing in better condition (not exhibited) is also in the Muniment Room at Badminton House.
[2] Muniment Room Badminton House: letter from Rysbrack to Elizabeth, Dowager Duchess of Beaufort, 14 April 1766, quoted by Physick, 1969, p. 100.
[3] G.R.O. Schedule to Badminton papers. These papers and the 4th Duke's diary were not available during the preparation of this exhibition.
[4] Rudder, 1779, p. 257.
[5] Little, 1955, p. 183.
[6] Evans, *circa* 1823b, pp. 57–8.

fig. 46 Monument to the 2nd and 3rd Dukes of Beaufort, St. Michael's, Badminton.

157

71

MICHAEL RYSBRACK

71 A finished design for the monument to the 4th Duke of Beaufort, St. Michael's, Badminton

Pen and ink and watercolour, $15\frac{1}{4} \times 10\frac{13}{16}$ in, 387×275 mm

Inscribed with a scale and on the back in ink: *The Height 14 Feet 9 in Width 8:2 Projection 3:3 The Width of the Table for the Inscription is 4ft 11 in The Height is 2:6$\frac{3}{4}$*

Lent by His Grace the Duke of Beaufort, K.G.

fig. 47 Monument to the 4th Duke of Beaufort, St. Michael's, Badminton.

The figure of the 4th Duke is the same as the figure on the left in Cat. No. 68. It is suggested here that the figure had been completed as part of a grander scheme for the monument to the 2nd and 3rd Dukes commissioned by the 4th Duke before his death in 1756, and that on his death, his widow and executors asked for the figure to be adapted for a separate monument to his memory. This monument may therefore be a rare case of the design post-dating the carving of the figure. This would mean that whereas the dates of the terracotta bust (Cat. No. 63) and the figure on the monument (fig. 47) are probably 1754 or 5 or earlier, this design is after 1756. If this is so, it would explain the apparent weakness of composition and the lack of significance in the Duke's gesture, commented on by modern critics.[1]

The 4th Duke's widow, Elizabeth, daughter of John Berkeley of Stoke Gifford in Gloucestershire and sister of Lord Botetourt, was probably responsible for the adaptation of her husband's earlier scheme. Rysbrack's letter addressed to her is dated 1766, that is after he had virtually retired, and when he was, the letter suggests, in ill health.[2] She was absent in Italy from 1769 to 1774, and the monuments were probably not set up until after the new church was completed (see Cat. No. 70).

The poor condition of this drawing and the remains of smears of plaster on the back suggest that it was used as a guide for the erection of the monument.

[1] Webb, 1954, p. 172; Whinney, 1964, p. 118.
[2] See Cat. No. 70 fns 2 and 3.

MICHAEL RYSBRACK

72   Hercules   1744

Terracotta, 23½ in, 597 mm
Signed and dated: *Mich: Rysbrack 1744*
Provenance: 1770, bequeathed by the artist to
Henry Hoare
Literature: Webb, 1950, Sculpture by Rysbrack
at Stourhead, *Burlington Magazine*, XCII, pp.
307–15, fig. 2; Webb, 1954, pp. 121–3 and 217, fig.
52; Whinney, 1964, *Sculpture in Britain 1530–1830*,
pp. 116–17, pl. 94A; Fedden, 1976, *Treasures of the
National Trust*, p. 54, pl. 32
Lent by the National Trust, Stourhead

Vertue describes at some length the making
of the Hercules model in 1744, and includes a
sketch of it in the margin of his notes:

> Finding himself somewhat at leisure.
> busines not being so brisk (as had been
> with him for some years before.) He
> therefore set himself about a Model of
> Hercules
>
> with the intention to show all the skill
> therein he was Master of. therefore prop-
> oseing the Antique Hercules of Farnese to
> be his rule of proportion – but to make his
> Model standing but in a different attitude.
> & the limbs otherways disposd –
>
> in order to his improvement in this
> study, he had found out a strong well made
> proportiond man. being one of the famous
> fighting boxers – (George the Coachman)
> – of Broughtons Amphiater – by this man
> he planted his whole figure. and as it is sd
> of the Antient Greek statuarys – from
> several human bodies. they formd an
> Intire Model best of the proportions the
> best scimetry. & parts accumulated
> together in one figure.
>
> so when Rysbrake had well disposd &
> planted his Model of Clay. in due propor-
> tions – he had the bodies of several other
> men stood naked before him in order to
> form the body, Limbs. arms legs &c to
> chuse the most beautyfull, or the most
> perfect parts. for example – the (1) head
> (coachman) of Hercules he had several
> antient Medals – for the (2) neck & breast
> (Taylor). for the belly & (3) lower parts
> another. (broughton) for the back of (4)
> the neck & shoulders (Hussey) another.
> for the Armes (5) to the wrist (Ellis) for the

> thighs (6) and leggs (&c.). the lower part
> of the (7) back another – besides modelld
> hands & feet from the best chosen life. or
> antique – at least seaven or 8 different men
> & altogether. is surely an excellent
> Model for truth correctnes & excellentcy
> of stile. (about 2 feet hi.) truely compara-
> ble to the ancient statue of Hercules.
> so much for the Honour of England.[1]

Hoare must have seen the model in Rysbrack's studio. In 1747 he signed an agreement
with Rysbrack for "a Hercules in Statuary marble
six feet three inches high . . . and that the same
shall be finished according to the model agreed
on." Rysbrack was to be paid £300 and the statue
was to be finished in two-and-a-half years. He was
paid £150 immediately and £150 on 9 July 1752.[2]
Vertue records "the noble statue of Hercules
finisht now" in August of that year, and goes on to
describe it as "a Master peece of Art – not to be
paralelld. scarcely by any artist hearetofore for
the Greatness & nobleness of the style – the
Antient Greek or Roman study and tastes – of rare
merit & excellent Skill will be to him a monument of lasting Fame to posterity –".[3] It was not
finally finished, however, until 1756, the year in
which it was signed and dated.

Rysbrack had taken as much care with the
marble version as he had with the model; a very
fine terracotta model of the full-size head is now at
the Yale Center for British Art (fig. 48).[4] His
industry was rewarded. Hoare planned a building to receive the statue, called the Temple of
Hercules.[5] In the event the building became
known as the Pantheon (fig. 49). He paid Rysbrack a gratuity of £50 "beyond y Contract".[6]

'Hercules' was regarded as Rysbrack's
masterpiece, "an exquisite summary of his skill,
knowledge and judgement", said Horace
Walpole.[7] Charles Rogers, too, claimed it would
"acquire him the greatest fame to the latest
posterity . . . a figure of which Glycon the Athe-
nian would have been pleased to be esteemed the
sculptor."[8]

The colossal statue of the 'Farnese Hercules'
was discovered in Rome in 1540. Until 1786, it
stood in a courtyard of the Palazzo Farnese, from
which it took its name. One of the most copied of
ancient sculptures, it became, particularly after
Shaftesbury's *Characteristics*, symbolic of all that
was noble about the classical world. Hogarth
based much of his theory of beauty on its tapering
legs, but ironically these were restoration work by
della Porta.[9]

Rysbrack's was not the first life-size marble statue after the 'Farnese Hercules'. In 1722 his rival Delvaux had completed a statue for Lord Castlemaine, which is now at Waddesdon Manor, in Buckinghamshire.[10] Rysbrack himself owned Plumière's terracotta statuette,[11] together with several other versions, including "a laying *Hercules*, by *Algardi*".[12] At his sale in 1765 there was a figure "of Hercules reposing; on a Plinth of Dove Marble".[13] This is probably the sleeping 'Hercules' now in the Fitzwilliam Museum, Cambridge.

Rysbrack was particularly proud of his terracotta model of Hercules, for it appears in Soldi's portrait of him (fig. 20). It failed, however, to find a purchaser at his sale in 1765,[14] and in his will he left it to his greatest patron, Henry Hoare.[15]

[1] Vertue, III, pp. 121–2; Webb tells us that Broughton, a Thames waterman, was the founder of modern prize-fighting: Webb, 1954, pp. 121–3.
[2] W.R.O. Stourhead papers 383.4; quoted in full by Webb, 1954, p. 122.
[3] Vertue, III, p. 162.
[4] Yale Center for British Art, Paul Mellon Collection: B1977.14.28.
[5] W.R.O. Stourhead papers 383.6: entry "Sep 29 1753".
[6] W.R.O. Stourhead papers 383.6: 16 July 1757.
[7] Walpole, 1798, III, p. 479.
[8] Rogers, 1778, II, pp. 227–8.
[9] Haskell and Penny, 1981, p. 230.
[10] Avery, 1980, pp. 155–6, fig. 4.
[11] Langford and Son sale catalogue, 25 January 1766, lot 68.
[12] Langford and Son sale catalogue, 18 April 1767, lot 47.
[13] Langford and Son sale catalogue, 20 April 1765, lot 71.
[14] *Ibid.*, lot 45.
[15] Somerset House P.C.C. Jenner 28; quoted by Webb, 1954, p. 190.

fig. 48 Hercules, terracotta, The Yale Center for British Art, Paul Mellon Collection.

fig. 49 Hercules, Stourhead, Wiltshire.

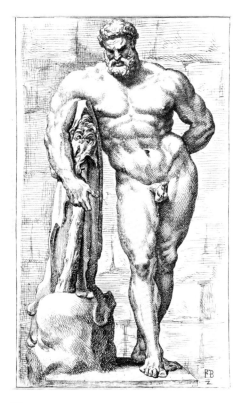

73a

73c

73b

FRANCOIS PERRIER

73 **Hercules**

From Perrier's *Segmenta nobilium signorum
et statuarii*, Paris, 1638
(a) Engraving, $8\frac{7}{8} \times 5\frac{1}{10}$ in, 223×131 mm
   Inscribed within the plate with monogram
   FPB and *2*
(b) $9\frac{1}{10} \times 5\frac{3}{10}$ in, 230×137 mm
   Inscribed within the plate with monogram
   FPB and *3*
(c) $8\frac{3}{5} \times 5$ in, 220×127 mm
   Inscribed within the plate with monogram
   FPB and *4*
Lent by B. Weinreb Ltd, London

163

MICHAEL RYSBRACK

74 Flora 1759

Terracotta, 22 9/16 in, 573 mm
Signed and dated: *Mich: Rysbrack Feb. 1759*
Provenance: *circa* 1762, purchased by Sir Edward Littleton; 1932, sold London, Spink and Son Ltd; 1969, purchased under the Bequest of Dr W. L. Hildburgh, F.S.A.
Literature: Webb, 1950, Sculpture by Rysbrack at Stourhead, *Burlington Magazine*, XCII, pp. 307–15, fig. 3; Webb, 1954, pp. 126, 199, 202, 208; Charleston and Wills, 1956, The Bow "Flora" and Michael Rysbrack, *Apollo*, 63, pp. 125–7, fig. 1; Whinney, 1971, *English Sculpture 1720–1830*, No. 11, p. 50 (illus.); Haskell and Penny, 1981, *Taste and the Antique*, fig. 43
Exhibited: London: Spink and Son Ltd, 1932, 'The Art of Rysbrack in Terracotta', Cat. p. 42, pl. VIII
Lent by the Victoria and Albert Museum, London (A9–1961)

In March 1759 Henry Hoare commissioned from Rysbrack a large marble statue of Flora, "from the antique", for which this terracotta is the model.[1] It is argued here that Sir Edward Littleton, Rysbrack's other great patron of his later years, purchased this terracotta very soon after its execution.

In January 1758 Rysbrack had written to Sir Edward Littleton that "the little Figure of Flora, I Expect to work after sometime or other and therefore cannot part with it because it would be a Detriment to me."[2] The following December he wrote again "I have made a Model of Flora (which I am glad Every Body approve of) I have followed the Model of the Flora which I had by me, and likewise a Flora in Plaster, only altering some Places according to Mr. Hoare's Desire for whom I am going to do it in Marble; and hope when Your Honour comes to Town You will do me the Favour to Come and see it."[3]

It is likely that the "little Figure of Flora" Rysbrack first refers to and which he did not wish to sell to Sir Edward, was a terracotta partly by Duquesnoy known as 'Il Fiammingo'. This figure was sold on 25 January 1766 under lot 65: "A figure of *Flora*, the *trunk after the antique* by *Fiamingo*, the head, arms and hands, legs and feet, by Mr. *Rysbrack*". A few days after the sale Rysbrack wrote to Sir Edward saying that he had safely packed some busts[4] and he continues: "I heartily wish You much Joy of them, and they are

bought cheap as they were such Great Men, and done by so great Masters; [Littleton has endorsed the letter "two Models of 2 Popes by Algardi, & the Model of a Cardinal by Bernini"] they are not to be had every Day, for which reason I am sorry You did not buy the Flora."[5] It would be entirely out of character for Rysbrack to refer to his own work in the same sentence and with such sentiments, and it is clear that he was here referring to the Duquesnoy terracotta which he had just sold. It is possible that Littleton had not acquired this figure because he had already responded to Rysbrack's letter of December 1758 and had purchased Rysbrack's own terracotta of Flora as soon as it was no longer required for the execution of the marble for Stourhead.

Rysbrack was paid £200 on 9 December 1760 for the marble 'Flora' and another £200 a year later.[6] It stands in the Pantheon at Stourhead with the 'Hercules' (figs. 49 and 50).

Horace Walpole made a note, after a visit to Stourhead, that 'Flora' was "much inferior to the Hercules: the head particularly flat and without grace".[7] He even wrote to tell Henry Hoare that he thought the face "too short and compressed".[8] Hoare in a letter to his son-in-law, Lord Bruce, said that "Mr Rysbrack will return with me . . . in order to examine & [illegible] the Head of Ceres He left unfinishd till he saw it in its place with the skylight."[9]

Rysbrack's model and statue are much more faithful to their classical prototype than either the 'Hercules' or the 'Bacchus' (Cat. Nos. 72 and 87), where he had allowed himself a personal interpretation. This is no doubt the result of the changes "according to Mr Hoare's Desire" and the stipulation in the agreement that it should be "from the antique". The antique prototype was the 'Farnese Flora', whose history parallels its companion, the 'Hercules'.[10] It was famous for the delicacy and beauty of its drapery, and was much copied. Rysbrack would certainly have been familiar with engravings after the antique, and quite probably with the gilded lead version in the Cupola Room at Kensington Palace, which had been designed by William Kent to display a series of statues after the antique, and for which Rysbrack had done one of his earliest reliefs, a 'Roman Marriage' in 1723.[11]

Rysbrack was not the only sculptor to copy the 'Farnese Flora',[12] but his own 'Flora' became the subject of popular reproduction. John Cheere, who produced versions of the 'Farnese Hercules' and 'Flora',[13] also produced at least one life-size lead statue for the gardens at Longford Castle, for

which he was paid eight guineas.[14] The factory at Bow produced coloured and plain white porcelain versions.[15]

[1] W.R.O. Stourhead papers 383.4; quoted in full by Webb, 1950, p. 311.
[2] Fitzwilliam Museum Library, Cambridge; quoted in full by Webb, 1954, p. 199.
[3] Fitzwilliam Museum Library, Cambridge; quoted in full by Webb, 1954, p. 202.
[4] Langford and Son sale catalogue, 24 January 1766, lot 74 "A bust of Pope *Innocent* the XIth. by *Algardi*" and lot 75 "A ditto of Pope *Clement* the Xth by *ditto*"; 25 January 1766, lot 72 "A bust of a *Cardinal*, by *Bernini*".
[5] Fitzwilliam Museum Library, Cambridge; quoted in full by Webb, 1954, p. 208.
[6] W.R.O. Stourhead papers 383.4 and 383.6; Webb, 1950, p. 311 notes the payment of a further £82 for 'Flora' in January 1762, presumably for the pedestal.
[7] Walpole, 1927–8 (published), Visits to Country Seats, p. 41; quoted by Webb, 1954, p. 126.
[8] W.R.O. Stourhead papers 241, reported in Henry Hoare's letter to Lord Bruce, 17 July 1762.
[9] W.R.O. Stourhead papers 241: 17 July 1762.
[10] Haskell and Penny, 1981, pp. 217–18.
[11] Webb, 1954, p. 43, pl. 29.
[12] An ivory 'Flora', signed and dated *P Scheemaker 1732* was advertised for sale in 1979 by S. Stodel, Amsterdam: *Connoisseur*, Vol. 200, p. 210; Rysbrack, himself, owned a "*Flora*, by Mr. *Scheemaker*": Langford and Son, 18 April 1767, lot 78.
[13] Leeds: Temple Newsam House, 1974, Cat. Nos. 30 and 33.
[14] Longford Castle Muniment Room: 'Extracts from the private Account Book of Jacob, 1st Viscount Folkestone 1722–1761'.
[15] V.A.M. 533–1868; Leeds, Temple Newsam House, 1974, Cat. No. 35.

fig. 50   Flora, Stourhead, Wiltshire.

75

166

FRANCOIS PERRIER

75 Flora

From Perrier's *Segmenta nobilium signorum et statuarii*, Paris, 1638
Engraving, plate mark $8\frac{3}{4} \times 5\frac{1}{4}$ in, 222×133 mm
Inscribed within the plate with monogram *FPB* and *62*
Lent by B. Weinreb Ltd, London

MICHAEL RYSBRACK

76 John Milton   1738 or 9

Marble, 26 in, 660 mm
Inscribed: *MILTON*
Provenance: *circa* 1739, William Benson; passed to Benson's nephew, Henry Hoare;. thence by descent
Literature: Webb, 1950, Sculpture by Rysbrack at Stourhead, *Burlington Magazine*, XCII, pp. 307–15, fig. 7; Webb, 1954, pp. 112–15 and 221; Woodbridge, 1970, *Landscape and Antiquity, Aspects of English Culture at Stourhead, 1718 to 1838*, pp. 71–2; Kenworthy-Browne, 1980, *National Trust Studies*, pp. 72–6, fig. 11
Exhibited: Brussels: Palais des Beaux Arts, 1973, 'Treasures from Country Houses', Cat. No. 83 (illus.)
Lent by the National Trust, Stourhead

Vertue reported in 1740 that "Mr Rysbrake Statuary. the first Bust of Marble that he made of Mr. John Milton was done for Mr Tho. Serjeant Esq of the Tower. after his death it was sold to Sr. Joseph Eyles for 35 pounds – and after wards bought by Mr. Auditor Benson who set it up in Westminster Abey. with the Monument – and pd Sr. John Eyles [£]40 for it and to Mr. Rysbrack [£]70 for the other part of the Momt. – also Mr Rysbrake made for the Auditor another Marble Bust which the Auditor carryd to his Country house wch he has built. and also another Bust of young Milton – from the Speakers picture (the Hon. Arth. Onslow)".[1] William Benson (1682–1754), the Palladian architect who succeeded Wren as Surveyor of the Works, commissioned the Milton monument in Westminster Abbey, which was completed in 1737.[2] The pair of busts which he then commissioned for himself must date from 1738 or 9, for 'Old Milton' is identical to the terracotta bust now in the Fitzwilliam

Museum, Cambridge, which is signed and dated 1738.[3]

The "Country house" referred to by Vertue was the house Benson designed for himself at Wilbury in Wiltshire. Benson's sister, Jane, married Henry Hoare I[4] and was the mother of Henry Hoare II, Rysbrack's patron.

The cult of Milton was fostered by Rysbrack's friends, the Richardsons, who published *Explanatory Notes and Remarks on Milton's 'Paradise Lost'*, in 1734/5. Vertue tells us that the elder Richardson "was alwayes in great raptures" about the poet.[5] Richardson painted a portrait of himself and his son "in the presence of Milton", in about 1734.[6]

Rysbrack had executed a bust of Milton for the Temple of British Worthies at Stowe as early as 1728.[7]

[1] Vertue, III, p. 100.
[2] There is a design by Rysbrack in the Department of Prints and Drawings, Victoria and Albert Museum (V.A.M. E422–1946).
[3] The model was bought by Sir Edward Littleton: Esdaile, 1932, pp. 34–5, pl. I.
[4] The monument to Henry Hoare I in the church at Stourton has a bust which, though very high up, looks as though it might be by Rysbrack.
[5] Vertue, III, p. 74.
[6] Bromley-Davenport collection, Capesthorne; Kerslake, 1957, pp. 23–4, fig. 27. An anonymous painting, after Faithorne, once in the collection of Sir Charles Wakefield looks very much like the work of Richardson: illus. in *Connoisseur*, XLVI (1916), p. 12.
[7] Kenworthy-Browne, 1980, p. 74, fig. 14.

76

GEORGE VERTUE

77   John Milton   1725

Line engraving, plate size $14\frac{3}{8} \times 9\frac{3}{10}$ in, 365×236 mm

Inscribed within the plate: *IOANNES MILTON Aetat: 62. A.D. 1670.Illustrissimo Dno. Dno ALGER-NON Comiti de HERTFORD Dno PERCY &c. &c. Obsequeatissime D.D.D. G. Vertue. Geo: Vertue Sculp: 1725.*

> *Three Poets in three distant ages born,*
> *Greece, Italy, and England did adorn:*
> *The First, in loftiness of thought surpast;*
> *The Next, in majesty; in both the Last,*
> *The force of Nature cou'd no further go;*
> *To make, a Third, She joyn'd the former Two. Dryden.*

Provenance: 1877, purchased

Literature: O'Donoghue, 1912, *Catalogue of Engraved British Portraits*, III

Lent by the Victoria and Albert Museum, London (27865.4)

This engraving is based on William Faithorne's engraving of Milton, drawn from the life and first published as the frontispiece to the poet's *History of Britain* in 1670.[1]

Vertue used Faithorne's image several times: as the frontispiece to Milton's *Works* in 1720, to *Paradise Lost* in 1732 and again in 1747.

---

[1] Vertue, I, pp. 55, 79 and 142; Kenworthy-Browne, 1980, p. 74, figs. 8, 9 and 16.

77

78 Young Milton

Marble, $22\frac{13}{16}$ in, 580 mm
Inscribed: *Johs. Miltonis Aets. 18₀*.
Provenance: *circa* 1738, William Benson; passed to Benson's nephew, Henry Hoare; thence by descent
Literature: Webb, 1950, Sculpture by Rysbrack at Stourhead, *Burlington Magazine*, XCII, pp. 307–15, fig. 6; Webb, 1954, p. 221; Woodbridge, 1970, *Landscape and Antiquity. Aspects of English Culture at Stourhead, 1718 to 1838*, pp. 71–2; Kenworthy-Browne, 1980, *National Trust Studies*, pp. 72–6, fig. 19
Lent by the National Trust, Stourhead

Almost certainly commissioned at the same time as Cat. No. 76, the 'Young Milton' is based on an anonymous portrait of the poet at the age of 21.[1] The portrait was then in the possession of Arthur Onslow, Speaker of the House of Commons.[2] Vertue, who had seen it in 1728 and thought it "like the manner of Corn. Jansen", had engraved it in 1731 for Bentley's edition of *Paradise Lost*, but thought that he looked about fourteen.[3] Rysbrack's 'Young Milton' certainly looks about this age, which perhaps explains the discrepancy in the inscriptions on the portrait and on this bust, which read respectively "aetatis suae 21" and "Aets. 18₀.".

[1] Vertue, III, p. 100.
[2] NPG 4222: Piper, 1963, pp. 394–7, pl. 33a; a version attributed to "C. Jonson", was sold out of the Shaftesbury collection, Christie's, 27 June 1980, lot 141. Another painting by "Cornelius Johnson" of Milton at the age of 10 is now in the Pierpont Morgan Collection, U.S.A. (Piper, 1963, pp. 237–8).
[3] Vertue, II, pp. 54–5 and IV, p. 22; Kenworthy-Browne, 1980, fig. 18.

79 Alfred the Great 1764

Marble, 28 in, 711 mm
Signed and dated: *Michl. Rysbrack Sculp 1764*, the socle inscribed: *ALFRED THE GREAT*
Provenance: 1764, purchased by Henry Hoare
Literature: Webb, 1950, Sculpture by Rysbrack at Stourhead, *Burlington Magazine*, XCII, pp. 307–15, fig. 9; Webb, 1954, pp. 116 and 210, fig. 46; Whinney, 1964, *Sculpture in Britain 1530–1830*, p. 88; Kenworthy-Browne, 1980, *National Trust Studies*, pp. 77–9, fig. 22
Lent by the National Trust, Stourhead

Rysbrack was paid "in full for a Bust & pedesl. of Alfred £100" by Henry Hoare on 12 May 1764.[1] Rysbrack was now seventy years old and 'Alfred' was the last work he completed for Hoare, the patron who employed him consistently over thirty-five years. He wrote touchingly to his patron from Vere Street, Oxford Chapel, on 15 May:

> "I have been out of Town to take the air till Wednesday, for the benefit of my health, and think myself something better for it, but my Rheumatism continues that I cannot walk well, or else I would have returned you my hearty thanks in Person for Your Generous Bounty, sooner, which I shall always retain a grateful sense of. When the Pedestal is finished and Packed up, with the Bust. I shall let you have the Bills of the Packing Cases according to your desire".[2]

Rysbrack was to retire at the end of this year.

Alfred, like William III, the Black Prince (fig. 44) and Queen Elizabeth I (Cat. No. 51) became a symbol of English liberty in the second quarter of the eighteenth century and all of them appear in the Temple of British Worthies at Stowe. Queen Caroline had commissioned a series of Kings and Queens of England, which, because of her death in 1737, never went beyond the completion of the terracotta models.

The 'Alfred' in this series (fig. 51) is very close indeed to Rysbrack's marble of nearly thirty years later. Rysbrack also executed a pair of marble busts for Frederick, Prince of Wales, for which he was paid £105, with additional payments for, no doubt, suitably patriotic inscriptions.[3]

It was in this spirit that Hoare first considered erecting a tower to Alfred's memory on

79

Kingsettle Hill near Stourhead.[4] Hoare considered incorporating Rysbrack's 'Fame' but the idea came to nothing.[5] The Tower was eventually finished ten years later, two years after Rysbrack's death. The inscription composed by Hoare succinctly expresses the historical sense of patriotism of the eighteenth century: "ALFRED THE GREAT AD. 879 on the summit erected his standard against Danish invaders. To him we owe the origin of juries and the creation of a naval force. Alfred, the light of a benighted age, was a philosopher and a Christian; the father of his people, and the founder of the English monarchy and liberty".[6]

A bust of King Alfred appears in the background of Hogarth's portrait of the blue-stocking, Mary Edwards (1742), now in the Frick collection in New York. It is paired with a bust of Queen Elizabeth.

In the eighteenth century it was believed that Alfred had founded University College, Oxford, and in 1771 Jacob, Viscount Folkestone, presented his old college with a bust of Alfred by Joseph Wilton after this bust.[7]

1 W.R.O. Stourhead papers 383.6.
2 See Appendix No. 4; W.R.O. Stourhead papers 383.6.
3 Duchy of Cornwall Voucher 1736, quoted by Webb, 1954, p. 156. The *General Evening Post* for 22–24 July 1735 reported that they were to be set up in the Prince of Wales' Octagon in the garden in Pall-Mall: B. L. Burney 313b; for an account of the political activities of Frederick, Prince of Wales, see *Frederick, Prince of Wales and his Circle*, Gainsborough's House, Sudbury, Suffolk, 1981: Introduction.
4 Letter from Henry Hoare to Lady Bruce, 23 October 1762, quoted by Woodbridge, 1970, p. 53.
5 Letter from Henry Hoare to Lord Bruce, 18 November 1762, quoted by Woodbridge, 1970, p. 53; see Cat. No. 88.
6 Quoted by Webb, 1954, p. 116.
7 Lane-Poole, 1912, II, No. I. Inscribed: *ALFREDUS REX FUNDATOR D.D. Jb: Vics: FOLKESTONE A:B:1771*, it is now outside the Library, University College, Oxford. A Bath-stone bust after the Stourhead 'Alfred' is above the portico of Alfred House, Alfred Street, Bath.

fig. 51   King Alfred, terracotta, formerly at Windsor Castle; destroyed in 1906. Reproduced by gracious permission of Her Majesty The Queen.

173

GEORGE VERTUE

80 Alfred the Great

Line engraving, plate size $11\frac{3}{16} \times 7\frac{1}{2}$ in, 285×190 mm
Inscribed within the plate: *AELFREDUS MAGNUS REX ANGL. Desig. et Sculp. G. Vertue*
Provenance: 1874, purchased
Literature: O'Donoghue, 1908, *Catalogue of Engraved British Portraits*, I, p. 34; Kenworthy-Browne, 1980, *National Trust Studies*, pp. 77–9, fig. 20
Lent by the Victoria and Albert Museum, London (27178.2)

This plate was included in the folio edition of Rapin and Tindal's *History of England*.[1] Vertue based his image of Alfred on a painting at University College, Oxford, now known to be of seventeenth-century date. His image became the standard representation of Alfred for other engravers.

[1] Rapin-Thoyras, P. de, 1725–31.

MICHAEL RYSBRACK

81 The Sacrifice of a Bull

Terracotta, $19 \times 30\frac{3}{4}$ in, 483×781 mm
Provenance: 1767, purchased by Henry Hoare
Literature: Webb, 1950, Sculpture by Rysbrack at Stourhead, *Burlington Magazine*, XCII, pp. 307–15, fig. 10; Webb, 1954, p. 128, pl. 59
Lent by the National Trust, Stourhead

A model for a marble relief in the Stone Hall at Houghton Hall, Norfolk, this sacrificial scene is based on the so-called 'Vota Publica' relief in the Medici Gardens in Rome (Cat. No. 84). Rysbrack would probably have been familiar, too, with Raphael's 'quotation' from the same source, in the 'Paul and Barnabas at Lystra' cartoon, at Hampton Court, which Jonathan Richardson the elder had drawn or traced.[1]

For a fuller discussion of the importance of these reliefs and their classical sources, see Malcolm Baker's essay in this catalogue.

Henry Hoare purchased this and Cat. Nos. 82 and 83 at Rysbrack's sale on Saturday, 14 February 1767, lots 50, 49 and 62 respectively.[2] He recorded the purchase on 19 February as "By Mr Rysbrack's Sale 5 Drawings and 3 Bass Relievos £41.9.6".[3]

The reliefs are listed in the "Inventory of Furniture and Effects Rescued from the Fire on April 16th 1902" as "carved stone groups in painted wood frames".[4] Four are listed, though in fact the fourth is a reduced plaster version of Rysbrack's signed marble relief in the Hall at Clandon Park, Surrey. The plaster is probably the "large basso relievo" for which Cheere was paid ten guineas in 1766.[5]

[1] Vertue, III, p. 13. For a fuller account, see Watson, 1944, On the Early History of Collecting in England, *Burlington Magazine*, LXXXV, pp. 223–8.
[2] Langford and Son sale catalogue.
[3] W.R.O. Stourhead papers 383.6.
[4] W.R.O. Stourhead papers 383.22.
[5] W.R.O. Stourhead papers 383.4. A fifth relief, a curious, small plaster, may safely be discounted as the work of Rysbrack.

81

82

MICHAEL RYSBRACK

82 The Hunt of the Trajans

Terracotta, 22¾×30 in, 578×762 mm
Provenance: 1767, purchased by Henry Hoare
Literature: Webb, 1950, Sculpture by Rysbrack
at Stourhead, *Burlington Magazine*, XCII, pp.
307–15, fig. 11
Lent by the National Trust, Stourhead

This is a model for the marble relief in the
Stone Hall at Houghton. It was described as "An
Hunting, after the Antique" in the catalogue to
Rysbrack's sale in 1767.[1] Rysbrack has subtly
recomposed the 'Hunt of the Trajans' relief on the
Arch of Constantine, probably using engravings
from his own copies of P. Santi Bartoli's *Römische
Antiquitäten in Basso-rilievo* (pls. XXII and XXV)
and Bellori's *Veteres Arcus Augustorum* (Cat.
No. 85).

[1] Langford and Son sale catalogue, 14 February 1767, lot
49.

83

MICHAEL RYSBRACK

83 A Sacrifice

Terracotta, $17\frac{1}{4} \times 28\frac{3}{4}$ in, 440×730 mm
Provenance: 1767, purchased by Henry Hoare
Lent by the National Trust, Stourhead

A very similar relief appears in one of the designs for chimney-pieces in Gibbs' *Book of Architecture*, pl. 92. The title for the plate given in the introduction (p. xxi) states "Three Designs of Chimneys done for Mess. *Clark* and *Young* at *Rowhampton*". The house at Roehampton was Elmgrove, burnt down about 1790, on what is now the site of Digby Stuart College.

Bartholomew Clark is shown in the Poor Rate until 1747, after which Hitch Young is recorded until 1759.[1] Clark was the father-in-law of Jacob Bouverie, 1st Viscount Folkestone of Longford Castle, Wiltshire. There is a bust of Hitch Young by Rysbrack at Longford Castle.[2] Rysbrack was commissioned to do the monument to Clark at Hardingstone, Northamptonshire. The monument, signed and dated 1746, includes a portrait medallion of Hitch Young.

[1] I am grateful to R. A. Shaw, Local History Librarian, Battersea, for this information.
[2] Folkestone records paying Rysbrack "200.0.0" on account, in December 1739, and annotates the entry: "The three busts of Jacob, Viscount Folkestone, his eldest son as a boy & Mr Hitch Younge are by Rysbrack": Longford Castle Muniment Room, 'Extracts from the Private Account Book of Jacob, 1st Viscount Folkestone, 1722–1761'.

FRANCOIS PERRIER

84 "Icones et Segmenta Illustrium e Marmore tabularum Quae Romae adhuc extant." Rome, 1645

Open at plate 48: Relief from the Medici Garden
Lent by B. Weinreb Ltd, London

84

J. P. BELLORI

85 "Veteres Arcus Augustorum . . ."
Rome, 1690

Engraved by P. Santi Bartoli
Open at plate 32: Relief from the Arch of Constantine
Lent by B. Weinreb Ltd, London

85

178

MICHAEL RYSBRACK

86 Nymph of the Grotto

Pen and ink, pencil, red chalk and brown wash, $9\frac{9}{10} \times 10\frac{1}{2}$ in, 252×267 mm
Laid on card; inscribed *M. Rysbrack, Sculptor* and on the back:

Hujus Nympha loci, sacri Custodia Fontis,
Dormio, dum blandae sentio murmur Aquae.
Parce meum, quisquis tangis cava Marmora, Somnum
Rumpere; sive bibas, sive lavere, tace.
Vide Jani Gruteri Corpus Inscriptionum, pag.
CLXXXII.3. et Monumenta aliquot
Sepulchralia, cura Marci Zuerij Bexhornij, Tab. 104

Nymph of the Grot, these sacred Springs I keep,
And to the murmur of these Waters sleep;
Ah spare my slumbers, gently tread the Cave!
And drink in Silence, or in Silence lave!
See Pope's Letter to Edwd. Blunt Esq. 2. June 1725.
Collector's mark: *CR*
Provenance: Charles Rogers; 1784, William Cotton, by descent; 1853, presented to Plymouth Public Library
Exhibited: London: Sotheby's, 1979, 'Old Master and English Drawings and European Bronzes', Cat. No. 63
Lent by the City Museum and Art Gallery, Plymouth

86

This unusual drawing by Rysbrack depicts the life-size lead figure of a sleeping woman, in the Grotto at Stourhead. The statue was, in all probability, from the yards of John Cheere or John Manning, at Hyde Park Corner. It was purchased by Henry Hoare about 1748, for G. Macey of Sarum was paid £2.11.8 for "Black Marble Slab for the Nymph and an old Bill for Wilberry in full" on 23 April 1748.[1]

We know Rysbrack went at least once to Stourhead, (see Cat. No. 74), and it is more than likely that he sketched the 'Sleeping Nymph' on such a visit.[2]

The classical source for the Stourhead 'Nymph' is the 'Cleopatra' now in the Museo Pio-Clementino, in the Vatican.[3]

It is interesting that the Stourhead 'Nymph' like its classical prototype, was set up as a fountain, and was also until the late eighteenth century in a grotto-like niche.

The popularity of the 'Borghese Cleopatra' and of the 'Farnese Hercules' in the eighteenth century is well demonstrated by Pompeo Batoni's portrait of Charles Crowle of Crowle Park in which small models of both these classical statues appear in the background.[4]

[1] Messrs. C. Hoare and Co: Wilberry Account Book, Lincolns Inn Fields Account, 1734–1749.
[2] It was probably on such a visit that Rysbrack drew Le Sueur's bronze bust of Charles I (V.A.M. D161–1886: Avery, 1979a, p. 134, fig. 8).
[3] Haskell and Penny, 1981, pp. 184–7.
[4] Christie's, 26 June 1981, lot 144. Another Batoni portrays Thomas Coke, 1st Earl of Leicester, standing before a life-size version of the 'Cleopatra': Oxford: Ashmolean Museum, 1981, *The Most Beautiful Statues*, Cat. No. 1.

MICHAEL RYSBRACK

87   Bacchus   1751

Marble, 46 in, 1168 mm
Signed and dated: *Michl. Rysbrack fecit 1751*
Provenance: 1751, purchased by Henry Hoare; 1883, sold Christie's, 1 and 2 June; E. A. V. Stanley collection (Lord Taunton Heirlooms), Quantock Lodge, Bridgwater; 1920, sold Sotheby's, 16 July, lot 29, acquired by Calouste Gulbenkian through Duveen
Literature: Webb, 1950, Sculpture by Rysbrack at Stourhead, *Burlington Magazine*, XCII, pp. 307–15; Webb, 1954, pp. 125–6 and 211

Lent by the Calouste Gulbenkian Foundation Museum, Lisbon (2216)

On 3 October 1751, Henry Hoare paid Rysbrack "in full" the sum of £71.18.10 for a 'Bacchus'.[1] Richard Colt Hoare records it in the Parlour in 1822,[2] while a watercolour of 1824 by J. C. Buckler, shows it paired with a 'Piping Faun' from Italy, in the room now known as the Little Dining Room.[3] In the trustee sale of 1883, when the then Sir Henry Hoare was a minor, the 'Bacchus' "by Rysbrack" was listed between "a pair of long necked Oriental bottles . . . and a pair of Derbyshire Spar Vases". It was sold to a Mr Denison for £63.2.0. Webb recorded it as missing in 1954.

Horace Walpole described it as "A young Bacchus, whole figure less than life, and composed by Rysbrack from different antiques, in marble, fine".[4] The possible sources were numerous and would have been to hand in his own copies of Perrier, Sandrart and Bisschop (see figs. 52 and 53).

Rysbrack's friends, the Richardsons, recorded an antique 'Bacchus' in the Medici collection "leaning one arm upon a stump with a *patera*; Exquisitely good, and has a lovely sweep!"[5] In 'The Painter's Son' by Jonathan Richardson the elder, the younger Richardson is shown surrounded by books, paintings, a bust of Homer after the antique, and on the table beside him, a small model, probably of an Apollo, but very close to Rysbrack's 'Bacchus'.[6] Though perhaps brought back by Richardson from Italy, it is not inconceivable that this is a model such as made Rysbrack's reputation on his first arrival in England.[7]

[1] Messrs. C. Hoare and Co.: Henry Hoare, private ledger.
[2] W.R.O. Stourhead papers 383.9.
[3] British Museum, Print Room; reproduced in the guide-book to Stourhead, 1981, p. 20.
[4] Walpole, 1927–8 (published), Visits to Country Seats, p. 41; quoted by Webb, 1954, p. 126.
[5] Richardson, 1754 (2nd edn), *Account of Statues, Bas-reliefs and Drawings in Italy, France, etc.*, p. 127.
[6] 1938, Messrs Sawyer; present whereabouts unknown: Kerslake, 1957, pp. 23–5, fig. 25.
[7] Vertue, I, p. 76, and III, pp. 17 and 56.

87

MICHAEL RYSBRACK

88   Fame   1760

Terracotta, 22⅞ in, 581 mm
Signed and dated: *Michl. Rysbrack fecit 1760*
Provenance: 1969, purchased
Literature: Webb, 1954, p. 226; Whinney, 1971,
English Sculpture 1720–1830, pp. 54–5
Lent by the Victoria and Albert Museum, London (A1-1969)

This study for the figure of Fame or Victory on the monument to Admiral Vernon (1684–1757), in Westminster Abbey, was one of the sculptor's last works, yet it shows no diminution of invention or vitality. The monument was completed in 1763.[1]

The model, described as "a sketch of *Fame* for Admiral *Vernon's Monument*" was sold on 25 January 1766.[2] Rysbrack attempted very few figures in movement and it has been argued that 'Fame' reflects the influence of Roubiliac's more theatrical tomb sculpture.[3] But it is more likely that the inspiration was both classical sculpture and the French tradition of Plumière and Delvaux. The pose closely parallels the 'Discobolus' or 'Borghese Gladiator'.

Rysbrack executed another statue of 'Fame' which was sold as "a STATUE of FAME, (*7 feet high*) *holding a medallion of his* Royal Highness *the late Duke of* CUMBERLAND; which *Statue*, with the *pedestal*, are of *Portland stone*".[4] It was bought by another of Rysbrack's loyal patrons, Jacob Bouverie, 1st Viscount Folkestone, for £59 and set up at Longford Castle, Wiltshire. The medallion of the Duke of Cumberland has been replaced by one of Alfred, and it would seem likely that this was done almost immediately, for another account book entry reads "1767, June 26 Vanderhagen statuary, for a bust of Alfred 7.0.0.'[5] Vanderhagen was Rysbrack's assistant. The

figs. 52 and 53 Plates d and e from J. D. Sandrart, 1675,
Teutsche Academie . . .

Portland-stone plinth was inscribed, like Alfred's Tower at Stourhead, with a Latin inscription proclaiming Alfred's virtues in a similar vein.

Sir William Wyndham had originally commissioned the Longford Castle 'Fame' for his park at Orchard Wyndham.[6] On his death the commission was not taken up and Rysbrack, following the Battle of Culloden, changed the medallion portrait from Queen Anne to the Duke of Cumberland. Henry Hoare considered purchasing the statue for Alfred's Tower and proposed changing the portrait to King Alfred.[7]

[1] There is a design for the Vernon monument at the Mellon Center at Yale (B1977.14.5719); another, less closely related, is in the Victoria and Albert Museum (E433-1946): Physick, 1969, pp. 108–9, figs. 73 and 74; yet another was one of three Rysbrack designs sold by Drewatt, Watson, and Barton of Newbury, Berks., May 1981.
[2] Langford and Son sale catalogue, lot 9.
[3] Whinney, 1971, pp. 54–5.
[4] Langford and Son sale catalogue, 18 April 1767, lot 87. The pose of 'Fame' closely resembles that of 'Time' on the monument to the Spinola family by Plumière in Notre Dame de la Chapelle, Brussels: see Avery, 1980, *National Trust Studies*, fig. 2; Rysbrack owned a figure of Time by Plumière, lot 45, Langford and Son sale catalogue, 18 April 1766.
[5] Longford Castle Muniment Room: 'List of Pictures from old Account Books', and 'Extracts from the Private Account Book of Jacob, 1st Viscount Folkestone, 1722–1761'.
[6] See Cat. Nos. 33 and 50; letter from Henry Hoare to Lady Bruce, 23 October 1762, quoted in full by Woodbridge, 1970, p. 53.
[7] Letter from Henry Hoare to Lady Bruce, *ibid*.

MICHAEL RYSBRACK

89 Charity

Pen and ink and red chalk, brown wash heightened with white body colour, $3\frac{7}{8} \times 2\frac{13}{16}$ in, 99×72 mm
Stamped with the collectors' marks of Nathaniel Hone and Charles Rogers
Provenance: Charles Rogers; 1784, William Cotton, by descent; 1853, presented to Plymouth Public Library
Lent by the City Museum and Art Gallery, Plymouth

"From time to time he would amuse himself with making high-finished Drawings in an admirable taste; these are generally of his own invention, designed with a smart pen, washed with bister, and heightened with white. This Amusement he continued to the last days of his life". So wrote the connoisseur and collector Charles Rogers in 1778.[1] J. T. Smith, the first keeper of prints at the British Museum who had trained as a sculptor under Nollekens excepted Rysbrack from his criticisms of the draughtsmanship of eighteenth-century sculptors, for, he said, Rysbrack's drawings "though certainly considerably mannered, possess a fertility of invention, and a spirit of style in their execution, seldom emanating from the hand of a Sculptor of modern times."[2]

Rysbrack's subjects were, in the main, classical or biblical, sometimes illustrative of an entire narrative, such as "out of the story of Joseph" or "from Homer".[3] Some, the religious ones in particular, were more personal, like the two moving scenes of the Entombment, at Stourhead and the Print Room of the British Museum,[4] or simply charming like 'The Rest on the Flight into Egypt' (Cat. No. 90). That most of them are "high-finished" is borne out by the number of studies and preparatory drawings that exist;[5] a few are after Old Masters or direct copies from engravings.[6]

The admiration of Rogers and Smith is indicative of the status Rysbrack achieved as a draughtsman. That the design for the Foley

89

monument (Cat. No. 39) should be contemporaneously mounted is another indication, while the inclusion of Rysbrack's 'Time' in Rogers' *Prints in Imitation of Drawings* is the final accolade. For though Reynolds, Adam and others are included as collectors, Rysbrack alone among British contemporary artists is represented by his own work.[7]

[1] Rogers, 1778, II, pp. 227–8.
[2] Smith, 1828 (reprinted 1949), p. 213.
[3] Christie's, 9 and 7 February 1774, lots 68, 69, 70 and 71.
[4] B.M. 1926-4-12-3.
[5] See Cat. No. 90.
[6] 'Woman with a Pitcher after Parmigianino' and 'Tobias and the Angel', Harris Museum and Art Gallery, Preston.
[7] Three drawings from Rysbrack's own collection are also included, two by Guercino, and a third, 'Two Soldiers', by Salvator Rosa. There is a very close parallel between the attitudes of the two soldiers, and Rysbrack's own 'Rubens' and 'van Dyck'.

MICHAEL RYSBRACK

90 The Rest on the Flight into Egypt

Pen and ink and red chalk, brown wash heightened with white body colour, $7\frac{1}{4} \times 10\frac{1}{2}$ in, 185×266 mm
Inscribed in ink on the old mount in a florid hand: *Rysbrack*
Provenance: 1964, purchased from Colnaghi's
Literature: to be included in Dr David Brown's forthcoming *Catalogue of the Collection of Drawings in the Ashmolean Museum*, No. 1649, pl. 461
Exhibited: London: P. & D. Colnaghi, 1964, 'English Drawings and Watercolours', No. 10
Lent by the Visitors of the Ashmolean Museum, Oxford

A preliminary study of St. Joseph holding the bridle of the ass, is in the British Museum (Fawkener 44.5211).

90

91   The Resurrection

Pen and ink and red chalk, and brown wash, $18\frac{5}{8} \times 11\frac{11}{16}$ in, 472×297 mm
Laid on card; inscribed *Michl. Rysbrack Sculptor*
Collector's mark: *CR*
Provenance: Charles Rogers; 1784, William Cotton, by descent; 1853, presented to Plymouth Public Library
Lent by the City Museum and Art Gallery, Plymouth

91

92   Moses striking the rock

Pencil, pen and ink, brown and grey wash heightened with white body colour, $10\frac{3}{4} \times 15$ in, 272×380 mm
Laid on card; inscribed: *Michl. Rysbrack Sculptor*
Collector's mark: *CR*
Provenance: Charles Rogers; 1784, William Cotton, by descent; 1853, presented to Plymouth Public Library
Lent by the City Museum and Art Gallery, Plymouth

Rysbrack owned a large engraving after Poussin's painting of the same subject, but he makes no specific reference to it here.[1]

[1] Christie's, 9 February 1774, lot 27.

92

93

MICHAEL RYSBRACK

93 The Surgeon extracting the dart from the wound of Menelaus

Pen and ink and red chalk, brown wash heightened with white body colour, $10\frac{11}{16} \times 14\frac{11}{16}$ in, 271 × 375 mm
Inscribed on the back in the artist's hand:

> *The heavy Tidings griev'd the Godlike Man;*
> *Swift to his Succour thro' the Ranks he ran:*
> *The dauntless King yet standing firm he found,*
> *And all the Chiefs in deep Concern around,*
> *Where to the steely Point the Reed was join'd,*
> *The Shaft he drew, but left the Head behind.*

Provenance: 1767, purchased by Henry Hoare at Rysbrack's sale, 14 February, lot 28, for £1.11.6.[1]
Lent by the National Trust, Stourhead

The title is taken from the sale catalogue entry for lot 28 on 14 February 1767. It and its pair "Menelaus wounded", lot 27, together with lots 68, 70 and 71 were the five drawings purchased by Henry Hoare, at Langfords' Auction House. They were listed as "DRAWINGS *framed and glazed*."[2]

They remained framed and glazed until comparatively recently. Alda Hoare's 'Catalogue of principal paintings at Stourhead' dated 6 July 1898 records "several compositions in bistre by the sculptor Rysbrack" in the "Old Library", now the Smoking Room.[3] Previous to that Sir Richard Colt Hoare mentions "several spirited original compositions in bistre by Rysbrack the sculptor" in the South Room.[4] Long exposure to light, particularly in a south-facing room, would explain the present blanched appearance of many of the Stourhead drawings. The verse inscribed on the back of this drawing is taken from Pope's *Homer*, lines 242–8.

94

[1] Langford and Son sale catalogue.
[2] W.R.O. Stourhead papers 383.6; the entry in Hoare's accounts for 19 February 1767, reads "By Mr. Rysbrack's Sale 5 Drawings and 3 Bass Relievos £41.9.6."

[3] W.R.O. Stourhead papers 383.9.
[4] Hoare, 1822, p. 75.

MICHAEL RYSBRACK

94 The Labours of Hercules, the encounter with Cacus

Pen and ink and red chalk, brown wash heightened with white body colour, $17 \times 14\frac{3}{4}$ in, 432×373 mm
Lent by the National Trust, Stourhead

This drawing may have been presented by the artist to his patron. On 19 May 1764, Rysbrack had written to Henry Hoare about the 'Alfred' commission (Cat. No. 79) and concluded "I hope you will not forget my request which I begged of You, that I may make a Drawing or two of Some Subjects which you shall think of which are Great & Noble, and something surprising, and that you will be so Good to send it to me in Writing, which will give me the Greatest Pleasure in the World".[1]

In this drawing of the encounter with Cacus, Rysbrack has included the Nemean Lion, the Hydra of Lerna, the Stymphalian birds, Prometheus and his vulture, Cerberus, and a Gorgon, while Athena supports the right arm of Hercules.

[1] W.R.O. Stourhead papers 383.6: see Appendix No. 4.

MICHAEL RYSBRACK

95 The Triumph of Alexander

Pen and ink and red chalk, brown wash heightened with white body colour, $10\frac{11}{16} \times 13\frac{5}{8}$ in, 272×345 mm

Inscribed on original mount: *Michl. Rysbrack Sculptor*

Literature: Wilson, 1976, Rysbrack in Bristol, *Apollo*, CIII, pp. 22–5, fig. 5

The City of Bristol Museum and Art Gallery (K4017)

The Temple of Vesta, the *lictor* and *fasces*, and the curious but correct trumpets, all suggest a Roman triumphal procession. The triumphant victor's horse and its leader are taken from the pair of colossal figures known as 'Alexander and Bucephalus' that stand on the Quirinal at Rome.[1] Rysbrack would have been familiar with these figures from engravings in such publications as Perrier's *Segmenta nobilium. . . .*[2]

[1] Haskell and Penny, 1981, pp. 136–41, figs. 71 and 72.
[2] Perrier, 1638, pls. 22 and 23; Sandrart, 1675, pl. f.

MICHAEL RYSBRACK

96 Coriolanus

Pen and ink and brown wash heightened with white body colour, $11\frac{1}{4} \times 16$ ins, 286×408 mm

Provenance: 1767, purchased by Henry Hoare at the artist's sale, perhaps lot 22 for seven guineas

Lent by the National Trust, Stourhead

The subject of this drawing is probably Coriolanus receiving the entreaties of his wife and mother. It may therefore be identified with lot 22 "Coriolanus", in the artist's sale of 14 February 1767 and is one of the five drawings purchased at the sale by Henry Hoare.[1] Rysbrack owned a "*Coriolanus*, by *P. da Cortona, framed and glazed*". It was sold, lot 48, at the artist's sale on 25 February 1764.[2]

[1] Langford and Son sale catalogue; W.R.O. 383.6.
[2] Langford and Son sale catalogue.

96

ANDREA SOLDI 1703–1771
(Illus. fig. 20)

97 Michael Rysbrack with the terra-cotta statue of Hercules   1753

Oil on canvas, 45×35⅞ in, 1143×911 mm
Signed: *A. Soldi . . ./A . . . 175.*
Inscribed on the base of the statue: *Michael Rysbrack*
Provenance: Christie's, 10 April 1970, lot 94
Literature: Ingamells, 1974, Andrea Soldi, *Connoisseur*: part II, vol. 186, pp. 181–3, fig. 9; Kerslake, 1977, *Early Georgian Portraits*, p. 239, pl. 702; Ingamells, J, 1980, Andrea Soldi, a check list of his work, *Walpole Society* XLVII, pp. 14–15, No. 56
Lent by the Yale Center for British Art, Paul Mellon Collection (B1976.7.75)

Another almost identical version of this painting, now untraced, was sold at Sotheby's 24 June 1970, lot 109. It was clearly signed: *A Soldi/Ao 1753*. Soldi also painted two portraits of Louis-François Roubiliac, one dated 1751 (Dulwich College Picture Gallery) and the other 1757–8 (Garrick Club).[1]

[1] Ingamells, 1974, p. 181, figs. 5 and 6.

Appendix

1. *Agreement between Paul Methuen and Michael Rysbrack, 2 July 1744. W.R.O. Methuen papers, 3641:*

Memorandum   July ye 2th. 1744

That It is this Day agreed by and between Paul Methuen Esqr. and Michael Rysbrack in Consideration of the Sum of two Hundred and Seventy pounds, to make a monument four teen feet three Inchess High an Six feet nine Inchess – Brodt According to a Drawing agreed upon the Said Paul – Methuen Esqr. – Doth agree to pay the Said Michael Rysbrack the Sum of One Hundred pound in part there of now, the Receipt where of the Said Michael Rysbrack does here By acknoledge.

The Coullers of the marble for ye monument are to be, for the architett part is to be white an vene, the Shielts an two-Inscriptions Statuary, the two Collums purple, the Sr. Coffergus to be Blak and yellow, and to be finished by the Letter Endt of may next and Sett up in the parish Church of Bradford in the County of Wilts. and then the Remaining Sum of one Hundred and Seventy pound to be paid, the Said Michael Rysbrack is to be at no Expence for Boxing, Carraige, or Scaffolling, in Setting it up. In witness where of we have sett our Handss.

P Methuen
Mich: Rysbrack

Witness.
    J. Selfe

By Mr Methuen   100–0–0
    Mr Neele   230–0–0
                 330

Two Marble Boys added charged at 60£ more than above Contract.

2. *Agreement between Paul Methuen and Michael Rysbrack, 23 February 1758. W.R.O. Methuen papers, 5086:*

The Honble Paul Methuen Esqr Dr to
              Michael Rysbrack Statuary

	£. S. D.
1758	
Febry 23d: On an Agreement Signed this Day, that the Said Michael Rysbrack, should make a Monument; In memory of the late Honble Sir Paul Methuen Knight of the Bath. According to a Drawing agreed upon to be finished within the Space of a Year from the above Dates; and to be Erected in Westminster Abbey For the Sum of ---	372.00.00
To an Addition agreed upon of White and Vein'd Marble to Case the Bottom Portland Plinth, Containg 28 feet Superl at 5£ per foot –	7.00.00
Total	379.00.00

1758	
Febry 23d: Recd of The Honble Paul Methuen Esqr: in Part, the Sum of – – –	150.00.00
	229.00.00
Paid the Bill of Mr Bacchus the Carpenter to the Abbey for the Scaffolding	9.12
	£238.12

Recd of The Honble Paul Methuen Esq
the Contents of this Bill in full of all Demands
              By me Mich: Rysbrack

3. *Letter from Michael Rysbrack to the Duchess of Beaufort, 14 April 1766. Muniment Room, Badminton House:*

Vere Street Oxford Chapel
May it Please Your Grace   April 14th 1766.

According to Your Orders, received by a Gentleman who has been twice with me, I send the number of the Boxes, which are as follow. For the Monument of His Grace the late Duke of Beaufort: the Number of Boxes are Nine. – And remaining for the Monument of Duke Henry the Number is four, (all the other Boxes of that Monument are at Badminton) one Box contains the Laying figure of the Father of Duke Henry, holding the Medal of his Dutchess, one contains two Die's of the Pedestal with the two Coats of Arms, another contains part of the Pyramid & the last the Inscription table, which Boxes will make a Load for a Waggon.

I Beg Your Grace will be so Good to conclude upon the Inscription for the Monument, that it may be finished as speedily as Possible. Because I am not well, and if I should Die, I know what will become of the Monument, therefore hope your Grace will please to have the Boxes taken away with all convenient Expedition. I, Conclude with wishing You all health and Happiness, and am

Madam,
Your Grace's.
Most Respectfull
and most Obedient
humble Servant
Mich: Rysbrack

4. *Letter from Michael Rysbrack to Henry Hoare, 19 May 1764. W.R.O. Stourhead papers, 383.6 (loose):*

Vere Street. Oxford Chapel
May 19th 1764

Sir,

I have been out of Town to take the air till Wednesday, for the benefit of my health, and think myself something better for it, but my Rheumatism continues that I cannot walk well, or else I would have returned you my hearty thanks in Person for Your Generous Bounty, sooner, which I shall always retain a grateful sense of. When the Pedestal is finished and Packed up, with the Bust. I shall let you have the Bills of the Packing Cases according to your desire, – Sir. I hope you will not forget my request which I begged of You, that I may make a Drawing or two of Some Subjects which you shall think of which are Great & Noble, and something surprising, and that you will be so Good to send it to me in Writing, which will give me the Greatest Pleasure in the World.

And I remain, Sir
Always your most
Dutiful & Respectful
humble Servant
Michl Rysbrack

5. *Inscription on the monument to Andrew Innys, St. John's, Bristol.*

SACRED/To the Memory of ANDREW INNYS *alias* INNES, Gent./(SON of WILLIAM INNES, A.M./One of the Sons of Sr. ROBERT INNES of *INNES,*/In the SHIRE OF *MURRAY* IN THE KINGDOM OF *SCOTLAND*, Bart/By Lady GRISEL STUART DAUGHTER of JAMES EARL of *MURRAY,*)/WHO DIED THE XXIX. OF DEC. MDCCXXXIII. IN THE LXXXII. YEAR OF HIS AGE./He married JOAN the DAUGHTER of ROBERT RANDAL, Gent./By whom he had one SON RANDAL INNYS, deceas'd./SHE DIED THE III OF MAY, MDCLXXII./HE AFTERWARDS MARRIED/ELIZABETH the DAUGHTER of JEREMY MARTIN, M.D./SHE DIED THE XIII. OF SEPTEMBER, MDCCXI./By whom he had Eight SONS and Six DAUGHTERS, *Viz*/WILLIAM, HESTER, ANDREW,/EDWARD, AND JOSEPH, deceas'd,/ELIZABETH, MARY, MARTIN, ANN, JEREMY,/WILLIAM, SARAH, MARTHA, AND JOHN, now living./A.D. MDCCXXVI.

6. *Inscription on the monument to Sir Edward Seymour, Maiden Bradley, Wiltshire:*

Under this marble are deposited the/Remains of Sr. EDWARD SEYMOUR Bart./Late of Bury Pomroy in the County of Devon/and of this place;/A man of such Endowments/as added Lustre to his noble Ancestry,/Commanded Reverence from his Co:tempories,/and Stands the fairest pattern to Posterity./Being often chosen in Council and always called to Parliament/(a friend to his Prince, a Servant to his Country)/He advised the King with Freedom,/the Senate with Dignity;/That Senate, the Bullwark of English Liberty,/in which he presided for Several Years:/found his eloquence an advocate,/his Integrity a Guardian,/his Vigour a Champion for its Priviledges:/nor can any English man rejoyce/in that envied Portion of his Birth-right,/the HABEAS CORPUS Act,/without Gratitude to the ashes of this Patriot,/under whose influence/it became his Heritage./Born in the year 1633,/His Childhood felt not the Calamities/ which, in the succeeding years/the Spirit of Anarchy and Schism/spread over the Nation:/ His Manhood saw the Church Monarchy restored;/and he lived in Dutifull obedience to them both; Loaden wth Honour, full of years,/(amidst the Triumphs of his Country/raised to the highest point of Glory/by that Immortal Princess Queen ANNE)/He Died/in the Year 1707./FRANCIS SEYMOUR Esqr. in just Veneration/for the memory of his illustrious Grandfather/and in due obedience to the last Will + Testament/of Lieutenant General WILLIAM SEYMOUR,/ Second Son to the deceased Sr EDWARD,/Hath Caused this Monument to be erected.

7. *Inscription on the monument to Mary Edwards, St. James's, Bristol:*

Near this place
Lies Interred the body of
MARY, the Wife of WALTER EDWARDS Esqr.
and Daughter of the Right Honourable
RICHARD FREEMAN Esqr
of Battesford [Burresford] in the County of
Gloucester
Sometime Lord High Chancellor of Ireland
Distinguished
By her Birth, but much more by her Virtues:
Highly exemplary in the Character of Wife and
Parent:
Constant in her Devotions, Unblemished in her
Life:
She died the 12th of July 1736 in the 37th Year of
her Age,
leaving issue two Sons Walter and Thomas
WALTER EDWARDS Esqr who erected this
monument
in memory of MARY
His beloved wife died 24th of December 1758 and
lies interred near this place
In a steady conduct through Life, The strictest
Integrity and most
disinterested Benevolence directed and governed
all his Actions.
Also JANE EDWARDS sister of WALTER, who
died 11 December 1770
Her Life was one Uniform Pattern of Exemplary
Goodness and true Christianity.

8. *Inscription on the monument to the Reverend Sir John Tynte, Goathurst, Somerset:*

Sacred to the Memory/of the Reverend Sr. JOHN TYNTE Baronet/Rector of this Church./Who esteemed his Funchion [sic] to be his highest Honour,/and discharged the Duties of it with the greatest of pleasure: The ornaments of this Fabrick are publick Evidences/of the pious Regard He had for the Service of God;/His many Acts of Friendship and Charity, void of Ostentation/are more lasting Proofs of his good Will towards Men./This Small Testimony/of Gratitude/to a most generous Brother/was erected by/Sr. CHARLES KEMEYS TYNTE Baronet/1742.

9. *Inscription on the monument to John Wyndham, Alvediston, Dorset:*

To the Memory of *JOHN WYNDHAM* of Norrington Esq:/ and of Alice His Wife Daughter of THOMAS FOWNES/of Stepleton in the County of Dorset Esq: who are Both/buried near to this Wall, in the Churchyard/belonging to this Church, this Monument was placed by/the Order and at the Expence of The Right Honble/ THOMAS Lord WYNDHAM Baron WYND-HAM of Finglass,/and some time Lord High Chancellor of Ireland, their/Son, as a testimony of that Honour and Respect which/He had for them. June. 1746./The said JOHN WYNDHAM Esq: departed this Life/on the 29th of February 1723/4; aged 76. The said ALICE, his Wife departed this Life/on the 16th of May 1727; aged 70:

10. *Inscription on the Methuen monument, Bradford-on-Avon, Wiltshire:*

Ad Aedis hujusce Latus Boreale/Viri Praestantissimi/ANTONII METHUEN Arm:/Conduntur Exuviae/PAULI METHUEN de BRADFORD Arm/Filiu natu secundi/Antiquissimo/Stemmate de METHUEN in Regno SCOTIAE/Oriundi:/ et GERTRUDAE/Conjugis Pientissimae/THO-MAE MOORE de SPARGROVE in Com. SOMERSET Arm:/(EX ELIZABETHA uxore/ Filia Primogenita Dni JOHANNES BAMP-FYLDE/De POLTIMORE in Agro DEVON/ Baronetti/Filia et Cohaeredis)/Obierunt/Ille, Mai 10, 1717, Annos natus 67./Illa, Jni 20, 1699, Annos nata 40.

Juxta Proavorum Cineres/THOMAE METHUEN. Arm:/ANTONII et GERTRU-DAE/Filii Unici/Requiescit Depositum:/Qui Nihil non aequum et liberale/Et fecit semper et cogitavit,/Tranquillus, patiens, clemens, benignus,/Ingenio minimc vulgari,/Singulari prorsuis humanitate:/Et ANNAE Uxoris,/Filae ISAACI SELFE Arm:/De BEANACRE in Agro WILTO-NIENSI/(EX UXORE PENELOPE/Praehon orabilis CAROLI LUCAS Baronis de SHEN-FIELD in Com ESSEX:/Filia et Cohaerede)/ Cujus Formam inter primas venustam,/Et commendabant et superabant,/Ineffabilis morum suavitas,/Animiq. Cunetis Virtutibus Ornati/ Potentiores Illiciae./Obierunt/Ille Jan 2, 1737 Aet. 53/Illa, Maii 15, 1733, Aet. 37./Parentibus bene meritus/PAULUS METHUEN Arm. Heres et Filius unicus/P.

Bibliography to the Catalogue

Archibald, E. H. H. 1954. *Portraits at the National Maritime Museum*. London.

Atkyns, Sir R. (the younger). 1712 (reprinted in facsimile 1974). *The ancient and present state of Glostershire*. London.

Avery, C. 1979a. Hubert Le Sueur's Portraits of King Charles I in Bronze, at Stourhead, Ickworth and elsewhere. *National Trust Studies*, pp. 128–47. London.

Avery, C. 1979b. Sculpture at North Mymms Park. *Connoisseur*, 202, pp. 115–19.

Avery, C. 1980. Laurent Delvaux's Sculpture in England. *National Trust Studies*, pp. 151–70. London.

Barrett, W. 1789. *The History and Antiquities of Bristol*. Bristol.

Beaven, The Reverend A. B. 1899. *Bristol Lists: municipal and miscellaneous*. Bristol.

Bellori, J. P. 1690. See Santi Bartoli. 1690.

Bisschop, J. de. (*circa* 1670). *Signorum veterum icones*. Amsterdam?

Borenius, T. 1936. A Venetian Apotheosis of William III. *Burlington Magazine*, LXIX, pp. 245–6.

Bristol Record Society. 1932. vol. III.

Burke, J. 1976. *English Art, 1714–1800*. Oxford.

Carracci, A. 1670?. *Gallerie que l'eccelant Annibal Carrache a peinte à Rome dans le Palais de Farnese*. [Plates engraved by Le Fébure] Paris.

Carracci, A. 1690?. *Imagines farnesiani* . . . Rome.

Chancellor, E. B. 1911. *The Lives of the British Sculptors* . . . London.

Charleston, R. J. & Wills, G. 1956. The Bow "Flora" and Michael Rysbrack. *Apollo*, 63, pp. 125–7.

Charlton, J. & Milton, D. M. 1951. *Redland 791–1800*. Bristol.

Chilcott, J. 1840? (4th edn). *Descriptive History of Bristol, Ancient and Modern* . . . Bristol.

Christie's. See Rysbrack sale catalogues.

Collinson, The Reverend J. 1791. *The History and Antiquities of the County of Somerset* . . . 3 vols. Bath.

Colvin, H. 1968 (4 April). Georgian Architects at Badminton. *Country Life*, CXLIII, pp. 800–4.

Colvin, H. (ed.) 1978 (1st edn 1954). *A Biographical Dictionary of British Architects, 1600–1840*. London.

Constable, W. G. 1962. *Canaletto. Giovanni Antonio Canal, 1697–1768*. 2 vols. Oxford.

Croft-Murray, E. 1962 and 1970. *Decorative Painting in England 1537–1837*. 2 vols. London.

Cust, Sir L. H. 1908. A Terra-cotta Bust of Thomas Third Earl of Coventry, by John Michael Rysbrack. *Burlington Magazine*, XIII, p. 362.

Dening, C. F. W. 1923. *The Eighteenth-Century Architecture of Bristol*. Bristol.

Esdaile, K. A. 1932. See Exhibition catalogues, London: Spink & Son Ltd.

Esdaile, K. A. 1940. A Statuette of William III at South Kensington. *Burlington Magazine*, LXXVI, pp. 123–4.

Esdaile, K. A. 1946. *English Church Monuments, 1510 to 1840*. London.

Evans, J. *circa* 1823a (3rd edn; 1st edn 1814). *The New Guide, or Picture of Bristol with Historical and Biographical Notices*.   bound with

Evans, J. *circa* 1823b (2nd edn) *Beauties of Clifton; or, the Clifton and Hotwell Guide*. Bristol.

Fagan, L. A. 1888. *A Descriptive Catalogue of the Engraved Works of W. Faithorne*. London.

Fedden, R. (ed.) 1976. *Treasures of the National Trust*. London.

Gibbs, J. 1728 (2nd edn 1739). *A book of architecture, containing designs of buildings and ornaments*. London.

Gibbs, J. 1747. *Bibliotheca Radcliviana, or a short description of the Radcliffe Library, at Oxford*, . . . London.

Girardon, F. 1707? [A collection of engravings from designs by François Girardon by various engravers.] Paris.

Gomme, A., Jenner, M. & Little, B. 1979. *Bristol, an architectural history*. London.

Gunnis, R. 1953. *Dictionary of British Sculptors 1660–1851*. London.

Hall, J. 1974 (revised edn 1979). *Dictionary of subjects and symbols in art*. London.

Harris, C. n.d. Catalogue of the stock of Charles Harris. (Copy in the Victoria and Albert Museum Library.)

Haskell, F. & Penny, N. 1981. *Taste and the Antique*. New Haven (U.S.A.) and London.

Hirst, H. C. M. 1921. *History of the Church of St. John the Baptist, Bristol*. Bristol.

Hoare, Sir R. C. 1822–44, and 1843. *The History of Modern Wiltshire*, 14 parts. London.

Holderbaum, J. 1957. Notes on Tribolo-II: A Marble Aesculapius by Tribolo. *Burlington Magazine*, XCIX, pp. 369–72.

Honour, H. 1958. English Patrons and Italian Sculptors in the first half of the eighteenth century. *Connoisseur*, CXLI, pp. 220–6.

Houbraken, J. 1747. *The Heads of illustrious persons of Great Britain engraven by Mr. Houbraken and Mr. Vertue.*

Hussey, C. 1945 (8 June). Witley Court, Worcestershire I–The Church. *Country Life*, XCVII, pp. 992–5.

Hussey, C. 1948. (19 March). Lydiard Tregoz, Wilts–I. *Country Life* CIII, pp. 578–81.

Hussey, C. 1955. *English Country Houses. Early Georgian, 1715–1760*. London.

Ingamells, J. 1974. Andrea Soldi, Parts I & II. *Connoisseur*, 185, pp. 192–200; 186, pp. 178–85.

Ison, W. 1952. (reprinted 1978). *The Georgian Buildings of Bristol*. London.

Kemp, B. 1980. *English Church Monuments*. London.

Kenworthy-Browne, J. 1980. Portrait Busts by Rysbrack. *National Trust Studies*, pp. 67–79. London.

Kerslake, J. 1957. The Richardsons and the Cult of Milton. *Burlington Magazine*, XCIX, pp. 23–4.

Kerslake, J. 1977. *National Portrait Gallery: Early Georgian Portraits*. 2 vols. London.

Landais, H. 1961. Some Bronzes from the Girardon Collection. *Connoisseur*, CXLVIII, pp. 136–44.

Lane-Poole, Mrs R. 1912, 1925. *Catalogue of Portraits in the possession of the University, Colleges, City, and County of Oxford*. 3 vols. Oxford.

Langford and Son. See Rysbrack sale catalogues.

Latimer, J. 1900, 1893, 1887. *The Annals of Bristol in the Seventeenth Century, Eighteenth Century, and Nineteenth Century*. 3 vols. Bristol.

Little, B. 1955. *The Life and Work of James Gibbs, 1682–1754*. London.

Liversidge, M. J. H. 1980. *William Hogarth's Bristol Altar-Piece*. Bristol Branch of the Historical Association.

London: National Portrait Gallery. 1979. *Report of the Trustees, 1978–9.*

London: Westminster Abbey. 1977. *Official Guide.*

McKenzie, D. F. (ed.) 1978. *Stationers' Company Apprentices 1701–1800*. The Oxford Bibliographical Society.

Maffei, P. A. See Rossi, D. de.

Manchee, T. J. (ed.) 1831. *The Bristol charities, being the report of the Commissioners for Inquiring concerning Charities in England and Wales, as far as relates to the Charitable Institutions in Bristol*. 2 vols. Bristol.

Mariette, P. J. 1768. *Description des travaux qui ont précédé, accompagné et suivi la fonte en bronze d'un seul jet de la Statue équestre de Louis XV, . . .* Paris.

Mathews, W. 1794. *New history, survey and description of the City and Suburbs of Bristol*. Bristol.

Mendez. 1981. See Exhibition catalogues, London: Mendez, C.

Michaelis, A. T. F. 1882 (translated by C. A. M. Fennell). *Ancient Marbles in Great Britain*. Cambridge.

Montfaucon, B. de. 1719. *L'Antiquité expliquée et représentée en figures*. 5 vols. (Supplement 5 vols.) Paris.

O'Donoghue, F. M. 1908–1925. *Catalogue of Engraved British Portraits preserved in the Department of Prints and Drawings in the British Museum*. 6 vols. London.

Overbeke, B. van. 1708. *Reliquiae antiquae Urbis Romae, . . .* 3 vols. Amsterdam.

Panofsky, E. 1964. *Tomb Sculpture . . .* London.

Penny, Nicholas. 1977. *Church Monuments in Romantic England*. New Haven (U.S.A.) and London.

Perceval, S. G. (ed.) 1898. "Journal of an Excursion to Eastbury and Bristol, etc., in May and June, 1767" by Sir Joseph Banks. *Proceedings of the Bristol Naturalists' Society*, IX, part 1, pp. 6–37.

Perrier, F. 1638. *Segmenta nobilium signorum et statuarii . . .* Rome and Paris.

Petrov, V. n.d. *Equestrian statue of Peter I by Carlo Rastrelli*. Leningrad.

Pevsner, N. 1958a. *The Buildings of England: North Somerset and Bristol*. Harmondsworth.

Pevsner, N. 1958b. *The Buildings of England: South and West Somerset*. Harmondsworth.

Physick, J. F. 1967. Some 18th century designs for monuments in Westminster Abbey. *Victoria and Albert Museum Bulletin*. London.

Physick, J. F. 1969. *Designs for English Sculpture 1680–1860*. London.

Piper, D. 1963. *Catalogue of the Seventeenth Century Portraits in the National Portrait Gallery*. Cambridge.

Plomer, H. R. 1922. *A Dictionary of the Printers and Booksellers who were at work in England, Scotland, and Ireland from 1668 to 1725.* London.

Plumb, J. H. 1950. *England in the Eighteenth Century.* Harmondsworth.

Potterton, H. 1975. *Irish Church Monuments: 1570–1880.* Belfast.

Pryce, G. 1861. *A Popular History of Bristol . . .* Bristol.

Raines, R. 1976 (24 June). An Art Collector of many parts. *Country Life*, CLIX, pp. 1692–3.

Ralph, E. [1973]. *Government of Bristol 1373–1973.* Bristol.

Rapin-Thoyras, P. de (translated by N. Tindal). 1732. *History of England.* 15 vols. London. See also Vertue, G. 1736.

R.I.B.A. 1969–74. *Catalogue of the drawings collection of the Royal Institute of British Architects.*

Richardson, J. [the elder]. 1715. *An Essay on the Theory of Painting.* London.

Richardson, J. [the elder]. 1719. *An Essay on the art of Criticism (so far as it relates to Painting).* London.

Richardson, J. [the elder] & Richardson, J. [the younger]. (1722 2nd edn 1754). *An Account of some of the statues, bas-reliefs, drawings and pictures, in Italy, etc.* London.

Roberts, Sir S. C. 1956. *The Evolution of Cambridge Publishing.* Cambridge.

Rogers, C. 1778. *A Collection of Prints in Imitation of Drawings.* 2 vols. London.

Roper, I. M. 1931. *The Monumental Effigies of Gloucestershire and Bristol.* Gloucester.

Rossi, D. de. 1704. *Raccolta di Statue antiche e moderne data in luce . . . da D. de Rossi. Illustrata colle sposizioni a ciascheduna immagine de P. A. Maffei.* Rome.

Rudder, S. 1779 (reprinted 1977). *A New History of Gloucestershire, . . .* Cirencester.

Rysbrack sale catalogues:

Langford and Son. 15 to 25 February 1764 (British Library).

Langford and Son. 20 April 1765 (Art Library of the Rijksmuseum, Amsterdam).

Langford and Son. 24 and 25 January 1766 (British Library).

Langford and Son. 14 February 1767 (Rijksbureau voor Kunsthistorische Documentatie, The Hague).

Langford and Son. 18 April 1767 (Messrs Colnaghi).

Langford and Son. 6 to 9 April 1772 (British Library).

Christie's. 7 to 9 February 1774 (Christie's).

Sandrart, J. von. 1675. *Teutsche Academie der edlen Bau-Bild-und Mahlerey-künste.* Nuremberg.

Sandrart, J. von. 1680. *Sculpturae veteris admiranda, sive delineatio . . . perfectissimarum eminentissimarumque statuarum, una cum artis hujus . . . theoria, . . .* Nuremberg.

Santi Bartoli, P. 1690. *Veteresarius Augustorum triumphis insignes ex reliquiis quae Romae ad huc supersunt cum imaginibus triumphalibus restituti, antiquis nummis notisque I. P. Bellorii illustrati . . .* Rome.

Santi Bartoli, P. 1693 (1st edn 1685?). *Admiranda romanarum antiquitatum . . . Notis J. P Bellorii illustrata.* Rome.

Santi Bartoli, P. 1697. *Gli Antichi Sepolcri; . . .* Rome.

Santi Bartoli, P. (ed. J. J. von Sandrart). 1699. *Petr. Sanct. Bartoli Römische Antiquitäten, in Basso-rilievo* (with notes by G. P. Bellori) *und Henr. Testelini Anmerckungen von der Mahlerey.* 2 parts. Nuremberg.

Shepherd, T. 1927. *Catalogue of the Wilberforce House Collection, Hull.*

Shiercliff, E. 1789, 1793 (2nd edn). *The Bristol and Hotwell Guide; . . .* Bristol.

Smith, J. T. 1828 (reprinted 1949). *Nollekens and his Times.* London.

Souchal, F. 1981. *French Sculptors of the 17th and 18th centuries.* 2 vols. Oxford.

Sparrow, J. 1960a. An Oxford Altarpiece. *Burlington Magazine*, CII, pp. 4–9.

Sparrow, J. 1960b. An Oxford Altarpiece: A further Note. *Burlington Magazine*, CII, pp. 452–5.

Stewart, J. D. 1963. Some Unrecorded Gibbons Monuments. *Burlington Magazine*, CV, pp. 125–6.

Stewart, J. D. 1978. New Light on Michael Rysbrack: Augustan England's 'Classical Baroque' Sculptor. *Burlington Magazine*, CXX, pp. 215–22

Stourhead, Wiltshire. 1981. *Guidebook.* The National Trust.

Strong, R. 1963. *Portraits of Queen Elizabeth I.* Oxford.

Strong, R. 1972. *Van Dyck: Charles I on Horseback.* London.

Sutton, D. 1981. *Apollo*, CXIV, No. 237 ('British Collecting' issue).

Trevelyan, G. M. 1946 (2nd edn; first published 1942). *English Social History.* London.

Vertue, G. Notebooks. I–VI. *The Walpole Society*. XVIII, XX, XXII, XXIV, XXVI, XXX; index XXIX. Published between 1930 and 1955. Oxford. (Reprinted 1968).

Vertue, G. 1736. The heads of the Kings of England proper for Rapin's History, translated by N. Tindal . . . London.

Waagen, G. F. 1838 (translated by H. E. Lloyd). *Works of Art and Artists in England*. 3 vols. London.

Walpole, H. 1762a(–1771). *Anecdotes of Painting in England*, 4 vols. . . . Strawberry Hill.

Walpole, H. 1762b. *The Life of George Vertue* (bound in with vol. III of *Anecdotes of Painting*).

Walpole, H. 1798. *Anecdotes of Painting* in vol. 3 of *The Works of Horatio Walpole*. London.

Walpole, H. 1927–8 (published; written 1762). Journals of Visits to Country Seats. *Walpole Society*, XVI. Oxford.

Ware, I. 1757? *Designs of Inigo Jones and others*. London.

Waterhouse, E. K. 1953. *Painting in Britain 1530 to 1790*. Harmondsworth.

Waterhouse, E. K. 1977. Sculpture from the Paul Mellon Collection at the British Art Center at Yale. *Burlington Magazine*, CXIX, pp. 351–2.

Waterhouse, E. K. 1981. *The Dictionary of 18th Century British Painters*. Woodbridge, Suffolk.

Watson, F. J. B. 1963. A bust of Fiammingo by Rysbrack rediscovered. *Burlington Magazine*, CV, pp. 441–5.

Webb, M. I. 1950. Sculpture by Rysbrack at Stourhead. *Burlington Magazine*, XCII, pp. 307–15.

Webb, M. I. 1954. *Michael Rysbrack, Sculptor*. London.

Webb, M. I. 1956 (24 May). Portraits of Bolingbroke. *Country Life*, CXIX, pp. 1131–2.

Whinney, M. D. 1964. *Sculpture in Britain, 1530–1830*. Harmondsworth.

Whinney, M. D. 1971. *English Sculpture 1720–1830*. (Victoria and Albert Museum Monograph). London.

Wibiral, F. 1879. *L'Iconographie d'A van Dyck d'après les recherches de H. Weber*. Leipzig.

Wilkins, H. J. 1920. *Edward Colston, 1630–1721 A.D. A chronological Account of his Life and Work. Together with an account of the Colston societies and memorials in Bristol*. Bristol.

Wilkins, H. J. 1924. *Redland Chapel and Redland*. Bristol.

Wilson, A. 1976. Rysbrack in Bristol. *Apollo*, CIII, pp. 22–5.

Wilson, A. n.d. *Sculpture from the City Art Gallery, Bristol*. Bristol.

Wittkower, R. 1958. *Art and Architecture in Italy, 1600 to 1750*. Harmondsworth.

Woodbridge, K. 1965. Henry Hoare's Paradise. *The Art Bulletin* XLVII, No. 1 (published by the College Art Association of America).

Woodbridge, K. 1970. *Landscape and Antiquity: aspects of English Culture at Stourhead, 1718 to 1838*. Oxford.

York (City of) Art Gallery. 1973. *Preview* 103. York.

Exhibition Catalogues

Birmingham: City Museum and Art Gallery. 1953. *Works of Art from Midland Houses*.

Brussels: Musée d'Art Ancien. 1977. *La Sculpture au siècle de Rubens*.

Leeds: Temple Newsam House. 1974. *The Man at Hyde Park Corner. Sculpture by John Cheere 1709–1797*.

Liverpool: Walker Art Gallery. 1958. *Paintings and Sculpture in England 1700–1750*.

London: Iveagh Bequest, Kenwood House. 1968. *The French Taste in English Painting during the first half of the 18th century*.

London: Iveagh Bequest, Kenwood House. 1979. *Thomas Hudson, 1701–1779*.

London: Mendez, C. 1981. *Dutch and Flemish Prints*.

London: Sotheby's. 1974. *Exhibition of Old Master and English Drawings and European Bronzes from the Collection of Charles Rogers and William Cotton*. (Loan exhibition from the City Museum and Art Gallery, Plymouth.)

London: Spink & Son Ltd. 1932. *The Art of John Michael Rysbrack in Terracotta* (catalogue by Mrs Arundell Esdaile).

London: Victoria and Albert Museum. 1950. *William and Mary and their time*.

Oxford: Ashmolean Museum. 1981. *The Most Beautiful Statues. The Taste for Antique Sculpture 1500–1900* (catalogue by F. Haskell & N. Penny).

Sudbury, Suffolk: Gainsborough's House. 1981. *Frederick, Prince of Wales and his circle* (catalogue by Stephen Jones).

Manuscripts

Beaufort papers: Gloucestershire Record Office, Gloucester, and Muniment Room, Badminton.

Burney Collection: The British Library, London.

Chancery Masters Exhibits: Public Record Office, London.

Common Council Proceedings: Bristol Record Office.

Gough MSS, 'Somerset': The Bodleian Library, Oxford.

Halsewell Tynte papers: Somerset Record Office, Taunton.

Henry Hoare's private ledgers and account books: Messrs C. Hoare and Co., 37 Fleet Street, London.

Innys, J. Biographical Memoranda arranged alphabetically, from the Innys Library, Redland Court, 3 vols: Avon County Reference Library.

Merchant Venturers, The Society of, Books of Proceedings: Avon County Reference Library, microfilm.

Methuen papers: Wiltshire County Record Office, Trowbridge.

Peel MSS: Fitzwilliam Museum, Cambridge.

Radnor family papers: Muniment Room, Longford Castle, Wiltshire.

Redland Chapel Trust Papers: Osborne Clarke, Solicitors, Bristol.

Rogers, Charles, Esq., 'Memorials and Correspondence of Charles Rogers, Esq., F.R.S. and F.S.A.': The City Museum and Art Gallery, Plymouth (W.B.104).

St. John's Church, Wardens Accounts 1699–1730, Vestry Meeting Minutes 1676–1726, Parish Accounts 1710–1752: Bristol Record Office.

Seymour papers: Wiltshire County Record Office, Trowbridge.

Smith, Richard. 'Bristol Infirmary Biographical Memoirs', Vols 1–3; Bristol Record Office.

Stourhead papers: Wiltshire County Record Office, Trowbridge.

Tottenham House Archive: Wiltshire County Record Office, Trowbridge.

Webb, M. papers: Victoria and Albert Museum, London, Department of Sculpture.

Lenders

Her Majesty The Queen, 51.

Charles Avery, 3.

Duke of Beaufort, 61–68, 70, 71.

Viscount Cobham, 53, 54.

Private Collection, 55, 56.

Earl of Harrowby, 57.

Bryan Little, 11.

B. Weinreb Ltd, 27, 73, 75, 84, 85.

Bristol, City of Bristol Museum & Art Gallery, 6–9, 58, 95.
> Corporation of Bristol, 5.
> Diocese of Bristol, 15–20.
> Lord Mayor's Chapel, 32.

Kingston upon Hull, City Museums and Art Galleries, 25.

Lisbon, Calouste Gulbenkian Foundation Museum, 87.

London, British Architectural Library, R.I.B.A., 34.
> British Library, 21–24.
> National Maritime Museum, Greenwich, 29.
> National Portrait Gallery, 1, 2.
> St. Martin-in-the-Fields, 10.
> Victoria and Albert Museum, 4, 12, 14, 30, 31, 33, 35, 36, 39, 40, 42, 43, 69, 74, 77, 80, 88.
> Warburg Institute, University of London, 28.

Melbourne, National Gallery of Victoria, 26.

Oxford, Ashmolean Museum, 13, 52, 59, 60, 90.

Plymouth, City Museum and Art Gallery, 37, 38, 41, 44–49, 86, 89, 91, 92.

Stourhead, National Trust, 72, 76, 78, 79, 81–83, 93, 94, 96.

Swindon, Borough of Thamesdown, Lydiard Mansion, 50.

Yale Center for British Art, Paul Mellon Collection, 97.

Photograph sources

Ashmolean Museum, Oxford, 13, 52, 59, 60, 90.

City of Bristol Museum & Art Gallery, frontispiece, fig. 2, fig. 3, fig. 4, fig. 5, fig. 6, fig. 7, fig. 14, fig. 21, fig. 22, fig. 25, fig. 26, fig. 27, 3, 4, 5, 6, 7, 8, 9, 11, fig. 28, fig. 29, fig. 30, fig. 31, fig. 32, 12, fig. 33, 14, 15, 16, 17, 18, 19, 20, 27a, 27b, 30, 31, 32, 33, fig. 34, fig. 35, 34, fig. 36, 35, 36, fig. 38, fig. 39, 37, 38, 39, 40, 41, 42, 43, 44, 45, 46, 47, 48, fig. 43, 49, 50, 57, 58, 62, 63, 64, 65, 66, 67, 68, 69, 70, 71, 73a, 73b, 73c, 75, 77, 80, 84, 85, 86, fig. 52, fig. 53, 89, 91, 92, 93, 94, 95, 96.

University of Bristol Department of Diagnostic Radiography, fig. 23, fig. 24.

British Architectural Library, R.I.B.A., 34.

British Library, 21, 22, 23, 24a, 24b, 24c.

The Lord Chamberlain, St. James's Palace, fig. 51.

Christie's, 26.

Country Life, fig. 17.

Courtauld Institute of Art, London, fig. 19, fig. 40, fig. 41, 51, fig. 44, fig. 45, 53, 54, 61, fig. 46, fig. 47, 72.

Dr Terry F. Friedman, fig. 1.

G.L.C. Photographic Unit, Department of Architecture & Design, 10.

Calouste Gulbenkian Foundation Museum, Lisbon, 87.

Kingston upon Hull Museums & Art Galleries, fig. 13.

National Maritime Museum, Greenwich, 29.

National Monuments Record, London, fig. 18, fig. 37.

National Portrait Gallery, London, 1, 2.

National Trust, Stourhead, fig. 49, fig. 50, 76, 78, 79, 81, 82, 83.

Sabin Galleries Ltd, 55, 56.

John Trelawny-Ross, fig. 8, fig. 9, fig. 10, fig. 11.

Victoria & Albert Museum, London, fig. 15, fig. 42, 74, 88.

Warburg Institute, University of London, fig. 16, 28.

Yale Center for British Art, Paul Mellon Collection, cover, fig. 12, fig. 20, fig. 48.